Marwan Adeeb Dwairy, DSc

Cross-Cultural Counseling
The Arab-Palestinian Case

Pre-publication REVIEWS, COMMENTARIES, EVALUATIONS . . .

"*Cross-Cultural Counseling* is written by one of the pioneer clinicians amongst Palestinians in Israel. Dr. Dwairy skillfully and successfully uses his rich experiences as an Arab who acquired Western tools of psychotherapy to put psychopathology and psychotherapy within an appropriate cultural context. It is an illuminating book for all therapists, especially for those who deal with patients coming from diverse cultures."

Shafiq Masalha, PhD
Clinical Psychologist Supervisor, Counseling Services, Hebrew University of Jerusalem

"Many psychotherapists give lip service to the cross-cultural experience, but when faced with a cross-cultural client are at a loss as to how to proceed. At times, therapists routinely apply time-honored strategies without carefully being attuned to the nuances of the client's culture. It is clear, then, from Dr. Dwairy's writings, that in some instances the therapy has to be dramatically altered and that the basic premise of treatment must be modified. Given that Dr. Dwairy, a Christian who is a Palestinian living in Israel, has experienced the confluence of several cultures, he is in an excellent position to provide a guide for treating Arab-Palestinians. This book should definitely be read by students enrolled in cross-cultural counseling classes."

Michel Hersen, PhD, ABPP
Professor and Dean, School of Professional Psychology, Pacific University, Forest Grove, OR

Cross-Cultural Counseling
The Arab-Palestinian Case

THE HAWORTH PRESS
Advances in Psychology and Mental Health
Frank De Piano, PhD
Senior Editor

Beyond the Therapeutic Relationship: Behavioral, Biological, and Cognitive Foundations of Psychotherapy by Frederic J. Leger

How the Brain Talks to Itself: A Clinical Primer of Psychotherapeutic Neuroscience by Jay E. Harris

Cross-Cultural Counseling: The Arab-Palestinian Case by Marwan Dwairy

The Vulnerable Therapist: Practicing Psychotherapy in an Age of Anxiety by Helen W. Coale

Cross-Cultural Counseling

The Arab-Palestinian Case

Marwan Adeeb Dwairy, DSc

Jane Jagelman
Editorial Assistant

The Haworth Press
New York • London

The Haworth Press, Inc., 10 Alice Street, Binghamton, NY 13904-1580

Cover design by Monica L. Seifert.

Library of Congress Cataloging-in-Publication Data

Dwairy, Marwan.
Cross-cultural counseling : the Arab-Palestinian case / Marwan Dwairy ; Jane Jagelman, editorial assistant.
p. cm.
Includes bibliographical references and index.
ISBN 0-7890-0481-X (alk. paper).
1. Cross-cultural counseling. 2. Palestinian Arabs—Counseling of. 3. Palestinian Arabs—Psychology. I. Title.
BF637.C6D85 1998
158′.3′0899274—dc21 97-37271
CIP

To
the memory of my parents, Louris and Adeeb,

and to my family,
who raised me to be a proud Palestinian,

and to my lovely children, Nasim and Mona,
two promising Palestinian kids

ABOUT THE AUTHOR

Marwan Adeeb Dwairy, MA, DSc, has been a Visiting Professor in the Graduate Program of the Center for Psychological Studies at Nova Southeastern University in Florida since 1994. In this capacity, he has taught classes on psychological intervention in somatoform disorders, on the diagnosis and treatment of dissociative disorders, and on cross-cultural counseling. He was the Director of the Municipal Psychological Services Center for Nazareth, Israel, from 1978 until 1994, and the Director of a private clinic specializing in psychosomatic and stress disorders from 1980 until 1994. Through sixteen years of practice, he has acquired extensive experience in psychodynamic therapy, helping parents and teachers cope with children's behavioral and emotional problems, and in Cognitive-Behavior Therapy. A former lecturer of cognitive, developmental, and social psychology at TECHNION—The Israeli Institute of Technology, Dr. Dwairy was a Chairperson on the Arab-Palestinian Mental Health Association in Israel (1991–1994) and of the North section of the Israeli Association of Behavior-Cognitive Therapy. He has spoken at three international peace conferences and delivered and published numerous papers and articles on Arab-Palestinian mental health and national identity, special education in Arab-Palestinian schools, and sexual abuse in the Arabic community.

CONTENTS

Figures

Tables

Author's Note

While I was writing this book, affected by Western terminology, I referred spontaneously to people who are not part of the so-called West (North America and Europe) as "non-Westerners." During the review of the first chapters with my spouse Khawla, a family therapist who studies the cultural issues in family therapy, she drew my attention to the term non-Westerner as reflecting a disrespectful attitude. As Palestinians, it reminded us of the term "non-Jews" by which the Israeli government referred to the Palestinian Israeli citizens. We always felt that this term represents the centrality that the government attributes to Jewish citizens and the marginality that is attributed to us. It serves to establish our identity in relation to the Jewish one as if we do not have an identity independent from the others. Similarly, to refer to the people in Asia, Africa, and South America as non-Westerners is to deny their culture and heritage. It is to consider them as nothing but non-Westerners, despite the fact that in numbers they greatly exceed the Europeans and the North Americans, and they have very rich cultures that could never have been understood and appreciated through the Western perspective or criteria.

In comparison to Western society, people in Asia, Africa, and South America share many cultural features. To refer to these features in general, and at the same time to avoid labeling these cultures as non-Western, I will use in this book the terms *Southern* cultures for African and South American areas, and *Eastern* cultures for Asian and Middle Eastern areas. In a shortened combination of the two terms I will use the term *South/Eastern* cultures, without undermining the uniqueness of every nation, race, and ethnicity in these areas in the world.

Foreword

Historians of medicine reported that Ar-Razi, a physician well known during the medieval Arab-Islamic civilization, was the first to use the term psychotherapy, *Al-Ilaj Annafsani.* After a golden age in the history of Arab psychiatry and psychology, Arab science had gone into a long slumber, which was reinforced by European colonization. However, during the last four decades there has been an intellectual revival among Arab scholars that has contributed to the international scientific endeavor in the area of mental health. Arab psychology and psychiatry follows Western theoretical models and is still in search of its own identity. *Cross-Cultural Counseling* is one of the rare attempts at an Arab psychology or psychiatry independent of Western domination. In this volume, Dr. Dwairy challenges the assumptions that theories and practices in the West can be transplanted to the Arab culture or to other Asian, African, and South American cultures without radical modifications.

It has long been recognized that traditional psychotherapy is only suitable for white YAVIS (young, attractive, verbal, intelligent, and successful) clients. The theory and practice of psychotherapy have excluded lower-class persons and people from various ethnic backgrounds from psychotherapeutic intervention. A significant contribution of the present volume is to present critical evaluation of the main psychotherapeutic systems and to present the reader with real live cases to illustrate the problems related to the therapeutic process in dealing with Arab patients. Dr. Dwairy has clearly demonstrated how psychological factors interact with the social context in determining therapeutic outcome. An important message of the volume is that regardless of the therapeutic approach (e.g., insight, client-centered, behavioral-cognitive), psychotherapy that is divorced from the social context, particularly the family, is doomed to failure with Arab patients as well as with patients from other collectivist societies. In these societies, individualism, which is often considered the ideal in the West, has to be sacrificed for the sake of harmony in the family and the society at large.

Dr. Dwairy provides detailed discussion of how the sociocultural context affects psychotherapeutic processes such as insight, transference, and the client-therapist relationship. In addition to the sociocultural context of psychotherapy, it is important that the therapist be familiar with the idioms of distress used by patients. The reader is provided with a thorough review of the literature on mental illness and its manifestations in the Arab countries. Although traditional methods of socialization in the Arab culture and their role in the reaction of patients in therapy are discussed, Dr. Dwairy warns the reader against generalizations to all Arab patients. He gives excellent illustrations of how therapists have to be cautious in dealing with patients undergoing different degrees of acculturation and Westernization. Even in a small Arab-Israeli town, Dr. Dwairy treated cases ranging from the most to the least traditional. It required much flexibility and practical ingenuity to modify his techniques to suit individual cases.

A major contribution of the volume is the application of the biopsychosocial model to the theory and practice of psychotherapy. Readers are of course familiar with the biopsychosocial perspective, particularly in the area of health psychology. However, its application to psychotherapy with supportive case studies of ethnic groups is almost nonexistent. The discussion of the biopsychosocial model within the framework of collectivist societies by Dr. Dwairy not only applies to Arab patients but also to other ethnic groups.

Cross-Cultural Counseling is an original and unique contribution to the psychology of cultural diversity. It is also a humanitarian appeal against prejudice and discrimination not only against Arabs and other ethnic groups in Israel but also against culturally different people all over the world. Readers can seek and find abundant intellectual nourishment but should not miss the human passion throughout the book.

Ihsan Al-Issa
General Secretary,
International Arab Psychological Association

Preface

If Arabs are the people most misunderstood by the West, Palestinian Arabs are the most misunderstood Arab people. Political conflicts and historical events have dehumanized them and overshadowed their national tragedy, culture, and other human aspects of their lives. Publications about Arabs in English are focused on either sociopolitical or mental health issues, usually from a Western perspective. Publications that make the connection between Arab mental health and sociopolitical issues are very rare. It is hoped that this book will shed some light on the cultural and human aspects of Arabs in general, and of Palestinian Arabs in particular, and in connection with that, will help readers to comprehend mental health issues and limitations of Western psychology and psychotherapy in understanding and treating Arabic clients' behavior.

Today, there are approximately three million Arabs living in the United States. As with many other immigrants, they face various psychosocial problems. Due to cultural barriers, reports about psychotherapy with this sector are not encouraging. Arab clients feel alienated from the American mental health system. American clinicians find it difficult to understand Arabs' behavior and to accomplish change. This book analyzes the difficulties in the therapeutic encounter and suggests a model of treatment for Arab clients.

Although this book focuses on Arabs, it is about cross-cultural psychology and psychotherapy. Most of the mental health issues, especially the difficulties of Western psychotherapy with Arab clients, as well as the suggested model of treatment, can be applied to all South/Eastern clients, such as Africans, South Americans, Asians, and Native Americans, who share with Arabs a collective/holistic way of living, rather than an individualistic/dualistic one. Therefore, readers who are not particularly interested in Palestinians may consider them as a case that exemplifies the cultural limitations of Western psychology with other South/Eastern clients.

Who are the Palestinians? How are they related to Arabs and Muslims? Chapter 1 introduces the Palestinian Arabs in relation to Arab and Islamic history. It describes how Arab life has transformed from one historical stage to another, from *Aljahiliyya* (see Chapter 1) before the seventh century to the Islamic empire that lasted for approximately seven centuries. This was followed by the stagnation period in the fourteenth century when Arabs lost their empire and were ruled by Mamluks and Ottomans. In the past two centuries a new revival period began, in which Arabs regained their independence and resumed the national debate concerning basic social and political issues, such as traditionalism versus modernity, and authenticity versus Westernization.

The history of a nation represents the collective experience of the people, through which their culture is developed and modified. In Chapter 2, Arabic cultural features are discussed. Based on the four periods of Arab history, a two-dimensional cultural field is described: authority-ruled, and individualistic-collectivistic. The chapter describes the sociopolitical developments that took place in Western Europe and the United States that led to the emergence of individualism. It then shows how different sociopolitical situations in the Arab countries maintain an authoritarian collectivistic culture.

Chapter 3 presents empirical studies concerning socialization in Arabic families and schools. The results show the authoritarian methods of rearing and education. Arab parents use verbal explanations and punishment interchangeably to make their children acknowledge their authority. Schoolteachers implement violent and oppressive methods of education. The educational climate in homes and schools actually narrows the field of experimentation for Arab children and conditions them to absorb and obey the adults' directives.

Differences in the collective experience of Arabs, compared to Westerners, generate personality differences. Chapter 4 describes the characteristics of the Arabic personality, including the differences in development of Arab children compared to the process of individuation and independence in the West. In addition, it describes the structure and dynamics of the collective Arabic personality that are controlled by social factors, compared to the personal internal factors that Western theories use to explain behavior. Social means of coping, as opposed to intrapsychic defense mechanisms, are described in detail.

Chapter 5 presents epidemiological psychiatric studies in the Arab world and highlights differences in the prevalence and manifestation of the psychological disorders compared to what is known in the West. This chapter challenges the universality of the *Diagnostic and Statistical Manual of Mental Disorders,* Fourth Edition (DSM-IV), as a diagnostic instrument. In Chapter 6, the traditional Arab theory of psychopathology is presented, as well as the attitude of Arabs toward mental health and psychotherapy. Also, it describes the help-seeking behavior of Arabs and the poor mental health services delivery system in the Arab countries.

Chapters 7 and 8 focus on psychotherapy. Chapter 7 challenges Western insight psychotherapy when applied within South/Eastern societies. It analyzes the cultural barriers that psychotherapy may face. Therapeutic goals and techniques are questioned and found unsuitable for South/Eastern clients. In Chapter 8, a model for making therapeutic decisions is presented. A model that considers the cultural identity of the client and his or her family to tailor the therapy is proposed. Given that Arabs and most of the South/Eastern societies adopt a collective identity and a holistic perspective toward health, a biopsychosocial approach is recommended in Chapter 9. In addition, based on the metaphoric language that characterizes Arabs and South/Eastern clients, metaphor therapy is proposed.

Six Arab cases that exemplify the presence of culture in psychotherapy are presented in Chapter 10. These cases display the typical client's behavior and the barriers that psychotherapy faces. In addition, the cases help to identify the factors that should be taken into account when making therapeutic decisions and tailoring the therapy for the client.

Finally, I hope this book will undo the dehumanization that has surrounded Palestinian Arabs and help clinicians understand the behavior of the Arabic client and come to know the person within.

Acknowledgment

I wish to thank my spouse Khawla Abu Baker for her support and to acknowledge her valuable comments on the content of the book.

PART I:
THE ARAB-PALESTINIAN CULTURE

Chapter 1

The Palestinian Arabs

As a Palestinian living in Israel, I frequently face various difficulties in introducing myself to Western people.

When I say "I am Palestinian," people find it difficult to know my country because Palestine does not exist as an independent state yet. Then the conversation usually proceeds in the following way:

> "Oh, from Pakistan," attributing the misunderstanding to my accent.
>
> "No, I am from Israel."
>
> "You are a Jew then."
>
> "No, I am an Arab." Then I explain, "Palestinians are Arabs like Egyptians, Syrians, Saudies."
>
> "So, are you Muslim?" They show signs of surprise, which I have learned are related to my blond hair and fair skin that do not fit the stereotype of Muslims.
>
> "No, I am a Christian. Among Palestinians there are Muslims, Christians, and Drouzes."

After this confusion, it becomes clear that it is difficult to understand my background. Some people find it easier to end the conversation with a silly smile and a head nod, while others realize it is complicated and ask for more explanation.

THE PALESTINIANS' STORY

Palestinians have been associated for a long time in the West with terrorism, first because of the dominance of Jewish propaganda in the Western mass media. Second, the Jewish tragedy of the Holocaust justifiably gains the sympathy of the West toward Israel, making the country appear to be a victim that is defending itself. Therefore, the Palestinian attacks against Israel overshadow the Palestinian tragedy and casualties that have been caused by Israel. Third, for historical and political reasons, Western countries have built a strategic alliance with Israel to serve their interests. Fourth, the Palestinians have failed for decades to gain access to the Western media and to communicate to the Western mainstream in a language consistent with Western culture. They have mistakenly assumed that their cause is obvious enough to speak for itself and to justify their military struggle. For these reasons, the Palestinians are known to the West by their struggles against Israel, rather than by their history, culture, and human aspects. Therefore, there is a need to dispute the misunderstanding that surrounds the Palestinian people and their tragedy.

Before the establishment of the state of Israel, Palestinians lived in their homeland, Palestine, under the British mandate. They were the majority, while the Jews, who immigrated to Palestine during the nineteenth and early twentieth centuries, were a minority. During the war in 1948, more than 70 percent of the Palestinians were expelled from their homeland and became refugees. The state of Israel was then created on land that was 75 percent of Palestine. The other parts of Palestine were divided; the West Bank was appended to Jordan, and the Gaza Strip to Egypt. Jerusalem was divided between Israel and Jordan. As the result of an intensive Jewish immigration immediately after the creation of the state of Israel and because many Palestinians abandoned their land, the few Palestinians who stayed in their homeland became a small minority living under a military regime in Israel, and the others became refugees in Arab countries such as Jordan, Syria, Lebanon, and Egypt. The Israeli government refused to take back any substantial number of Palestinian refugees; they expected that they would sooner or later be absorbed into the populations of the countries where they had found refuge.

In 1967, during the Six-Day War, Israel occupied the West Bank and Gaza Strip in addition to other parts of Syria, Egypt, and Lebanon. During this war, some Palestinians became refugees for the second time, while the others stayed in the West Bank and Gaza Strip, known as the occupied territories, and lived under the Israeli occupation. In December 1987, the Palestinians in the occupied territories started a national popular uprising, *Intifada*, against the Israeli occupation. This uprising, sustained for more than five years, made it clear that the occupation of another nation's lands cannot last. World governments became aware of the injustices that were being done to Palestinians and pushed toward a solution to this problem. A peace process between the Israeli government and the Palestinians, which was initiated in Madrid in October 1991 and simultaneously in Oslo in the early 1990s, accomplished a peace agreement between the two parties. According to that agreement, in 1994 the Israeli army started to withdraw gradually from the main cities in the occupied territories and submitted those cities to the Palestinian Liberation Organization (PLO). Negotiations are still taking place concerning the other occupied territories as well as the permanent solution. The Palestinians demand an independent state, while Israel is still not ready to accept this solution. The status of Jerusalem in the permanent solution seems to be one of the toughest issues in the negotiation.

Demographic Data

The number of Palestinians today is about eight million; 43 percent of them are living in Israel and the occupied territories, 44 percent are living in surrounding Arab countries such as Jordan, Syria, Lebanon, and Egypt, and the rest, 13 percent, are spread over different countries around the world.

Sixty percent of the Palestinians are still living as refugees, away from their villages and cities, under foreign regimes in different places: in the occupied territories that are ruled by the Israeli military regime, the Arab countries, and many other non-Arab countries in Europe and America. Most of the refugees are living under miserable socioeconomic situations.

Today Palestinians live in small villages and towns or in refugee camps. Before 1948, the vast majority of the Palestinians were peasants who worked on their lands. After they lost their land, the vast majority became laborers. Among those who live in Israel or the occupied territories, about 80 percent are working as laborers far away from their villages. Most of them are working on a temporary basis. The rate of unemployment among men (who are usually the breadwinners in Arab families) is very high, ranging from 20 percent to 50 percent. Only a small portion of Palestinians have successful businesses, which are mainly in the Arab countries, especially in the Arab oil countries.

The Palestinian family is a traditional one, with an average of six children in the nuclear family. The population is young; about half are children and teenagers. Due to this fact, and because the vast majority of women are homemakers, the Palestinian society is a consuming rather than a producing one.

Many factors have threatened the unity of the Palestinian family. The expulsion and deportation of Palestinians have physically torn many families apart. For instance, some brothers or sisters are living in Jordan, while others are in Lebanon, and still others remain in their homeland. For many decades they have not been allowed to meet or correspond because of the state of war between Israel and the Arab countries. During the occupation of the West Bank and Gaza Strip since 1967, half of all Palestinian men have been arrested and imprisoned for months or years by the Israeli army, which has left thousands of families without providers. In the refugee camps in the Arab countries, men have been obligated to leave their families for months or years looking for ways to earn a living in other areas or countries. As a result, the Palestinian father has become removed from his family, which makes the mother more central in raising the children and caring for their needs.

THE ARAB/ISLAMIC COLLECTIVE EXPERIENCE

As Arabs, Palestinians share the Arab culture that stems from the collective Arab/Muslim experience. Therefore, to understand the cultural background of the Palestinian Arabs, it would be helpful to present Arab history.

Looking back at Arab/Muslim history, we may identify four major periods, each representing a distinct layer in the Arab cultural structure (Dwairy, 1997b).

Aljahiliyya

In the period that preceded the emergence of Islam in A.D. 622, Aljahiliyya, Arabs lived in tribal systems in the Arabian peninsula,

Syria, and Iraq. Many of them were nomads, traveling in the desert, looking for water and a livable climate. Some were settled cultivators, tending their grain or palm trees in the oases; some were traders and craftsmen in small market towns; some combined more than one way of life. An ethos of courage, hospitality, loyalty to family, and pride of ancestry was dominant. Arabic poetry flourished, reflecting this ethos. Poetic language, with refinement of grammar and vocabulary, emerged out of formal Arabic language.

Collectivism and authoritarianism were the main cultural characteristics of that social system. People submitted to the authority of the tribe to survive in the tough desert climate. Age and gender were the main factors in the authority hierarchy. Young people submitted to older people, and women submitted to men. Collectivism included the nuclear and extended family, as well as the whole tribe. All of them shared the property and destiny and adhered to the authority of the tribe, the *shikh'*. The collective stand against other tribes was known as *'asabiyya.* Honor belonged to an individual through membership in a large whole. Much of that honor depended on the wealth of the tribe, as well as the behavior of the women. Women were expected to be submissive, modest, and decent. Women who deviated from these norms would hurt the so-called "honor of the family" and, therefore, would face severe punishment.

Islamic Empire

Immediately after the emergence of Islam in the Arabian peninsula in the early seventh century, Arab/Islamic armies conquered the surrounding countries and founded a new empire. This empire expanded from Iran in the east, through North Africa, to Spain in the west. At that period, the style of living changed from nomadic to peasant and town life. Trade flourished from the Indian Ocean through the Mediterranean Sea to Spain. Large cities, mosques, and palaces were built according to a distinctive Arab/Islamic style with pleasure pavilions set amid gardens and running water. They developed a system of irrigation that would bring water to the inhabitants of the cities (Hourani, 1991). Transportation and mail systems and hospitals were built during this period. The first mental health hospitals in the world were built in Baghdad, Iraq in A.D. 750, followed by hospitals in Cairo in A.D. 800, and Damascus in A.D. 1270 (Okasha, 1993).

From the beginning of Islam until the middle of the fifteenth century were the glory days of the Islamic Empire. During that period new Islamic values entered Arab culture. Although Islam brought new values as well as laws to Arab society, it did not challenge its classical collectivism and authoritarianism. Collectivism and authoritarianism were no longer limited to only within the tribe but extended to the Islamic state as well. People submitted to both tribal and Islamic law within a tribal and Islamic collectivism. The gender relationship did not change; the men continued to be responsible for looking after land or livestock. The women were responsible for cooking, cleaning, and rearing children, but they would also help in the fields or with the flocks. Men were exclusively responsible for dealing with the outside world. When a woman grew older and had produced male children, she could acquire great power in the family. The *'asabiyya* did not cease either; the tribal structure was involved in the structure of the state. Tribal considerations affected the army structure and the political authority (Al-Jabiri, 1991a, 1991b).

Because the revelation sent by God was to an Arab prophet, Muhammad, and the *Qura'an* (the Islamic holy book, Koran) was written in Arabic, Arabs held a special status in the Islamic empire. They became the rulers of the state, and their cultures and language became dominant. The Arabic language spread and became the official language; later it became the medium of expression in the whole empire and a symbol of educational status.

This period was the Arab renaissance. The tradition of poetic composition continued to flourish. During the eighth and ninth centuries, called the "documentation era," *a'sr elttadwin*, the state employed scholars, philosophers, and wise men to document the knowledge that they had gained from earlier Arab culture and from other developed cultures such as the Greeks, Indians, and Egyptians. During this period, Arabs contributed greatly to human knowledge in the areas of philosophy, mathematics, medicine, astronomy, occult sciences, astrology, alchemy, and magic. Because the language of the *Qura'an* was a figurative and metaphoric Arabic, the Islamic doctrine was open to various interpretations. Therefore, the Arabs gave much thought to the linguistics of their language, in an attempt to impose rules of interpretation. They developed the science of language, *I'lm el bayan,* which deals with the relationship between language and meaning.

Actually, the *Qura'an* did not cover the whole range of human life; it was most precise on questions of personal status such as marriage, divorce, and inheritance, less so on commercial matters, and least of all on penal and constitutional questions (Hourani, 1991). In a society that was generating a new way of living under Islamic values, these unresolved questions challenged the state and the scholars to find answers. Therefore, they were obliged to address basic questions of life concerning authority, constitutional law, truth, and so on.

While looking for answers, Arabs contributed much to basic philosophical epistemological questions. Three main Islamic epistemological streams appeared: (1) *Sunnism*, postulating that the literal meaning of the *Qura'an* and *H'adith* (sayings of the Prophet Muhammad) is the way to reach the truth; (2) *Shi'ism* and *Sufism*, claiming that the *Qura'an* and *H'adith* should be interpreted to understand the truth behind the words (it is believed that a Sufist can experience a revelation as well as the Prophet); and (3) the logical stream, affected by Aristotle, which looked for objective evidence to prove the truth. Two modern versions of the debate concerning these three streams exist today. One is between objectivism and phenomenologism and the other between religion and science.

To appreciate the contribution of Arabs, we should place their achievements in the context of that time: during the seventh to the fifteenth centuries Europe was immersed in its dark ages. Interestingly, by the end of the Arab renaissance in the fourteenth and fifteenth centuries, Europe started its renaissance, which coincided with the stagnation period of the Arabs. The European renaissance led to a technological revolution and to democracy.

Stagnation Period

Between the fourteenth and eighteenth centuries, the Arabs were ruled by other nations. In the thirteenth century, the eastern part of the Islamic Empire fell to the Mamluks, then to the Ottomans, who were non-Arab Muslims who ruled until the end of the eighteenth century. The western part of the Islamic Empire (Andalusia) fell into European hands during the end of the fifteenth century. In the beginning, Arabs felt that the Ottoman occupation, which was also Muslim, was saving the Islamic empire from the European threat. Gradually, they realized that their political and social status had deteriorated and that they were suffering under Ottoman rule. During this period, the Arabic identity became distinct from the Islamic one. Arabism became the ideology of many organizations that emerged to fight for the independence of the Arabs from the Ottomans.

This period is considered a time of stagnation because of the deterioration of culture and political status. Nationally, the Arabs were ruled rather than rulers. Mosques were built in Ottoman style: large courtyards led to domed prayer halls above which rose one, two, or four minarets that were long, thin, and pointed. The prayer hall might have been decorated with colored tiles or with flower designs in green, red, and blue. As the language of the *Qura'an*, Arabic was not completely diminished. Works of religion and law might have used Arabic, but poetry and secular works were written in the Ottoman language, Turkish, which developed during this period as a medium of high culture.

In the eighteenth century, the political power of the Ottoman Empire and its culture had a great influence on the Arab provinces. For example, local Ottoman families and groups within the cities retained positions in the Ottoman service from one generation to another. Generally, Ottomans gained status and control over social life in the Arab world. Some Ottomans held positions in the local administration, while others became wealthy through the acquisition of tax farms. They obtained posts in religious and legal services and, through them, acquired control over the property of the Islamic state: *Waq'fs*. By the late eighteenth century, therefore, there were powerful and more or less permanent families of local Turkish "notables" in the Arab state (Hourani, 1991).

During the stagnation period, authoritarianism and collectivism continued. In addition to the controlling authority of the family and of Islam, Arabs also surrendered to the will of the Ottoman rulers. When the Ottoman rulers of the state were abusing the Arabs and their property, collectivism (national and familial) was necessary to face the dangers; the interest of the collective exceeded the interest of the individual.

The New Revival Period

Since the nineteenth century, the Arab world has been exposed to European culture in a variety of ways. Some parts of the Arab world were ruled by Britain and France. Many missionary schools brought Western values into the curriculum. Several Arab scholars were educated in Europe and became impressed by the liberalism and humanism that emerged after the French Revolution. In the twentieth century, as a result of the development of communication and mass media, Western culture invaded almost every section of the Arab world, introducing the ideas of individualism and liberalism. Books, periodicals, and newspapers were channels through which knowledge of the new worlds of Europe and America came to the Arabs.

The exposure of the Arab world to Western liberalism challenged the fundamental authoritarianism and collectivism of Arabic society. In the last two centuries, the cultural debate has focused on the questions of traditionalism versus modernity, and authenticity *(asala)* and specificity *(khususiyya)* versus Westernization. These issues are raised in various areas: education, interpersonal relationships, familial style, entertainment, and many other social-political aspects. Arab leaders and scholars discuss the authenticity-Westernization continuum. Some extremists call for Westernization, and others call for Islamic fundamentalism. The majority of Arabs fall somewhere in the middle; they are looking for reforms in the traditional culture that maintain the uniqueness of Arab/Islamic life but also follow the rise of democracy in the world. There is a division of opinion about the basis of authority: whether authority should lie with officials who are responsible for their own sense of justice and the interests of the state or with a representative government created by elections.

By the end of the Second World War, Britain and France had become weak; therefore, their rule in the Arab world ended but not before creating a sectarian region divided into several independent states. The Arab states today are varied in their political systems and economies. Some, such as Jordan, Saudi Arabia, and Morocco, adopted a royal system, while others including Egypt, Syria, and Iraq adopted a republican system. Some of them, mainly the oil countries such as Saudi Arabia and the Gulf States, are rich, while others have poor economies. Even within one country, the degree of economic division is very high; in the rich quarters of the bourgeoisie, people live in a European style, while in the poor quarters and in the countryside, they have a traditional lifestyle. At the state level, rich countries such as Saudi Arabia and the Gulf States are more traditional and less open to Western liberal values concerning social life and the status of women. Some other countries such as Egypt, Lebanon, and Syria are more liberal and contribute greatly to intellectual and cultural Arab activity.

Despite the independence of Arab states, most Arab regimes are not democratic and are not meeting the needs of their people. Many areas are lacking basic civil institutions and services such as schools, clinics, hospitals, transportation, banks, social insurance, and so on. People feel they are marginalized; are not allowed to criticize the political regime. They have been denied the basic right to participate in the political process. The affairs of the community and society have ceased to be their own. Arab governments do not guarantee their citizens the fundamental human rights of freedom of conscience, expression, association, and assembly (Barakat, 1993). Some Arab governments use religion as a mechanism of control. They have cultivated religious, sectarian, and tribal orientations to governing. On the other hand, they forbid modern vehicles of struggle and expression such as political parties, labor unions, and popular movements. People find refuge in traditional institutions including religion, sect, tribe, family, and ethnicity to express their discontent. These institutions solidify rather than diminish the conditions of dependency, patriarchal and authoritarian relationships, socioeconomic disparities, and alienation that have endured since independence. Barakat (1993) points out some features that summarize the main characteristics of the Arab world today:

> . . . integration of the area into the world capitalist system; social and political fragmentation; the centrality of religion, or, conversely, the loss of religious faith and return of the *jahiliyya*; the absence of scientific and future-oriented rationalism; repressive family socialization and neopatriarchy; the subjugation of women; the dominance of traditionalism over creativity and modernity; duality of Westernization and *salafiyya* (ances-

tralism); disequilibrium in the Arab ego; and the prevalence of a traditional mentality. (Barakat, 1993, p. 270)

Christianity in Palestine

Christianity preceded Islam in Palestine. Christian Arabs existed in all of the Middle East, mainly in Palestine, ancient Syria (which included parts of modern Palestine, Lebanon, Jordan, and Iraq), Iraq, and Egypt. After the emergence of Islam, some Christians converted, but basically they remained a minority within the Islamic Empire. Both Islamic and Christian Arabs share the same language and collective experience, and therefore have a similar culture today. Christian Arabs see themselves as Arabs and tie their destiny to that of the Arab nation. When the Arab empire was attacked by Christian Europeans (during the eleventh to thirteenth centuries), as well as by Muslim Mamluks and then the Ottomans (during the thirteenth to nineteenth centuries), Christian Arabs shared the national struggle for Arabism and Arab interests.

Christian Arabs were exposed more than Moslems to the Western culture that Christian missionary schools and churches brought to the East; therefore, they contributed much to cultural progress. Many famous Arab thinkers, writers, poets, and scholars were Christians. They played a central role in bringing liberal humanistic values to Arab culture and into the cultural political debate over democracy and socialism.

Among Palestinians today, there is a Christian minority that lives in peace with Muslim Palestinians; they share the struggle against the Israeli occupation and work toward establishing a democratic Palestinian state.

Arab Families and Arab States

Familial systems have lasted even when substantial political change took place in Arab history. Political changes transformed rather than diminished the collective-authoritarian structure. Actually, the political system has been affected by, more than it has affected, familial structure. Political authority in the Arab-Islamic world actually stems from a coalition of tribes (Al-Jabiri, 1991a, 1991b). In the stagnation period, after the loss of Arab political sovereignty, the tribal-familial entity became the main affiliation. Today, the Arab states still rely on this structure. Most of the Arab states are built on ruling family systems based on sectarian-tribal alliances. Economic and political power, especially in the Arab oil countries, has been the privilege of a few families and tribal chiefs. Some Arab kings and presidents address the residents of their state as family members (e.g., Egyptian family, or Jordanian family), and consider themselves to be the patriarchs of that family. Sharabi (1992) proposed the term "new-patriarchism" to describe the Arab world structure, suggesting that, in essence, it had not changed much from the former traditional social structure despite some cosmetic signs of modernization.

Social dynamics within the Arab states resemble those within Arab families. Both of them are hierarchical authoritarian structures that prevent members from taking control of their own destinies. Political authority controls and suppresses individuals in the name of collective interests, facing the enemy, national unity, comprehensive development, liberation, or socialism. The authority of the family also works in the name of love, in the name of the family, for the protection of the family, and so on. Both state and family are interested in maintaining the system much more than in individual development. Arab leaders, similar to family authority, decide what is best for the country and punish citizens who disobey the rules in the name of the interests of the state.

Palestinians are the only Arabs who have not yet acquired an independent state and are still ruled by foreign regimes, inside Israel, under the Israeli occupation, or in exile. In unstable political conditions, in temporary residences, and under unsupportive governments, the Palestinian family has been the only social structure that has helped people to survive. Despite the fact that many families have been torn apart by becoming refugees, the parts of the family that have remained together have cooperated in order to survive; hence, the cohesiveness of the Palestinian family remains.

The Palestinian story and Arab history describe the collective experience of the people. Through this experience, the Arabic culture, norms, values, and lifestyle have developed. The four historical stages are crucial to understand Arab culture. In the next chapter, I will address the relationship between these stages of history and Arab culture.

SUMMARY

Palestinians are part of the Arab people. They lost their homeland, Palestine, to Israel in 1948. Since then, the majority of them have become refugees far from their homes. Since 1967, Israel has occupied the West Bank and Gaza Strip in addition to parts of Syria, Egypt, and Lebanon, which forced more Palestinians to become refugees. Today, 43 percent of Palestinians are living under the Israeli regime in their homeland; the rest are refugees in the Arab countries.

Palestinians share the collective experience of Arabs. They passed through four historical periods, and each had its own sociocultural characteristics. During the *Aljahiliyya* period, before A.D. 600, Arabs lived in tribal systems. Collectivism and authoritarianism were the main characteristics of the culture. The golden age of the Islamic empire, based on Islamic law, took place between the seventh century and the fifteenth century. This period, in which the culture and economy flourished, has been considered the Arab renaissance. In the fourteenth century, parts of the Arab empire started to collapse. Until the eighteenth century, the Arabs were ruled by other nations, and their culture stagnated. In the last two centuries, a new revival has taken place, in which Arab scholars and thinkers are debating essential issues concerning the future of the nation. This debate is focused on traditionalism versus democratization of the social and political systems. Despite the process of urbanization and industrialization taking place in many areas of the Arab world, the political systems in Arab countries remain based on a tribal authoritarian mentality that does not ensure the basic human needs of citizens.

Chapter 2

Psycho-Cultural Features of the Palestinian Arabs

THE ARABIC CULTURAL FIELD

Contemporary Arabic culture stems from the collective Arab experience during the course of history. Each period of Arab/Islamic history (*Aljahiliyya*, empire, stagnation, and revival) represents different collective experiences. New periods added new layers of values that interacted with the former ones. Actually, each period represents an end of a two-dimensional cultural field, within which the Arabs vary (Dwairy, in press a).

Collectivism-Individualism

Collectivism stemmed from the tribal *Aljahiliyya* period, and individualism emerged after the exposure to Western culture, during the revival of the last two centuries. This dimension explains the diversity in the relationship between the individual and the collective. In a collectivistic style, the individual relinquishes the self and obeys the will of the in-group that is represented in norms and values. The individualistic style is more pluralistic, egalitarian, and liberal. It recognizes the individual's needs, opinions, and values, and allows expression.

Authority-Ruled

This dimension represents the extremes Arabs have experienced during the course of their history. Historically, during the Islamic Empire, Arabs were the rulers (or authority); whereas since the stagnation period, until the second half of the twentieth century, they

FIGURE 2.1. Two-Dimensional Cultural Field of Arabs

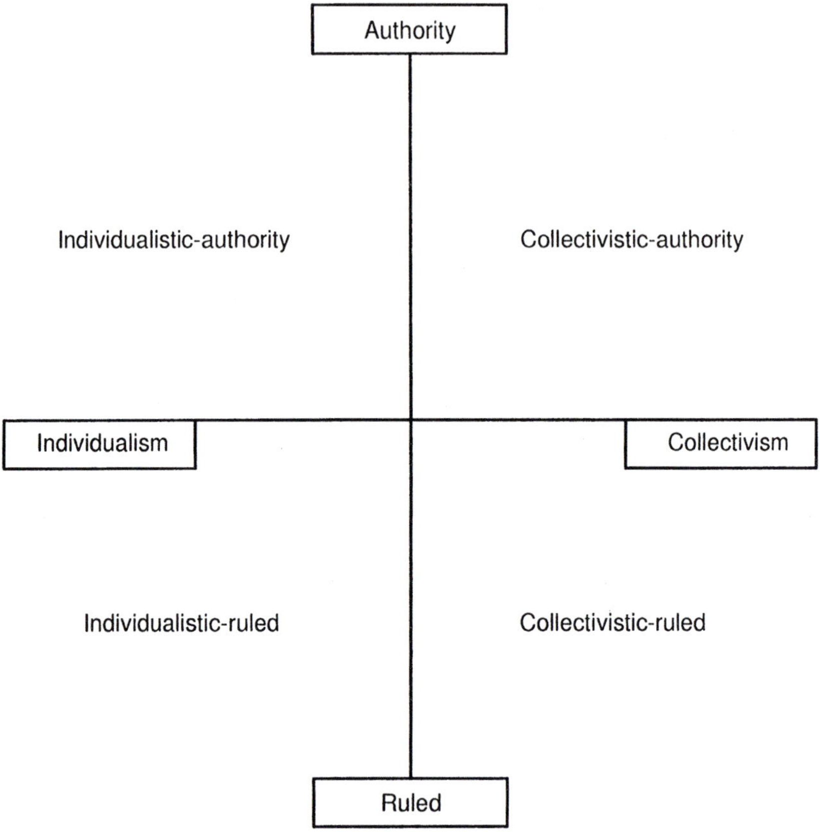

Authority

Individualistic-authority

Collectivistic-authority

Individualism

Collectivism

Individualistic-ruled

Collectivistic-ruled

Ruled

were ruled by others. On the personal level, living for centuries in a hierarchical society, Arabs alternate during life between these two statuses, authority or ruled, depending on age, gender, and social context. They move from being ruled as children and youngsters, to being rulers when they get older and establish families. Women submit to men's authority, while they still hold their own authority over their children (see Figure 2.1). Unlike Western culture, the transition from being a ruled child (or woman) to an authority when an adult (or mother) is extreme.

Depending on personal/familial experience, individual experience may vary from the collective Arab experience; therefore, people may adopt different cultural identities. At the same time, that identity may vary at different ages or in different social contexts. The two dimensions help to clarify both the cultural identity of a person or group as a relatively stable trait, and the variability of the cultural identity across periods of life and social contexts, the contextual cultural identity. Four types of cultural identity (and/or contextual cultural identity) may be identified within these dimensions (Dwairy, 1997b; in press a).

Collectivistic-Authority

Collectivistic-authority is an authority in a collective culture, such as the father of a traditional family (or a teacher in a traditional village, or a religious or political leader). The father expects full obedience of his family; he rules the family according to the traditional collectivistic norms and values. He does not consider individual tendencies of family members. He has the authority to punish any member who disobeys the rules.

The cultural identity of the father may change from one social context to another. For instance, when he is among his extended family in the presence of his parents, he may behave as a collectivistic-ruled person, obeying his father as his children do him. In another social context, such as a professional or social one, the father may behave in an egalitarian way toward others but still hold collectivistic authority in his family. For instance, since Arab political organizations have become more democratic in the last few decades, many political leaders and activists in these organizations seem very egalitarian and liberal in their social political behavior but still use collectivistic authoritarian styles at home.

Collectivistic-Ruled

Collectivistic-ruled are the ruled people in a collective culture, such as women and children in a traditional family (or pupils in school, or citizens in a country). They learn how to submit to norms and rules at the expense of denying themselves. Collectivistic-ruled people accept the hierarchical structure of society and express alliance with the authority in power.

Depending on the circumstances, a person may move from being an authority to being ruled and vice versa. A woman who is ruled by men and social norms may behave like a collectivistic-authority as a mother rearing her children, trying to impose norms, controlling the children, and punishing them for their misbehavior.

Individualistic-Authority

Individualistic-authority is an authority in a democratic culture, such as many liberal, educated parents (or teachers) who have adapted in one way or another to a Western style of living based on egalitarian values that respect the children's needs, feelings, and rights. The father and mother share authority and allow space for personal opinion and a democratic process of decision making. Many of these parents may use collectivistic authority when it comes to a sensitive issue that is still far from being accepted in Arab society, such as unacceptable sexual behavior. In other circumstances, such as in the relationship with their own parents, these parents may act as collectivistic-ruled people, respecting the norms and values of their own parents and adhering to their will.

Individualistic-Ruled

Individualistic-ruled people live in an individualistic culture, such as children (or pupils) within a democratic family (or class). They are encouraged to develop personal opinions and to express their own feelings. Some of these children may adopt two simultaneous cultural identities. Besides the individualistic-ruled identity at home, they may still face traditional authority at school and, therefore, adopt a collectivistic-ruled identity at those times.

Although Arabs apply all of the four cultural identity types across different social contexts in their lives, the vast majority of them are positioned as either rulers or ruled in the middle and to the right side (collectivistic) of the cultural field (see Figure 2.1). Only a few are located on the left side (individualistic). Therefore, the individualistic-authority and individualistic-ruled identities are the least common in Arabic society.

Acculturation in Arabic Society

The Arab world today is intensively exposed to Western values of individualism and liberalism. School and university curriculums are based on Western achievements in science and education. Children, as well as adults, are exposed to Western movies and TV series on a daily basis. Educators, intellectuals, and social leaders are influenced by Western humanism and have become agents for liberal individualistic values. Many Arabs have visited Western countries as tourists or students. For instance, the vast majority of medical doctors among Palestinians received their education in the West. These and many other educated people have adopted, at least partly, a Western way of living and thinking that affects their children, family, and friends.

Since the discovery of oil in the Saudi peninsula in 1937, rapid urbanization and sociocultural change have taken place in Saudi Arabia and the other Gulf Arab states. Many Americans and Europeans, as well as Arabs, immigrated to the Arab oil states. They came as experts or workers in search of economic advancement and to help these countries manage and operate many modern facilities, such as oil facilities, hospitals, schools, and so on. These immigrants brought Western culture to these countries that still had a traditional Islamic social system. As a result of these changes, a huge cultural polarity exists. On one side, there are millions of nomad Bedouin still living in the desert. They are completely neglected by the central authority and are still governed by centuries of tradition. On the other side, there are very modern facilities in the urban regions that seem to Richard Story, one of the American pharmacists who worked there, "to be prefabricated in the United States and dropped by some huge helicopter unto the desert" (Story, 1985).

Acculturation has taken place, at some level, in all the Arab countries. These changes are accompanied by intergenerational conflicts. New generations may oppose arranged marriages and cousin marriages, patterns of family relations, and the role of women in society, and they may seek freedom in choosing their own education, employment, or friends (Al-Issa, 1990; Al-Sabaie, 1989; El-Islam, 1982).

Considering individualism in the Arabic society as a result of acculturation, we may identify three groups with different levels of acculturation: *traditional, bicultural,* and *Westernized* groups (Dwairy, 1997b).

Traditional identity is the common cultural identity of rural areas. There, people live in a traditional agricultural or Bedouin way and maintain traditional collectivistic values and norms in their extended families and social life.

Bicultural identity is common mainly among middle-class/educated Arabs who live in urban areas. The main manifestation of biculturalism is seen when we compare materialistic and social contexts. Westernization is noticed mainly in business relationships and materialistic aspects of living, such as housing, furniture, clothing, entertainments, cars, and so on. Social relationships are least influenced by Western values; therefore, traditionalism is still the dominant identity in social life.

Only a very small portion of Arabs have adopted a completely Western cultural identity—those who received their education in the West or those who are exclusively exposed to Western society. Usually they are physically and socially detached from Arab society and have become completely immersed in Western societies. Westernized Arab people find it hard to keep in touch with their Arabic roots. On the other side, Arab society finds it difficult to trust and respect these people; therefore, if they maintain any relationship with Westernized Arabs, it will be limited to the elite.

Judging the cultural identity of Arabs exclusively in the context of social relationships, it seems that the vast majority of Arabs (traditional and bicultural) are authoritarian collectivists (Al-Sabaie, 1989). Many Arab countries, such as Saudi Arabia, remain very traditional, attempting to reconcile recent rapid development in material circumstances with the strict maintenance of Islamic values (Al-Khani et al., 1986). The vast majority of Arabs comply with the collective values at the expense of the self and accept the hierarchical structure of authority. They still adopt authoritarian collectivism in their familial, interpersonal, and social relationships. Education and socialization in homes and schools is still authoritarian (see Chapter 3). The relationship between gender in the family and society is still conservative. Therefore, shedding more light on the sociocultural roots of authoritarian collectivism and the process of transformation to individualism in the West will help clarify the Arabic culture.

FADING OF AUTHORITARIANISM/COLLECTIVISM IN THE WEST

An authoritarian collectivistic culture characterized preindustrialized Western societies as well as many South/Eastern (or non-Western) societies in the present. In the Middle Ages and the beginning of the Renaissance in Europe, individuals lived in a state of oneness with their families, without differentiation between individual and social environment. A person was identical to his or her role in society. One was conscious of himself or herself mainly as a member of a race, people, party, family, or corporation. During that time, society was characterized by authoritarianism and collectivism. Despite the submission to restricting rules and norms, this order provided feelings of security and belonging (Fromm, 1941, 1976). The state was the property of the ruler (king or emperor) and the ruler's family. The masses were exploited by a small minority. Individuals' rights were not recognized. The choices of individuals were limited. People spent all their lives working, socializing, and marrying within the appropriate social class, with little chance to move from one class to another. As adolescents, people simply adopted the rules as expected without examining options or choices. Sons of farmers became farmers, and sons of fishermen became fishermen. People were hardly free to move from one place to another or to choose their dress or food. This authoritarian order was perceived as natural. People served the interests of the ruler while the state did not take any responsibility for the welfare of the citizens. Therefore, the family was the main institution that took care of the individual. The relationship among family members was characterized by interdependency.

Sociopolitical and economic changes influenced the family's structure and personality. In the thirteenth century, Frederick II, Holy Roman emperor from 1215 to 1250, aimed at the complete destruction of the feudal state and at the transformation of people into a means of resistance (Burckhardt, 1921). The Protestant Reformation led by Luther and Calvin was the root of modern capitalism (Fromm, 1941, 1976). The Renaissance was accompanied by high development of commercial and industrial capitalism. The French Revolution in the eighteenth century accelerated the process of liberalization and democratization.

In this new order that reached its peak in the twentieth century, the relationship between citizens and the state changed. People no longer depended on their families for survival. The state took responsibility to provide jobs and developed various institutions and services to provide for the needs of the people. Actually, the five basic needs mentioned by Maslow (biological and safety needs, and the need for belonging, esteem, and self-actualization) (Maslow, 1970) have been provided for, since this change, by the state. Self-actualization could occur in the new society. The relationship between the state and the citizens became characterized by interdependency rather than one-way authoritarianism. The institutions of the state provide jobs and serve the needs of the citizens. In return, citizens are expected to work and obey the laws of the state. Many tasks that had been the duty of the family became the duty of the state. Ensuring food, housing, education, health care, social services, and protection became the responsibility of the state. In the last few decades, as a result of increased awareness of child abuse, the state has taken over responsibility for the welfare of children. Actually, parents have ceased to be ultimately responsible for their children and can even be punished by the state if they mistreat them.

This change in the role of the state freed the familial relationship from the economic interdependence that governed it before. Family became an institution for meeting psychosocial needs more than economic ones. Familial relationships became more egalitarian and democratic in that each party is expected to recognize the needs, rights, and attitudes of others. Relationships among family members became more a matter of choice than a normative obligation.

These sociopolitical changes allowed the emergence of the individual (and the *self*) as an independent entity. Democratic values and self-actualization became very popular. These dominant and widely accepted values and norms were transformed into laws enforced by the state, rather than the family. Since then, individuals have their own rights, attitudes, needs, and choices within the limitations of the state's laws. They live according to their own personal values and attitudes. As adolescents, people can form personal rather than collective identities after exploring many options (Cote and Levine, 1988). Pluralism in social life substituted for monism, laws substituted for social norms, and state executive authority (justice and police departments) substituted for familial authority. These changes actually removed authority from the backyard of the individuals and made it invisible, which gave people an illusion of full freedom and mastery over their own destiny.

The Western dream of self-mastery falters when people realize that they are cogs in the bureaucratic machine with their thoughts, feelings, and tastes manipulated by government, industry, and by mass communication, which is controlled by those powers (Fromm, 1976).

Indeed, democratic political systems give people the feeling of sharing in the process of political decision making and in determining the destiny of the state. But within this new social structure, much of the power that affects people is still invisible. For instance, the role of big companies in people's lives, public opinions, education, and the political system is still hidden behind democratic rules. The survival of the mass media, educational institutions, sports teams, and art groups depends on financing from large corporations. Therefore, they can survive as long as they serve, or at least do not contradict, the economic interests of big companies. Independence of education, media, art, and sports is far from reality. People are exposed intensively to commercials that modify public values and opinion. Political campaigns are financed by money raised from big companies that is not without a political price. Therefore, the cultural, educational, and political life of the people is indirectly influenced, if not controlled, by the big companies. Despite this fact, people still feel that they are masters of themselves and that they share the decision-making process that determines the destiny of society.

These changes in the relationship between the citizens and the state and the performance of familial responsibilities and duties by the state have not yet occurred in the majority of the Arab countries and other South/Eastern countries. In these societies, the state does not take complete responsibility for the citizens. The family still holds responsibility for the welfare of the individual. The family and its community are still responsible for finding jobs for its members, finding housing, raising and educating the children, providing protection from enemies, and providing economic help in critical times. Because of these political/economic differences between Western countries and the South/Eastern ones, the latter still has a lifestyle that does not rely on the state's support and is far from being liberal/democratic. Westerners who disregard the political/economic differences find it difficult to understand and empathize with some of the South/Eastern values. They cannot understand that, when the state does not take responsibility for the citizens, the people will find different ways to run their lives and to survive. Two examples may help clarify this point.

In many South/Eastern countries, people used to bribe officials to get governmental services. Many Western people consider this a primitive act opposed to their values. When we realize that the governments of these countries pay officials thirty to fifty dollars a month, we can understand that the bribes are part of the way the system works. Without bribes, officials cannot support their families, people cannot get official services, and the whole system will collapse without offering any better alternative. To make it more clear, consider the waiters in Western countries who have a similar situation. In order to get good service in Western restaurants, consumers pay tips to the waiters. Tips are another kind of bribe that people need to pay, not because they are lacking values, but because the owners of the restaurants do not pay the waiters enough money to survive. Therefore, the restaurant system developed the tip as a way to offer services to the people, to allow the waiters to survive, and to maintain the system.

The other example concerns punishment as a way of socialization in the South/Eastern societies. When a South/Eastern person is physically punished by his or her family, it is considered a brutal abuse by Westerners. When we realize that the state has not substituted for the family in these countries, things may be seen differently. With the transformation of the political/economic system in the West, social norms and values were transformed into state laws. The people have authorized the justice system to judge delinquent people and the police to punish them through imprisonment, restraints, fines, or even the death penalty. Western people justify these punishments and consider this system to be the only fair one. In South/Eastern societies, people still run their lives according to norms rather than state laws. State laws cover political and economic issues that are vital for the political regime to survive rather than for the welfare of the people. Police and courts are inefficient in imposing social justice. Therefore, the authority of the family is still responsible for social justice based on norms and values. This is the legitimate authority that functions similar to the court and the police of Western countries. Putting it this way, I wonder if the judge, juries, and the police are able to be more fair than the father and the family? I wonder if prisons or death penalties are more humane than physical punishment under the family's authority?

I hope that these two examples help to clarify that there is no good culture or bad culture. Every culture has developed within certain ecological, economic, and political systems in which people have found ways to live and survive. It is unfair to judge a culture while denying the ecological and economic system in which it developed. It is unfair to judge a culture through the lens of another culture. To clarify this point to my Western students, I used to ask them to discuss in small groups what changes may happen to their lifestyle, values, and norms if they were to lose one component of the Western sociopolitical system, such as police or transportation. After a few minutes of discussion, all of the groups usually describe changes toward an authoritarian/collectivistic way of living. They realize that, without transportation, they need to live in small communities and to act as a cohesive family to survive. Without a justice system and police, they need their family to ensure safety.

In summary, changes in the role of the state have enabled the emergence of individualism in the West. Interdependence is transferred from the relationship among family members to the relationship between citizens and state (see Table 2.1). Authority has become partly invisible. Individuals earn a limited freedom in familial and interpersonal life and an illusion of sharing the political system. Most of the South/Eastern countries did not pass through these changes; therefore, they still have an authoritarian/collectivistic lifestyle.

AUTHORITARIAN/COLLECTIVISTIC ARAB CULTURE

In this section, I will describe in detail only the authoritarian/collectivistic Arab culture; this does not include, as mentioned before, all Arabs. A small portion of Arabs do not fit these characteristics, especially Arabs from the middle/upper class, educated Arabs, and inhabitants of urban areas. This portion of the population may have some liberal individualistic characteristics.

TABLE 2.1. Sociocultural Changes in the West

Change	Middle Ages	After the Nineteenth Century
Sociopolitical structure	Feudal, totalitarian Unindustrialized	Capitalism, democratic Industrialized
Individual-state relationship	Individuals serve the ruler	Interdependence
Individual-family relationship	Interdependence	Independence Personal freedom
Cultural features	Authoritarianism Collectivism	Liberalism Individualism
Smallest socio-economic unit	Family	Individual

Interdependent Familial Relationship

Despite the similarity between the state and the family in the Arabic world that was mentioned in Chapter 1, one basic difference exists. Unlike Western democratic states, Arab states still do not provide for the basic needs of their citizens. Many areas, especially rural ones, are lacking jobs, transportation, schools, health services, banks, police, and social insurance; as a result, the family still fills these needs. This may explain why the Arab family has endured over centuries despite the political changes. Individuals find jobs within the familial economy, such as working in the fields or for merchants of the family. The family is responsible for rearing and educating children and then helping new couples to build their own houses and raise their children (Al-Haj, 1989; Barakat, 1993; Haj-Yehia, 1995; Hatab and Makki, 1978; Sharabi, 1975). Food is shared in the extended family. Family, rather than the police, protect the members from any assaults. Family, rather than social insurance, help the people in any economic disaster. The role of the Arabic family is not limited to psychosocial needs but to survival ones too.

The typical traditional Arab family consists of three or more generations with siblings living side by side and sharing domestic duties and economic responsibilities. Authority in these extended households usually rests with the grandfather. The grandmother plays a central role in child care. Up until the age of weaning, the mother has the main responsibility for care, after which the responsibility is shared within the family. Grandparents, uncles, and aunts as well as parents are all responsible for child rearing and education (Al-Awad and Sonuga-Barke, 1992). Despite fast urbanization, Arabs in the cities still live in extended families. Members of nuclear families maintain physical and emotional bonds with their extended families of origin (Abdelrahman and Morgan, 1987; Al-Sabaie, 1989).

The relationship between Arab family members is still characterized by interdependence: as youngsters they depend on their parents, and when old they depend on their sons. This interdependence makes the behavior of a family member directly affect the lives of all of the family. Accomplishments of a member of the family is a success for the whole family. Failure or shameful behavior of a family member causes trouble for the whole family. Hence, the alleged right to intervene and control another member's behavior to meet collective needs, is actually represented in the collective norms and values.

External Control

Unlike governmental laws, social norms cover every area of personal life. Arab children as well as adults are guided by strict norms. External authority such as parents and teachers are the agents that ensure fulfillment of the norms. These authorities allow very little space for personal choices. Almost everything is determined a priori. The only mission left to an individual is to learn what he or she is expected to do and to adhere to the norms. People in these societies do not have many personal choices and are not involved much in decision-making processes. Norms substitute for attitudes and personal decisions. Decisions concerning clothing, leisure activities, friendship, career, marriage, housing, size of the family, and ways of raising children are not personal ones.

Social rules cover everyday situations. Even the way of talking is highly determined. One has to choose words according to the other speaker's age, sex, and social status. In traditional Arab regions, even a greeting has its own rules; one should ask about the health of every member of the family, naming males and referring to females indirectly (Al-Sabaie, 1989; Chaleby, 1987).

To ensure control over personal behavior, secrets or privacy are not welcome in the Arabic family (Al-Sabaie, 1989). The social authority is hierarchical, within which the right to know and intervene is one-directional. Parents and elders of the family have this right while children and youngsters do not. Men have the right to control and know everything about women in the family, while women do not have this right to know about the men.

Although there are no secrets within the family, the family's affairs should be kept from strangers (Meleis and La Fever, 1984). To disclose family secrets to a stranger is considered a betrayal. Appearance to the outside world is very important for the esteem and honor of Arabs. Much effort is made to save face and to do what is expected at the expense of genuineness and fulfilling personal needs.

Gender Relationship

In general, Arabic women are controlled by men, primarily the father and older brothers. The adolescent female can expect increasingly watchful sanctions on her behavior as well as a protective attitude toward her. To break social rules is to risk alienation from the family and punishment for the female and confusion and insecurity for the male (Timimi, 1995). In rural regions, girls are brought up to accept and withstand frustration, are given little or no education, and express few opinions during decision making. In urban regions, primarily among new generations, there is a trend to terminate the suppression of women and the limitations on the education of girls (El-Islam, 1982), although only a small portion of Arabs in urban regions conduct an egalitarian style of life.

Interpersonal relationships are typically between persons of the same gender. Women socialize with women, and men with men. Relations between the sexes are strictly controlled. Dating between the two sexes is unacceptable. Premarital sexual relationships are absolutely prohibited. Much of the honor of the family depends on the modesty of women's behavior. Premarital sexual relationships and infidelity of women disturbs the so-called "honor of the family," *Sharaf el a'aela*. The family punishes every woman or girl that behaves in an unacceptable manner. In some rural Arab communities, the family may kill a woman who participates in sexual affairs that tarnish its reputation.

Marriage is almost totally a familial issue rather than a personal one. The opinion of the family about the bride or the bridegroom is central. Marriage that is not welcomed by one of the families will almost certainly lead to cancellation. Besides the typical marriage that is preceded by a period of courtship, several different kinds of marriage exist in Arab countries: arranged marriage, cousin marriage, forced marriage, and marriage of couples who have not met before consummation. Although polygamy is still sanctioned in many Arab countries, only a small percentage of marriages are polygamous (Al-Sabaie, 1989). In some extremely traditional communities, marriage may take place even without asking the opinion of the bride or the bridegroom.

In many traditional rural regions, the life of women is harshly constrained. They are expected to play a very strict role during their life; their destiny is to be married and to bear children. They are repeatedly reminded that woman is inferior to man and subject to his will (Al-Khani et al., 1986; Racy, 1980). Divorce is an ever-present possibility. Women who fail to bear children are almost like women who are sterile; both are likely to be replaced by other more favored wives. These conditions cause women to suffer continuous stress related to neglect by the husband, lack of money, social oppression, and conflicts with the institutional injustices (Racy, 1980).

Social Relationships

Social relationships are not a matter of choice either. Unlike Western society, an Arab is not free to choose his or her in-group. Extended family members, neighbors, and inhabitants of small villages are expected to have close relationships. The feeling of duty, *wajib*, motivates people to visit each other and help in times of crisis. Visits on some occasions are mandatory, such as marriage, the birth of a child, times of sickness, death, and before and after long travel. If one chooses not to meet this duty, *wajib*, he or she may be excluded from the community and may endanger the vital social and economic support that the family provides.

The need for affiliation is very central in Arab life. They give friendship high priority over schedules, work, and deadlines. They engage in daily family gatherings and visits. Men gather outside the home in a special house called *Diwan* or *Majlis,* or in cafés. Women have their gatherings in the home, especially during the daytime, before their husbands return from work (Meleis, 1981). Social relationships are more familial than personal. A person is expected to be a friend of his or her family's friends. A visit to an Arabic friend may turn into a visit to the whole family.

Norms and Values

Norms and values usually emerge to meet collective needs in certain socioeconomic circumstances. They serve to maintain the status quo and prevent change. Arabic hospitality is one example: Because many areas in Arab countries are lacking public transportation, restaurants, and hotels, Arab families open their homes for relatives and friends who travel from far away. Hence, hospitality is valued in Arabic culture, especially by nomad Arabs who inhabit the desert because it serves a basic need of the society. Hospitality is still maintained even in developed places and cities in which transportation, restaurants, and hotels exist. Food still plays a central role in the lives of Arabs. It is not only a matter of nutrition but is also a way to express feelings and attitudes. Love, care, and respect are expressed by providing food or invitations to meals (Meleis, 1981). Parents consider providing meals their major role. When visiting an Arab family, providing food is the way the family expresses its acceptance and respect toward the guests. Reluctance to eat may be considered an insult. Poor Arab families may provide food for guests even though they are not able to feed their own children.

Values of sharing are very common among extended family members and neighbors. They may share their harvest and home products. Men of the family and neighborhood share in building a house or in harvesting the fields for one family member. Women of the neighborhood work hard as a group to prepare feast meals when marriages take place. Family members are enlisted to rescue any one of them who is mired in economic or social problems. They are persuaded to protect family members from any enemy that threatens them.

Sacrifice is a central value in education. Parents encourage their children to sacrifice themselves for other family members. They act as role models for their children in this regard. Good parents are those who sacrifice everything for the good of their children.

Sharing and sacrifices seem to contradict authoritarianism. In fact, these two values exist because of obedience to social norms rather than empathizing with personal needs. Sometimes sharing and sacrifices occur as *wajib* (duty), despite the wishes of the individual. Sharing harvest with cousins, for instance, may happen not because of concern for the cousins and not because they are in need, but because people should comply to that norm that has enabled Arabs to survive.

Collective Identity

Arabs adopt collective identity. The self is an appendage of the familial identity. The family occupies a significant space in personal identity. Self-esteem depends on the family name and status more than on personal accomplishment. From the other side, the family reputation depends on the behavior of its members. When an Arab is asked to introduce himself or herself, the family will occupy a big part of the introduction, while the individual will undermine personal achievements. The name of the family contributes a lot to the reputation of the children. Children are considered an asset in the Arabic family. Their number, especially males, gives the parents pride. More children mean more hands for work, income, security, protection, and status. Fathers and mothers are proud to be called father of—"*abu* [first son's name]" or mother of—"*um* [first son's name]." Actually using a personal name when addressing a married person is considered insulting.

Harmony and integrity of the Arab family are much more important than confrontation. Saving the face of the family takes priority over fulfilling personal needs or wishes. The value of the family's integrity exceeds many other values. Moral values are submitted to and ruled by this primary value. To support the attitude of the family is more important than supporting abstract justice. In principle, family members should support other family members against their enemy regardless of the issue in conflict. One Arabic proverb says *Ana wa'khoy a'la ebin a'mi, wa'na wa'bin a'mi a'la elg'arib,* which means "I should be with my brother against my cousin, and with my cousin against the stranger." Accordingly, attitudes are ruled by familial relationships rather than morals. Social and political attitudes of individuals are hardly differentiated from those of the family. Patterns of vote in political campaigns among Palestinian Arabs in Israel are familial (Al-Haj, 1989).

In Arab collectivistic families, it is easy to identify differences in individual roles, but it is more difficult to identify individual characters or selves. To illustrate the differences between a collective family and an individualistic one, one of my doctoral students at Nova Southeastern University videotaped, as part of a course assignment, two families during dinnertime, one Hispanic family from Peru, and the other American. Despite the thousands of miles between Peru and the Middle East, I could not help but see the similarity between the Peruvian family and the Arabic family when the tape was presented in the class. The following observations were discussed in class.

> The Hispanic family was composed of grandparents, parents, and six children ranging in age from early childhood to late adolescence. Females (grandmother, mother, daughters) shared the preparation of dinner, while males sat talking. When dinner started, a tape of Hispanic music played loudly, and all members of the family were preoccupied with eating and listening to the music. The mother and grandmother fed and took care of the young children. They hardly sat for minutes to eat themselves. During the dinner, only a few sentences were spoken. The American family, on the other hand, was composed of parents and a teenage boy and girl. The wife and the husband prepared the table, while the boy and the girl were quarreling and arguing. During dinner, the mother and the daughter did not stop arguing about school, clothing, and weekend plans. Each side tried to convince the other of her point of view. The father and the son acted more like observers, and occasionally they expressed their opinions.

The immediate impression, when students watched the video, was that the Hispanic family is more close, cohesive, loving, and warm. This is true, but this unity was only around an event; all shared in the meal and music. In terms of personal conversation that involved an individual's self, feeling, opinions, or experience, the Hispanic family was far from being close. It reminded me of many Arab family meetings in which all of the family are together sharing a meal and talking about anything but personal feelings or experiences. Within this collective united family, the person or the self was absent. On the other hand, the American family did not seem united like the Hispanic one, but undoubtedly, the relations were much more personal and close. Every member contributed his or her self (experience, feeling, opinions) to the relationship. Noticeably, the conversation in this family included "I," "I am," and "you" many times, suggesting a direct personal conversation.

Regional Identification

In addition to the special relationship with the family, Arabs in the countryside have a distinctive relationship with the land. Typically, they are rooted in their villages. Mobility is uncommon unless a special necessity, such as the need to make a living, causes some people to move away from the village of origin. In the last few decades, the urbanization process has been taking place in the Arab world (Barakat, 1993). But the relationship with the village of origin remains physically and emotionally active. Many Arab families that move to new places become known by the name of the village or town of origin. Unlike the West, where interpersonal relationships or career may move a person from one state to another, interpersonal relationships and career in Arab society are determined by family affiliation and location. Leaving the village may happen only when life there has ceased to be bearable.

Normative Way of Thinking

In an authoritarian collectivistic society, things are determined by external authorities according to the norms of the community. Therefore, pluralism is very limited, and people think, feel, and behave almost in a standard way. Being smart or wise in this kind of society is to be aware of the social values and norms, to differentiate clearly between good and bad according to these values, to know how to control the self and delay gratification, and to gain knowledge about tradition and wise men. Mind, *a'ql* in Arabic, means control, and it has to do more with values than thinking. This concept of wisdom in Arabic society is far removed from the Western concept that is associated with reasoning, problem solving, and creative ways of thinking.

The major ways of socialization used by teachers and parents are lecturing, rote learning, and punishments. Arguing or debating are not encouraged, and may even be punished. In such an educational system, children memorize what they are to learn and may pass exams, but the content does not become an active part of their own individual system of thoughts. They still are unable to enrich their thoughts and use this knowledge to be creative. A well-educated child is an obedient, conformist one. Many parents and teachers consider a child impertinent if he or she argues, is curious, or creative. Children are not encouraged to develop their own values, thoughts, or opinions; they are expected to adopt their families'.

Repression of Authentic Feelings and Thoughts

To survive in an authoritarian collectivistic society, people learn to repress their personal needs and emotions. They are used to being detached from their internal feelings and, instead, focus on external demands and expectations. Social awareness substitutes for self-awareness. Physical symptoms of personal distress are very common among Arabs (Dwairy, 1997b; Gorkin, Masalha, and Yatziv, 1985; Racy, 1980). Implications of repression for mental health will be addressed later in Chapters 4 and 5.

Because of social sanctions, Arabs typically avoid overt emotional expression. They express what others expect them to express. Genuine feelings and attitudes are displaced or expressed privately, away from the public eye. Two main social coping techniques are common in Arabic society: *Mosayara* (to please others) and *Istig'aba* (to express one's needs or attitudes privately to avoid social sanctions). These two coping skills are vital for adaptation in an authoritarian collectivistic society and are important components of the Arab personality that will be discussed in Chapter 4.

In some Arab societies, women are not free to move outside their homes without an escort or observer. In these societies, the use of

Istig'aba is almost impossible or costs them severe punishment. Therefore, *Mosayara,* at the expense of neglecting the self, is the only option for women's adaptation.

External Locus of Control

According to Islamic beliefs, things happen according to the will of God; therefore, humans are helpless in the face of what is written, *maktoob*. These beliefs foster helplessness and weaken individual responsibility (Al-Khani et al., 1986; Bazzoui, 1970). In addition, authoritarian society renders the individual powerless. Therefore, it is not surprising that people who have been raised in an authoritarian society become passive, attributing change to external factors such as others, society, state, or God. Arabs, in general, do not feel capable of changing their lives. They blame external factors for their problems and deny their personal contribution. In a liberal individualistic society, in which people are more or less masters of themselves and their destiny, this external locus of control may be considered a kind of projection. But in a society such as the Arabic one, people are really not their own masters, and things are determined by external authority. Therefore, external locus of control describes the Arab social reality, rather than a person's psychological projection. It is a cultural characteristic that represents good reality testing rather than detachment from reality or flight from responsibility. If an Arab girl says, "My family prevents me from higher education," "they force me into this marriage," or "they destroy my life," she describes real, strict restraints of the family that made her helpless.

Two Choices: Conformism versus Self

Obviously, with the lack of governmental social services, familial support is vital for people to survive in Arab countries. In fact, four of the five basic human needs that Maslow mentioned in his five-step hierarchy (biological, safety, belonging, and esteem) are provided by the Arab family. Unfortunately, in an authoritarian collectivistic society, familial support is not unconditional. The family provides its support with three conditions: (1) to control the sexual drives and limit sexual behaviors to marriage; (2) to express respect and love for the familial authority and prohibit expressions of anger or hatred toward family members in general and toward parents specifically; (3) to relinquish self-actualization (the fifth need in Maslow's hierarchy) and fulfill the social norms that the family adopts (Dwairy, 1997a).

Actually, Arab society provides every person with two choices (Dwairy and Van Sickle, 1996):

1. *Conformist choice* is that in which a person adheres to the family's rules and values, and enjoys the family support that helps to fulfill the first four basic needs of Maslow but at the expense of the fifth need, self-actualization. According to this choice, one is not free to express one's feelings and ideas. A special restriction surrounds the expression of negative emotions toward parents and the expression of sexual drives before or outside of marriage.
2. *"Self" choice* is that in which a person defends the right to be himself or herself, which may conflict with the norms. In this case, familial support may be endangered and withdrawn, and the person will be excluded from familial life. In some cases, when the needs of the self conflict with essential values, the person may be physically punished.

Conformist Majority

Because conditional support is given from early childhood, typically, decisions about the two choices are made unconsciously in early stages of development, when the child is still helpless and before the ability to make decisions is acquired. Therefore, the majority of Arabs adopt the conformist choice. Only a few people who are raised in unusual circumstances may adopt the "self" choice, such as those who have been exposed to democratic values and empowerment by their parents or teachers. Intensive exposure to Western society usually pushes people toward the "self" choice.

In many strict Arabic societies, as in Saudi Arabia and Kuwait, individuals, especially women, are rendered completely powerless. They have almost no control over their lives. Women are physically controlled inside their homes and other places as well. Sanctions against disobedient women often extend beyond social isolation and termination of familial support. They may face home imprisonment and physical beatings. If they behave in a way that threatens the so-called "honor of the family," their lives may be threatened too. In these societies, women actually do not have the two choices mentioned (conformist or self), because the self choice is almost fatal.

Conformism and dependency of Arabs are frequently misinterpreted by Westerners as a sort of immaturity. In a society that enables people to be independent, dependent people are reasonably considered immature. When the society does not encourage independence and conditions the support of conformism, conformity and dependency are very natural results. They are a mature way to adapt and survive in this social system.

Approach to Nature and Society

Three main epistemological approaches can be identified in Arabic cultural history: *Sunnism, Shi'ism* (or *Sufism*), and the logical scientific approach. Among these approaches, *Sunnism* and *Shi'ism* are the most dominant ways of explaining how Arabs perceive and deal with reality. Even though many Arab countries have started to be industrialized and technology based on science has become a part of many areas of life, *Sunnism* and *Shi'ism* are still the dominant approaches that help explain personal and social behavior in the Arab world.

In fact, *Sunnism* and *Shi'ism* are religious streams within Islam. Considering the fact that Islam is not solely a spiritual issue but also a way of life and law, *Shari'a*, the two approaches have to do with daily life, ways of thinking, and values. Unlike the scientific, Aristotelian approach, both *Sunnism* and *Shi'ism* deny the laws of nature. They claim that the truth is found in religion. *Sunnis* claim that the truth is found in the *Qura'an* and *H'adith* (the Holy Book and the sayings of the Prophet Muhammad). *Shi'ists* deny reasoning and logic and claim that truth can be reached by *Sufic* meditation that brings the individual closer to God, the real reality. The religious leader in *Shi'ism* is the *Imam,* who is able to reach the truth by means of *Sufic* prayers. So, according to both approaches, truth is not in nature or objective reality, but in the *Qura'an* and the *H'adith* according to *Sunnism,* and in the *Imam* according to *Shi'ism.*

These two approaches actually discourage any interest in scientific research in nature or society. The only thing people should do to understand the world and know how to behave is to understand and follow what was written literally according to *Sunnism*, or to follow the *Imam*'s guidance according to *Shi'ism*. To put it another way, the truth is found in the words of an authority rather than objective reality or nature. Understanding what is written substitutes for the senses and reasoning. These philosophical approaches are in harmony with the authoritarian collectivism that dominates social life and education.

Much of the problem-solving techniques of Arabs rely on one of the *Sunnist* principles called *Q'ias*, which means to compare a new situation for which one needs an answer to a similar one for which there is an answer in the *Qura'an* and *H'adith*. Then, apply what was written. If one does not find a solution in the written references, he or she may adopt another technique called *Ijmaa'* or consensus of the religious authority. Again, we can see how much this epistemology fits authoritarian collectivism by discouraging personal opinion and creative thinking.

Salafeya (to rely on ancestors' points of view) is considered a major source of knowledge in Arabic culture. It is directives from the past, rather than present experience, that should help people make decisions and judge right from wrong. Therefore, being aware of the cultural heritage is more than a factor that contributes to the cultural identity for Arabs. It is a major source of guidance in daily life. Hence, it is safe to say that the past occupies a significant part of the Arab's experience in the present.

Unlike Western philosophy, which differentiates between objective reality and subjective experience, Arabic philosophy, in general, considers beliefs as reality. For many Arabs, visions, dreams, possessions, or other states of consciousness are real. Evil eyes, for them, are not delusions but are real and explain many problematic changes in people's lives. These cultural characteristics should not be misinterpreted as pathological delusions.

Arabs tend to describe their experiences in a metaphoric way. As a result, Arabic literature is rich in metaphors that act as modifiers of an Arab's thoughts and guidance for behavior. For many Arabs, metaphors may be more powerful than evidence for persuasion.

Sometimes metaphoric descriptions of a person's experience sound unclear or psychotic for a person who is not aware of the role of metaphors in Arab life. The role of fantasies and metaphors in psychopathology and treatment will be discussed later in Chapter 9.

One should keep in mind the diversity among Arabs (traditional, bicultural, Westernized) to realize that not all Arabs adopt a *Sunnist* or *Shi'ist* way of thinking. The vast majority have been affected, in one way or another, by these approaches but still are open to a scientific, Aristotelian approach. On the other hand, many traditional Arab scholars attribute the bad socioeconomic situation to the abandonment of the Islamic tradition and call people back to their roots, *Sunnism* and *Shi'ism,* and to be cautious about the Western way of thinking and living. The historical role that the West played in the stagnation of Arabs and the occupation and exploitation of their countries makes caution about the West look reasonable.

SUMMARY

Individualism-collectivism and authority-ruled constitute a two-dimensional field in which the Arab cultural identity varies. Because the Arab states do not provide for the basic needs of citizens, the family is still the institution that ensures these needs. Interdependence rather than independence characterizes relationships among family members. The vast majority of Arabs live in an authoritarian collectivism and behave according to social values and norms rather than personal opinion or decision. The self is not differentiated from the familial collective identity. *Mosayara* (to please others), sharing, and hospitality are highly valued in Arabic society. Listening to authority and understanding holy written references (*Qura'an* and *H'adith)* are the main epistemological approaches to gaining knowledge and reaching the truth.

Chapter 3

Socialization in Arabic Families and Schools

In the previous chapters, I explained the historical and socioeconomic roots of authoritarianism and collectivism in Arab society. On the macro level, socioeconomic interdependence may explain the submission of Arabs. Arab children learn to give up the self and meet certain norms and expectations because the survival of an individual in Arabic society depends on the vital support that the family provides. On the micro level, we still need to understand how this happens. How do parents and educators accomplish this goal? What are the methods that parents and teachers endorse to make children adhere to their expectations and rules?

To study the socialization process in an authoritarian collectivistic society, two empirical studies about socialization in Arabic homes and schools are presented. These two studies were conducted among Palestinian Arabs in Israel in the early 1990s.

PARENTAL METHODS OF SOCIALIZATION

The role of parents in the socialization process is important in any society. It is much more important in Arab society than in most because they are able to maintain control over external effects with almost no intervention by state regulations. Parents are able to prevent schooling of their children, control children's mobility when necessary, and control interpersonal relationships and the influence of peers. To study Arab parental methods, 96 mothers and 103 fathers were interviewed and asked to answer questions concerning their attitudes and methods of socialization. The mean age was 40.5 years. Average length of education was 10.4 years. Fifty-five percent of them were middle-class parents, 20 percent were lower class, and 25 percent were upper class.

Instrument Description

A questionnaire was used to inquire about the way parents deal with problematic behaviors. The questionnaire was administered by trained interviewers. It included four parts:

1. *Personal information:* This includes gender, age, occupation, education, economic status, and family members.
2. *Level of intolerance:* In this section, parents made a list of behaviors that may occur with their children and were asked to rate their level of intolerance on a 5-point scale that ranges from "I feel angry and intervene in all ways to change the behavior = 5" to "I accept and do not intervene = 1." To allow parents to tell us their responses to what they consider problems, behaviors offered were defined in abstract terms rather than objective concrete ones (e.g., "careless hygiene" or "violation of rules"). Therefore, the responses were to behaviors that crossed the limits that each parent defined for the behavior in question.
3. *Methods of socialization* (open-ended questions): In this section, parents were asked, "What will you do if your child (or adolescent) displays one of the intolerable behaviors?" After getting the parents' response, they were then asked, "And what will you do if your child proceeded in his or her way, denying your directions?" The second question helped to find out if there is a point at which parents would withdraw and let their children decide for themselves or learn from the natural consequences.
4. *Rating the means of socialization:* After the parents reported about their methods in open-ended questions, fifteen common methods were offered. Parents were asked to rate the frequency they use each of them on a 5-level scale (5 = always, 1 = rarely).

Parents' responses were taken separately for boys versus girls and for children versus adolescents.

Results

Level of Intolerance

The mean score of intolerance toward girls was 4.12, which was significantly higher than that toward boys, 3.97 (Table 3.1). No significant difference was found between fathers and mothers.

Without exception in all of the problems offered, parents show high levels of intolerance and gave rankings above 3 (Table 3.2). The highest intolerance (above 4) was toward careless hygiene, carelessness about school responsibilities, shyness and withdrawal, inappropriate social behavior, disregard of responsibilities, lying, dropping out of school, choosing inappropriate friends, violation of parents' rules in a social setting, and inappropriate behavior at a wedding. Intolerance was significantly higher toward girls in inappropriate choice of clothes, profession, and spouse, disregard of directives, violation of rules, and inappropriate behavior in social settings such as visits or weddings. No significant differences were found between fathers and mothers or between children and adolescents.

Methods of Socialization

When parents were asked to rate how often they use each of the 15 common means of socialization, the highest ratings (above 3) were given to explanation, verbal encouragement, redirection, positive promises, rewards, contracts, and allowing natural consequences. They denied the use of beating, time outs, and belittling (Table 3.3).

TABLE 3.1. Mean of Intolerance of Mothers and Fathers Toward Boys and Girls

	Boys			Girls			
	M	SD	n	M	SD	n	*p*
Mothers	3.97	0.56	98	4.09	0.63	98	.001
Fathers	3.96	0.48	103	4.16	0.51	103	.0001
Both	3.97	0.52	201	4.12	0.57	201	.0001

TABLE 3.2. Mean of Parents' Intolerance Toward Boys and Girls

Problem	Boys	Girls	*p*
Careless hygiene	4.47	4.59	n.s.*
Siblings fighting	3.93	4.03	n.s.
Carelessness about school responsibilities	4.61	4.58	n.s.
Disruptive behavior	3.69	3.86	n.s.
Shyness and withdrawal	4.10	4.10	n.s.
Fears and phobias	3.87	3.88	n.s.
Destructive behavior toward property	3.64	3.67	n.s.
Inappropriate social behavior	4.49	4.48	n.s.
Disregard of responsibilities	4.35	4.39	n.s.
Lying	4.59	4.66	n.s.
Slowness	3.60	3.58	n.s.
Forgetfulness	3.31	3.44	n.s.
Drop out of school	4.74	4.61	n.s.
Inappropriate leisure activities	3.89	4.01	n.s.
Inappropriate hobbies	3.34	3.54	n.s.
Choosing inappropriate clothes	3.17	3.75	.0001
Choosing inappropriate friends	4.39	4.53	n.s.
Choosing inappropriate profession	3.42	3.90	.0003
Choosing inappropriate spouse	3.46	4.04	.0001
Disregard of directives in a social setting	3.86	4.21	.0009
Violation of rules in a social setting	4.02	4.27	.0135
Inappropriate behavior at a wedding	4.33	4.57	.0090

*n.s. = not significant, $p < .05$

A 2 x 2 x 2 variance analysis of socialization methods according to parents' gender and children's gender and age revealed some differences between fathers and mothers, as well as differences between parents' methods toward children and adolescents. Fathers used more explanations, positive promises, and rewards, while mothers were more likely to yell and allow natural consequences (Tables 3.3 and 3.4).

It seems that parents apply socialization means according to the age of the children. The use of spankings, beatings, time outs, threats, negative punishments, rewards, and positive promises is more common with children than with adolescents, while the use of contracts is more common with adolescents. No significant differences were found between the methods of socialization used for boys and girls. Additionally, no significant interaction was found between parents' gender and children's gender and age (Tables 3.3 and 3.4).

TABLE 3.3. Mean and F Values of Variance Analysis for Socialization Methods According to Parents' Sex, Children's Sex, and Age

			F		
Method	**Mean**	**df**	**F/M**	**B/G**	**CH/AD**
Explanation	4.71	5	4.39*	0.05	0.76
Verbal encouragement	4.67	5	0.44	0.40	1.87
Redirection	4.13	5	1.41	1.76	1.20
Positive promises	3.83	5	5.22*	0.00	5.66**
Rewards	3.59	5	5.18*	0.71	6.85**
Contracts	3.43	5	1.05	0.90	3.62*
Allowing natural consequences	3.06	5	7.67**	3.51	1.37
Moralization and shame	2.93	5	0.18	2.99	1.05
Negative punishment	2.80	5	2.01	0.06	4.56*
Threats	2.50	5	0.01	0.15	9.00**
Yelling	2.35	5	6.64**	1.91	0.40
Spanking	1.67	5	1.98	0.79	40.36**
Belittling and insulting	1.25	5	0.76	0.41	0.14
Time out (isolation)	1.25	5	2.17	0.46	11.96**
Beatings	1.08	5	1.88	0.35	4.08*

$^{*}p < .05$ $^{**}p < .01$
F = Mothers; M = Fathers; B = Boys; G = Girls; CH = Children;
AD = Adolescents.

TABLE 3.4. The Extent of Using Different Methods of Socialization by Mothers and Fathers Toward Children and Adolescents

Method	**Mothers**	**Fathers**	***p***	**CH**	**AD**	***p***
Explanation	4.62	4.80	.036	4.68	4.75	n.s.
Verbal encouragement	4.64	4.70	n.s.*	4.72	4.61	n.s.
Redirection	4.21	4.05	n.s.	4.06	4.21	n.s.
Positive promises	3.61	4.04	.024	4.02	3.58	.020
Rewards	3.39	3.79	.025	3.79	3.33	.012
Contracts	3.54	3.33	n.s.	3.26	3.65	.057
Allowing natural consequences	3.33	2.81	.006	2.96	3.18	n.s.
Moralization and shame	2.97	2.88	n.s.	3.02	2.81	n.s.
Negative punishment	2.65	2.93	n.s.	2.98	2.56	.035
Threats	2.49	2.50	n.s.	2.76	2.17	.002
Yelling	2.57	2.15	.010	2.40	2.29	n.s.
Spanking	1.76	1.59	n.s.	2.00	1.26	.000
Belittling and insulting	1.21	1.29	n.s.	1.27	1.24	n.s.
Time out (isolation)	1.17	1.32	n.s.	1.40	1.06	.000
Beatings	1.05	1.11	n.s.	1.12	1.03	.037

*n.s. = not significant, $p < .05$

Factor analysis with orthogonal transformation revealed five main methods for socialization: behavioral techniques, punishments, acceptance and regard, explanation and moralization, and oppression (Table 3.5).

When parents were asked open-ended questions about the methods they use when their children display one of the behaviors that they do not tolerate, their responses were similar to those methods they rated high. Without exception, the parents stated that they will use verbal methods to direct or explain.

When they were asked, "And what would you do if your child continued to deny your directions?" 88.8 percent of parents reported that they will use *any means* to make the child stop. Their responses

TABLE 3.5. Factor Analysis of Socialization Methods: Orthogonal Transformation

Factor	**Eigen-value**	**% Variance**	**Methods**	β
Behavioral techniques	3.353971	22.36	Rewards	.81
			Positive promises	.86
			Negative punishment	.62
			Contracts	.47
			Threats	.41
Punishments	2.011812	13.41	Threats	.60
			Time out (isolation)	.70
			Spanking	.79
			Beatings	.50
			Yelling	.40
Acceptance and regard	1.392852	9.29	Natural consequences	.76
			Redirection	.73
			Contracts	.52
Explanation/ moralization	1.198428	7.99	Explanation	.65
			Moralization/shaming	.65
			Verbal encouragement	.63
			Redirection	.32
Oppression	1.089777	7.27	Yelling	.44
			Belittling/insulting	.74
			Beatings	.34

were very consistent, without differences between fathers or mothers, girls or boys, children or adolescents. The typical stages start with explanation, and, if that is not effective, they yell and shame, then threaten, then punish. Many of them responded by saying "there is nothing like this [disobedience]" or "he should" or "I will oblige her in any way." Some of them were more rude and stated, "I will use any means; I will kill her" or "I will smash his head" or "I will break his teeth."

Unlike the ratings that parents gave to the methods in the closed questions, punishments were more common methods in cases of disobedience than they reported in the open-ended questions (Table 3.6). While the parents' ratings of negative punishments, beatings, and yelling were 2.80, 1.08, and 2.35 respectively, these methods became very common when the parents' authority was challenged.

Discussion

Regardless of the behavior, Arab parents do not tolerate deviation from their expectations. To all of the behaviors offered in the questionnaire, they reported an intolerance level above 3, which was the midpoint of intolerance. Their intolerance was extremely high (between 4 and 5) toward behaviors that related to school and other responsibilities, social behaviors and appearance, and other behaviors that challenge parents' authority such as lying. Intolerance was higher toward girls, especially concerning appearance and social behavior. Both fathers and mothers displayed high levels of intolerance toward children and adolescents.

TABLE 3.6. Percentage of Parents Who Reported Using Each Method in Cases of Disobedience

Method	%
Punishments	60.2
Beatings	54.1
Yelling	25.5
Complain to the father*	28.7
Seek counseling	15.3
Rejection	14.3

*Exclusively a mother's method.

The most common methods for socialization reported by parents were positive ones, such as explanation, encouragement, redirection, promises, and rewards. The application of beatings and other aversive methods was very rare (Tables 3.3 and 3.4). Fathers seem to be more supportive, explaining to and rewarding their children, while mothers yell and allow natural consequences more frequently. Although the level of intolerance remained high in adolescence, many of the punitive methods decreased in adolescence, as well as the use of rewards and promises. Contracts that define rights and responsibilities are applied more often in adolescence.

Factor analysis revealed five general methods: behavioral techniques, punishments, acceptance and regard, explanation and moralization, and oppression. Behavioral techniques and punishments were the most distinct methods used among Arab parents. Acceptance and regard, as well as explanation and moralization, were less distinct and explained only 17.28 percent of the variance (Table 3.5). It seems that parents who use the last two methods are using other punitive methods that made these two methods less distinctive. Oppression methods are not distinctive either, which suggests that yelling, belittling, insulting, and beating are used in combination with other methods.

The vast majority of parents reported that they will use *any method* to make their children adhere to their authority (Table 3.6). It seems that Arab parents have two "drawer plans" to cope with children's unacceptable behavior. Verbal explanation is used for normal situations and punishments for disobedience. As long as children comply with the parents, parents apply explanation, encouragement, redirection, rewards, and other positive methods and avoid punitive methods. When a child disregards the parents' directives, punishments including beatings are used. Only 11.2 percent of the parents reported not turning to punishments when verbal explanations proved inefficient.

Parents did not consider the importance of the behavior when they resorted to punishments. It seems that disregarding parental authority is the most severe "felony" regardless of the type of behavior displayed. Further discussion will come after presenting the socialization methods used in Arabic schools.

VIOLENT BEHAVIOR IN ARAB SCHOOLS

After family, school is the second institution that modifies child personality and behavior. In order to learn about students' experience in Arab schools and the methods they are exposed to, 1,263 Arab students, 11 to 15 years old (717 girls and 546 boys), completed a questionnaire addressing teachers' methods of modifying student behavior, amount of aggressive behavior at school, and the way teachers and students handle these behaviors.*

Instrument Description

The questionnaire included two parts, each of which has three sections.

1. *Rating questions:* In three sections of the questionnaire, students were asked to rate the prevalence of certain behaviors on a 6-point scale. 1 = does not happen, 2 = happens every number of weeks, 3 = happens weekly, 4 = happens every number of days, 5 = happens daily, and 6 = happens every class. Section 1 included students' violent behavior toward other students. Section 2 included students' violent behavior toward teachers or school property. Section 3 included teachers' methods of dealing with problems.
2. *Open-ended questions:* In these three sections, students responded about behaviors that bothered the teachers, other students, or themselves and about the ways each reacted to these behaviors. Section 4 included students' behaviors that bother the teacher and how he or she reacts. Section 5 included teachers' behaviors that bother the student and how he or she reacts. Section 6 included other students' behaviors that bother the student and how he or she reacts.

---

*This research has been conducted by The Arab Mental Health Professionals in Israel. Thanks to the research team members, Faten Nahas Kamel (Coordinator), Dr. Hala Hazan, and Hanan Geraisy. Special thanks to Samia Jobran, who assisted in data analysis.

Results

As a starting point, we considered violent behavior that happens at least once a week (from level 3, weekly, to level 6, every class) as highly prevalent. The percentage of students that reported this high prevalence of violence toward teachers, as well as other students, was very high. Between 32.6 percent and 82.2 percent of the students reported that violent behaviors by students toward other students occurred at least once a week. Figure 3.1 shows that 82.2 percent of the students reported a high prevalence of yelling and screaming between students, and 57.9 percent reported beatings between students. When the kinds of beatings were specified, 24.3 percent of the subjects reported beatings that included an instrument like a stick or stone.

Students displayed violent behavior toward teachers and school property as well. The percentage of subjects who reported a high prevalence (at least once a week) of students' verbal violence

FIGURE 3.1. Percentage of Students Who Reported Students' Violence Toward Students

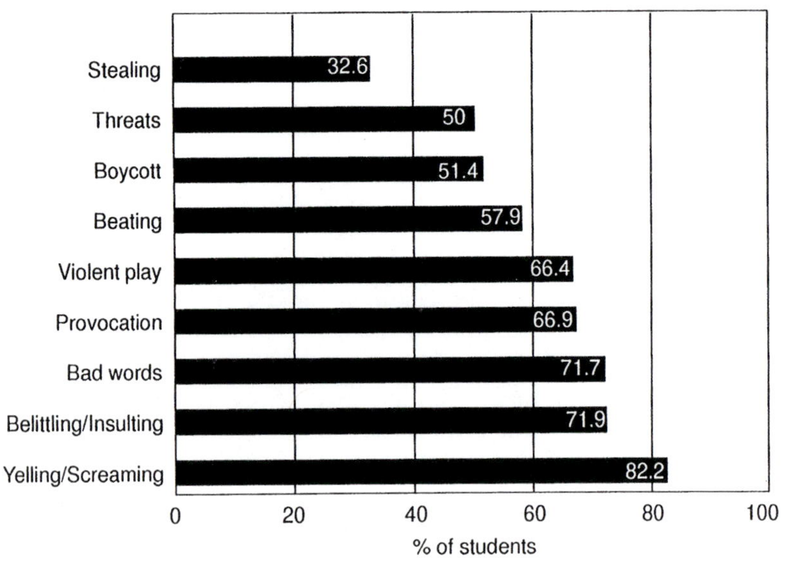

toward teachers was 44.1; vandalism, 35.2; stealing school property, 15.5; and physical violence toward teachers, 7.7.

It seems that teachers behave inconsistently toward students. Students reported a high prevalence of both positive and negative teachers' behaviors. For instance, 83.5 percent of the subjects reported encouraging behavior at least once a week, while 71.8 percent reported yelling and screaming (Figures 3.2 and 3.3).

Figure 3.4 shows the percentage of subjects who reported teachers' positive behaviors happening at least once a week. On the other hand, Figure 3.5 shows that teachers' negative behaviors are also frequent. A high prevalence of yelling was reported by 71.8 percent of the subjects, 65.4 percent reported removal from class, 60.2 percent moralization and shaming, 49.9 percent using bad words, 45.1 percent beating, and many other negative behaviors, such as standing in the corner, suspension, and detention.

When subjects were asked, in Section 4, about student behavior that bothered the teachers, 86.7 percent of them reported student violation of teacher orders. Only 45.3 percent of them reported problems that related to the learning process, 37.5 percent reported verbal violence, 23 percent violent behavior, 8 percent immoral behavior, and 7.6 percent vandalism. It appears that violation of orders bothers teachers much more than any of the other behaviors.

FIGURE 3.2. Frequency of Teachers' Encouragement of Students

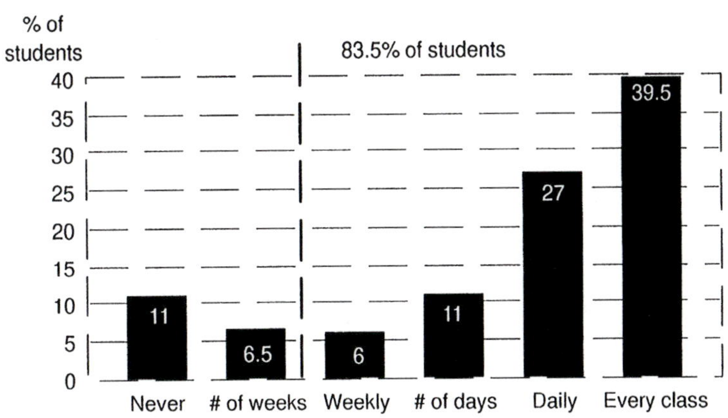

FIGURE 3.3. Frequency of Teachers' Yelling and Screaming at Students

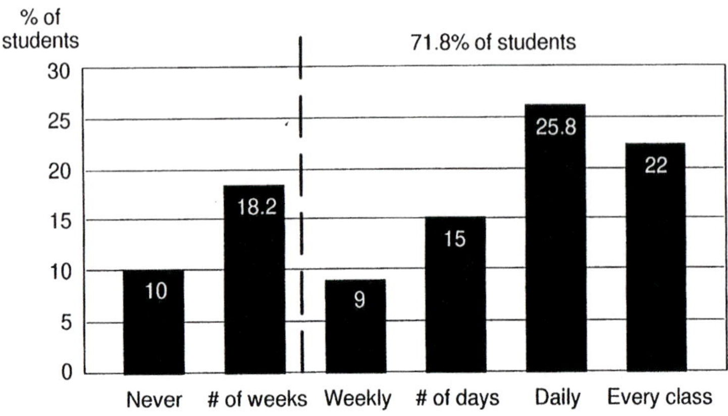

FIGURE 3.4. Percentage of Students Who Reported Teachers' Positive Behavior

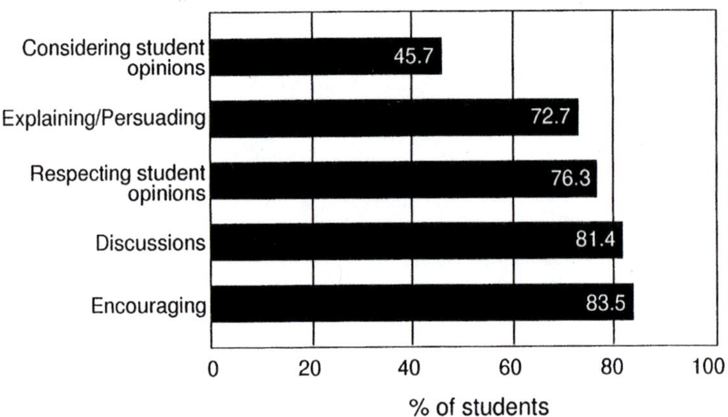

The methods that teachers used to deal with student behaviors are far from being tolerant. They used a wide variety of punitive methods, such as belittling (47.5 percent), removal from class (34.5 percent), and beatings (29.7 percent). None of the subjects mentioned positive humanistic methods of treatment such as contracts or discussions when there was a problem.

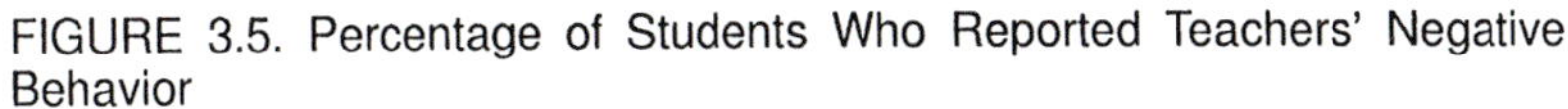

FIGURE 3.5. Percentage of Students Who Reported Teachers' Negative Behavior

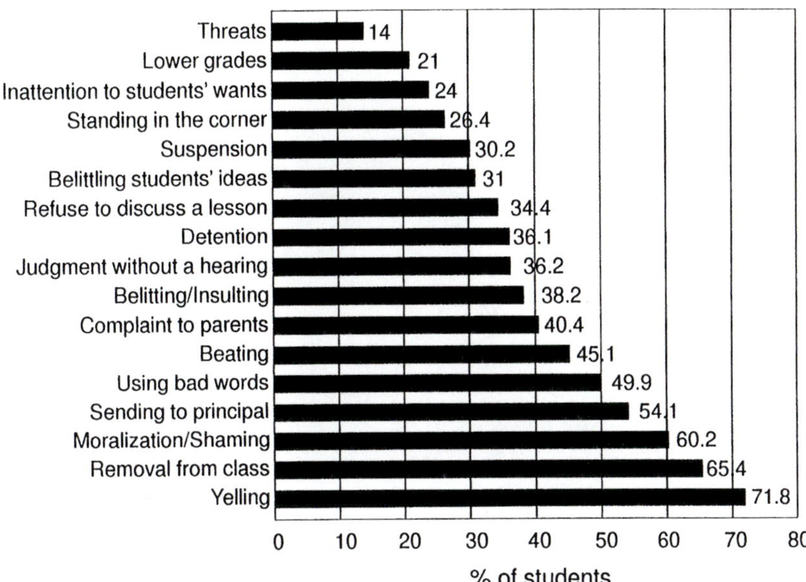

Interestingly, not all of the violent behaviors that teachers displayed (Figure 3.5) were considered responses to negative behaviors by students. When subjects were asked, in Section 4, about the way teachers react to students' bothering behaviors, they reported fewer violent methods than what they reported in Section 3. The percentage of subjects who reported teachers' punitive and violent behaviors as a response to student behaviors (white bar, Figure 3.6) was much lower than the percentage who rated a high prevalence of teachers' violent behavior in general (black bar). These differences suggest that part of teachers' violent behaviors, especially yelling or screaming and using bad words, are not related to student behavior, but to the teachers' own temperaments. More dangerous is the finding that the percentage of students who reported, in Section 5, teachers' negative behaviors that bother or insult them (striped bar, Figure 3.6) was lower than the percentage of students who reported about teachers' violent behavior in Section 3 (black bar). It seems that students consider teachers' violent behavior, especially removal

FIGURE 3.6. Percentage of Students Who Reported Teachers' Violent Behavior*

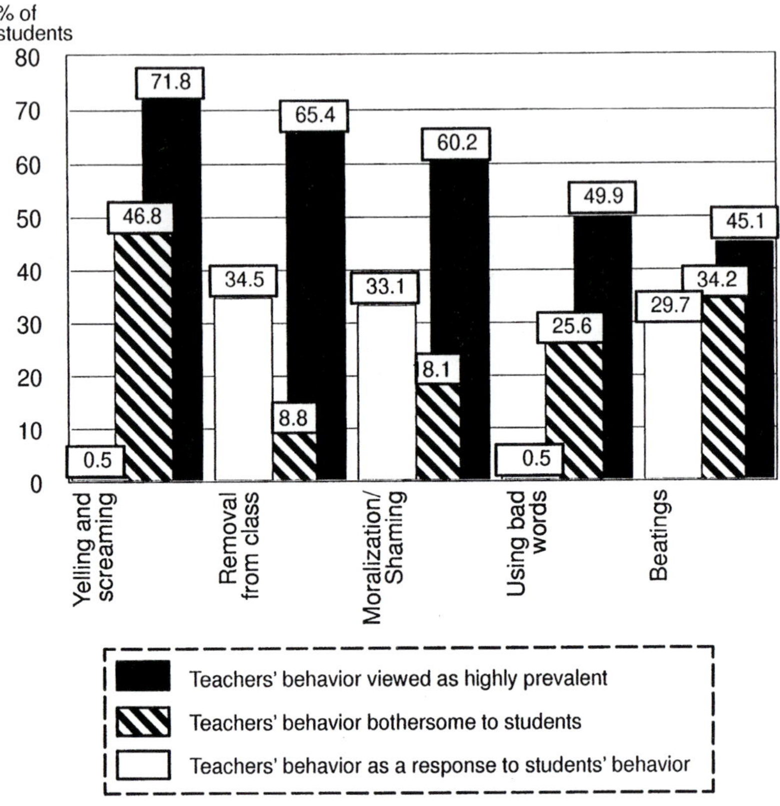

from class and moralization/shaming, to be normative and not a bother to them.

As with the normalization of teachers' violence noted above, students' violence toward other students seems to be normalized too. When subjects were asked, in Section 6, to report students' behaviors that bother them, fewer students reported violent behaviors than reported a high prevalence of violence in Section 1 (shown previously in Figure 3.1). For instance, while 82.2 percent of the subjects reported a high prevalence of yelling and screaming between students, only 53.4 percent of them mentioned that behavior among those that bother them.

Despite the high prevalence of violence displayed by teachers and other students, when subjects were asked how they responded to the bothersome behaviors by teachers, passive methods were the most commonly applied. Responses included "nothing" (43.7 percent), and "I feel inner distress" (37 percent). Only 29.8 percent of the subjects reported that they would discuss what bothers them with their teachers. When other students were the source of this behavior, 36.5 percent of the subjects reported reconciliation, 36.5 percent complaints to the teacher, 31 percent avoidance, 26 percent fight back, 21 percent passive emotional response, and 11.4 percent yelling and exchange of bad words.

Figure 3.7 summarizes the level and direction of violence in Arab schools. Violence between students was the highest, followed by the violence of teachers toward students. Students' violence toward teachers was the lowest, although students' verbal violence should still be considered high (44.4 percent).

FIGURE 3.7. Directions of Verbal and Physical Violence

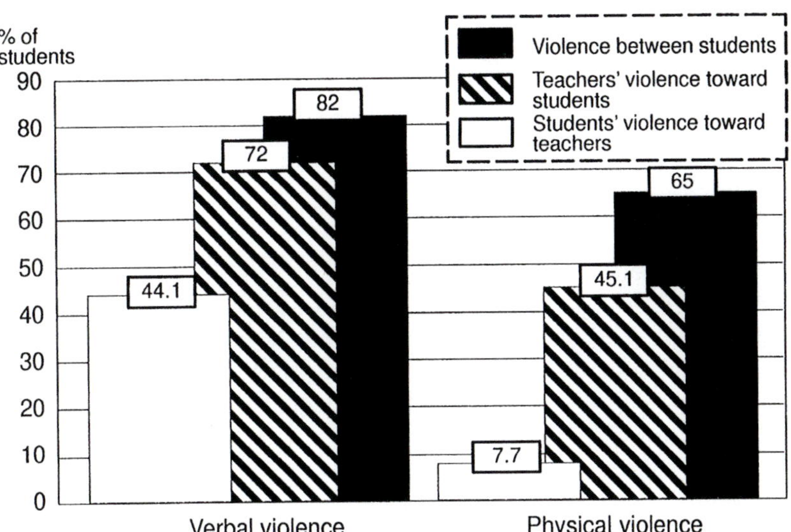

Discussion

Arab students and teachers display violent behavior frequently. A large percentage of students reported a high prevalence of verbal, as well as physical, violence displayed by teachers and other students. Obviously, the strict authoritarian methods adopted by Arab teachers do not control the students' violence. On the contrary, authoritarian methods may increase violence, in at least two possible ways: (1) students may learn violent methods through modeling from the teachers and (2) oppressive methods may increase frustration and anger that may then be displaced onto other students or school property.

These observations have two serious implications: (1) a part of the teachers' violence is viewed by students as unrelated to student behavior; rather, it is related to the teacher's temperament, and (2) a part of this violence is seen by students as normal or as a legitimate part of the teacher's role.

GENERAL TRENDS OF SOCIALIZATION

As in any collectivist society, parents and teachers believe in one way of living and reject or fight against any deviation from their way. The first research shows that Arab parents do not tolerate children's behaviors that do not match their expectations. Both studies show that Palestinian parents and teachers are capable of applying punitive violent methods when verbal methods fail. These findings are not different, in general, from other findings and reports about authoritarian socialization methods in other Arab countries, such as Egypt (Mohamad, 1985) and Lebanon (Hatab and Makki, 1978; Walker, Trimboli, and Trimboli, 1995).

Verbal methods, punishment, and very little room for experimentation are the three main characteristics of socialization in Arab society.

Verbal Methods

Verbal methods applied by parents and teachers include explanation, direction, and moralization. Content analysis of their explanations and directions revealed that they are the "do's and don'ts" rather than explanations that are based on reasoning. They tell the child what to do and how to behave without allowing discussion. When pushed into reasoning, they give moral explanations based on social norms and values. For many questions that children raise, parents and teachers answer *"a'eb,"* which means shame, or *"haram,"* which means forbidden by God. On many occasions, they make it clear that any deviation from their expectations will make the parents "lose face" and be publicly shamed, which will make them sad. Arab children are conditioned from an early age to feel responsible for the honor of their families.

Many directives are given without reasonable explanation. For instance, children are not given a reasonable explanation about why they should not argue with older people and why arguing is considered arrogant or rude. Children, who are less mature, do not know why they should learn to control their needs according to the will of adults, who are more able to control themselves. Restrictions on relations between sexes, as well as sex role differences, remain without reasonable explanations. When these and other questions come up, the answers are *"a'eb"* or *"haram."*

Therefore, explanation and direction, in a context that does not allow for discussion of choices and reasoning, remains a type of moralization and shaming. As a result, verbal methods in the Arabic family address the conscience (superego) rather than the reason (ego).

Punishment

When verbal methods do not prevent children from forbidden acts, punishments will be applied as an external and direct way to control and repress the children's drives and needs (id) that are not socially acceptable. As mentioned earlier, Arab parents will allow almost no unacceptable behavior to continue, regardless of its significance.

Physical punishment is not considered abusive and is appreciated in Arabic society. The majority of Arab parents and teachers consider it the most efficient method of discipline. Despite the law that prohibits physical punishment in schools in Israel, it is still frequently applied in Arab schools there. More surprisingly, Arab parents justify teachers punishing their children. In some extreme cases when students have been severely injured, parents have been reluctant to bring the case to court. In one typical case that has been recently reported in the media, the student lost consciousness. The father explained his reluctance to take any legal steps by saying, "Our morals and values force us to respect teachers and not to be dragged after our emotions. Teachers possesses a mission and grace. I do not believe a teacher beats a student without essential reason" (Koll El-Arab, 1996).

In many Arab communities, physical punishment is still used with adults as well. Women are frequently punished physically or at least threatened with it. Engaged Arab males are ready to use physical punishment on their future wives (Haj-Yahia, 1991). Surprisingly, Arabic women also justify violence against women (Shq'er, 1996).

Little Room for Experimentation

A narrow space for experimentation is an inevitable result of strict moralization and punishment. Arab children do not have trial and error experiences that can help them learn about the environment and the self from the natural consequences of their behavior. Parents' responses are the only consequences they know. Because of this, they lack the experience that helps to develop personal judgment and decision-making and problem-solving ability. Their egos are specifically constructed to understand and follow the rules and social codes of the Arab society and are unable to cope independently in new or novel situations without social directives.

This combination of moralization, which addresses the superego, and punishment, which addresses the id, prevents the development of internal self-control that parents wish to create; as a result, parents continue external control in adulthood. On one hand, values that are given without reasons and without discussion of choices will not be absorbed into a person's value system and personality. On the other hand, Arab children live in "punishment awareness"; they know that disobedience will be followed by punishment. Awareness of punishment remains more dominant than values transmitted by moralization. Therefore, ego calculation of profit and loss, rather than the superego, is the main source of control. Since the consequences of behavior are determined by the parents and the social environment, these external factors, rather than inner self-control, control behavior in the Arab society.

SUMMARY

Arab children grow up in a restrictive, oppressive educational environment. Parents and teachers apply punitive, violent means to control children's behavior. Parents have two plans. First, they apply verbal methods. As long as these methods are efficient, no punitive methods will be applied. If not, all punitive methods are open to make the child obey the parents, regardless of the significance of the behavior. Teachers display both verbal and violent behavior. Students, too, display high levels of violence toward teachers as well as toward other students. It seems that students have gotten used to teachers' violent behavior and consider it normal. Moralization, punishments, and allowing little room for experimentation are the major characteristics of the socialization climate in which Arab children grow up.

PART II: MENTAL HEALTH IN ARABIC SOCIETY AND OTHER SOUTH/EASTERN CULTURES

Chapter 4

Arabic Personality Development, Structure, and Dynamics

I have already described the Arab collective experience in four main historical periods: *Aljahiliyya*, Islamic Empire, stagnation, and revival (Chapter 1), explaining the authoritarian collectivism that is the dominant feature of Arab culture (Chapter 2). In Chapter 3, I show how these features lead to moralization and punishment as the main methods of socialization at home and at school (see Table 4.1). In this chapter, I will explain how these methods affect development and the personality structure and dynamic of the Arab individual.

Theories of personality developed in the West only after the emergence of the individual as an independent entity. These theories were developed to understand this newborn, the individual. The

TABLE 4.1. A Comparison of Western and Arabic Cultures

	Western societies	**Arab societies**
Sociopolitical regime	Capitalistic, industrial, democratic	Not industrial, totalitarian
Basic needs provider	Mainly the state	Mainly the family
Cultural characteristics	Liberalism/individualism	Authoritarianism/ collectivism
Familial relationship	Independence	Interdependence
Socialization methods	Mainly democratic	Mainly moralization and punishment

sociocultural climate within which Arab people grow up is different and does not lead to individualism; in fact, this climate rejects this trend. Therefore, significant differences are expected between the personalities of Arabic and Western people. To understand the uniqueness of Arab personality structure and development, I will describe it in conjunction with common characteristics of the personality as they are described by Western theories.

PERSONALITY DEVELOPMENT

Two main developmental issues seem to differ from what is known in Western society: the individuation process and the development of self-control.

Individuation of Personality

Many theories share the notion that, in the course of development, the child moves from a state of symbiosis to a state of independent individuated personality or identity.

Melanie Klein and Margaret Mahler describe development in terms of object relations (in psychoanalysis, the term *object* generally refers to persons, not things). Unlike Freud, they thought that the main psychological change that occurs after birth is in interpersonal relationships, rather than the expression of drives. Mahler believed that the life of an infant begins in a state of fusion with the mother. Development of the self involves separating from the mother and becoming an individual, independent of others (Mahler, 1968; Mahler, Bergman, and Pine, 1975). After the phase of normal autism (the first month of life), and normal symbiosis (the second to third months), a phase of separation-individuation is initiated and lasts until the end of the second year. During this stage, the child becomes differentiated from the mother and is able to explore the environment away from her. At the end of the second year, a phase of individuality and object constancy begins. In fact, this process of individuation continues, to some degree, during childhood and adolescence.

This idea of individuation is similar to what Erik Erikson described in his theory of social developmental stages. He, too, identified a process of individuation that he called the autonomy stage. This stage comes after the child has gained basic trust in the relationship with the mother during the first year of life. In the second and third years, children become autonomous and are able to feed and dress themselves, to look after their own hygiene, and so on. Like Mahler, Erikson believes that the process of individuation continues and reaches another peak in the identity stage, which takes place during adolescence (Erikson, 1963). In a less explicit way, Freud (1935/1960) addressed this notion when he discussed the process of forming an identity as a resolution of the Oedipus complex. He thought that, in this stage, the child starts to psychologically individuate and build his or her identity. Freud shares with Mahler and Erikson the observation of individuation during the course of development, although he believed that identity comes after the child resolves the Oedipal conflict and identifies with the same-sex parent.

Regardless of some specific details concerning the timing of individuation and the factors involved, almost all the theories of development agree that the child starts life in a state of symbiosis and achieves an individuated identity after adolescence (Figure 4.1).

One should keep in mind that individuation and formation of an independent identity became possible in the West only when the familial relationship became free from the interdependence that existed in the medieval period (Chapter 2). Considering the fact that Arab states do not ensure the basic needs of the individual, that the familial relationship in the Arabic family is still characterized by interdependence, and that Arab children grow up in an authoritarian collective community and are socialized by means of moralization and punishments (see Table 4.1), Arab children do not progress through the same individuation process described in the West. Arab adolescents do not reach a stage of independent identity. As adults, they maintain a collectivist unindividuated personality (Figure 4.2).

Arab children are oriented toward interdependence, accommodation, conformity, cooperation, and affection rather than toward individualism, intellectualization, independence, and compartmentalization (El-Islam, 1982). Separation of the individual's identity is not encouraged. Individuals are mainly perceived and valued as part of the unfolding history of their families (Gorkin, Masalha, and

FIGURE 4.1. Individuation Process in Western Society

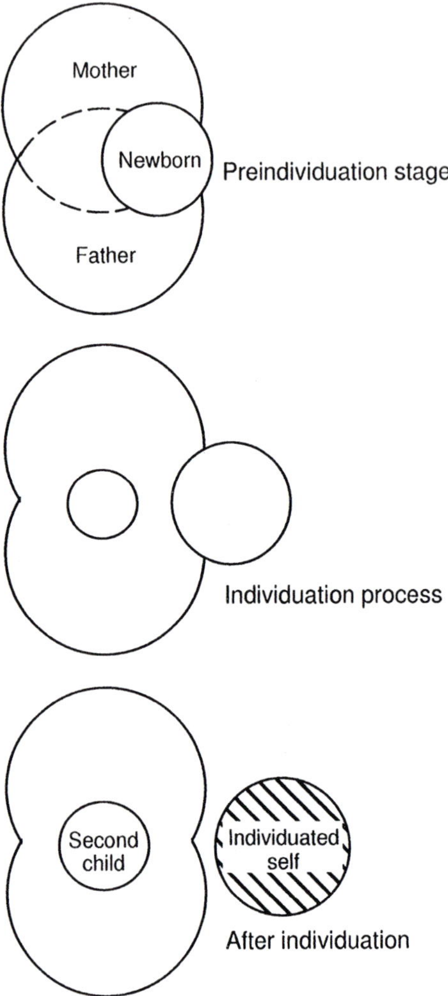

Reprinted from *Clinical Psychology Review*, Volume 16, Number 3, M. Dwairy and T. Van Sickle, Western Psychotherapy in Traditional Arabic Society, 1996, p. 232, with kind permission from Elsevier Science Ltd, The Boulevard, Langford Lane, Kidlington OX5 1GB, UK.

FIGURE 4.2. Collective-Unindividuated Arab Personality

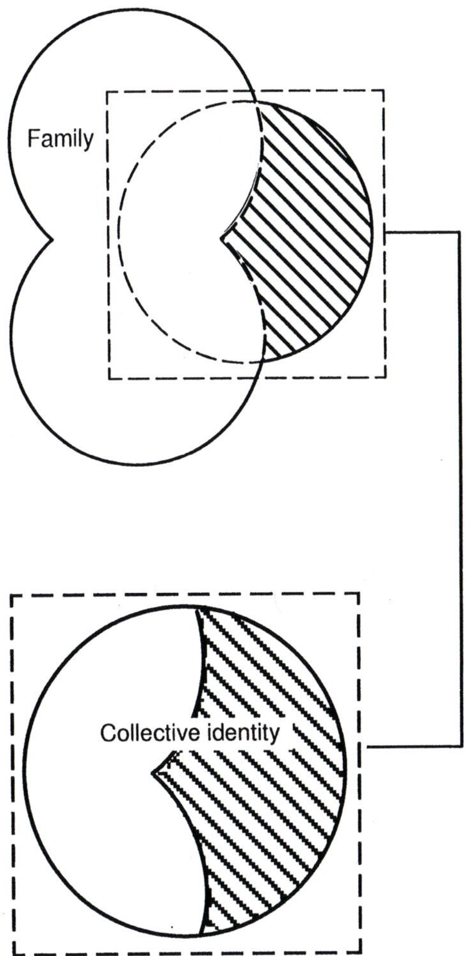

Reprinted from *Clinical Psychology Review*, Volume 16, Number 3, M. Dwairy and T. Van Sickle, Western Psychotherapy in Traditional Arabic Society, 1996, p. 232, with kind permission from Elsevier Science Ltd, The Boulevard, Langford Lane, Kidlington OX5 1GB, UK.

Yatziv, 1985). Psychological theories describing adolescence as a stormy stage that involves conflicts concerning autonomy and independence may bear only a limited relevance to common patterns of psychological maturation encountered in the Arabic culture. Arab adolescents shape themselves to fit their family's needs. Arab youngsters attach and reattach to their families, a process that continues throughout life. Roles and opportunities are defined for adolescents almost from birth, and the range of individual identity is limited (Budman, Lipson, and Meleis, 1992; Racy, 1970; Timimi, 1995).

In a study about the relationship between Arab youth and their parents, 50 to 70 percent of the youth reported that they follow their parents' direction in all areas of life, such as social behavior, interpersonal relationships, marriage, professional preference, and political attitudes. The vast majority of them reported that they are not suffering, that they are even satisfied with this way of life (Hatab and Makki, 1978).

Because of the continuous observation and control of others over children's behavior, Arab children learn how to behave appropriately in the Arabic environment. They learn *how* to behave but not *why.* They learn the accurate solutions for certain problems but not how to think about and solve problems. Arab children do not have problems answering *how* questions while they display significant difficulty in answering *why* questions.

In a comparison I have made between the WISC-R performance of Arab and Jewish students in Israel, I found very few differences in early ages (six to seven years), when both groups are still expected to be dependent. When I compared Arab and Jewish teenagers, significant differences were found, mainly in the subtests: information, similarities, and comprehension. Arab teenagers exceeded Jews on the information subtest that measures the amount of knowledge they have stored in their memories. They know more about their physical and social environment. This knowledge is absorbed from home and school environments that emphasize memorizing over thinking. On the other hand, Jewish teenagers exceeded Arabs on the similarities and comprehension subtests. These two subtests require analytical and flexible thinking, with which Arab students are not as familiar. For the similarities subtest, they are asked to compare two concepts to find a similar property. This kind of thinking is uncommon in Arabic classes, which adopt rote learning techniques rather than reasoning and discussion. On the comprehension subtest, students are offered problematic situations such as, What would you do if you saw smoke coming out of your neighbor's house? To answer this question, the student must evaluate the situation and the options to make a personal decision. Arab students, who are not used to this and are discouraged from evaluating situations and making personal decisions, will find these questions difficult to answer unless they have, by chance, been in similar situations before and were told what they should do.

The unindividuated self finds its expression in social relationships. In Arab society, social relationships are familial rather than interpersonal. A relationship with an Arabic person, in a friendship, business, or marriage context, is a relationship with his or her family. It is too difficult to remove the person from the family in which he or she is rooted and to develop a relationship without being involved with the family as well.

In summary, the survival of the Arab person depends on familial support. Therefore, the self of Arabic persons and the personality remain as dependent entities undifferentiated from the familial context. The values and attitudes of the person are almost synonymous with those of the family. While displaying high adaptability to Arab society, Arabs face difficulties in adapting to a foreign society in which individuals should make personal decisions.

Development of Self-Control

Developmentalists use the term self-control to refer to our ability to regulate our behavior to fit the social environment. Self-control is to learn to delay gratification and inhibit impulses. At birth, children are driven by impulses without any self-control. Social environments put external directions and restrictions on behaviors that interfere with impulses. Despite some overlap, three types of external control can be identified: (1) *logical control,* which relies on nature's laws (such as, "keep away from fire" or "do not climb a high fence"); (2) *moral control,* which relies on cultural values (such as, "do not say bad words," "respect elders," or "avoid sexual games"); and (3) *formal laws* of the society or the state (such as, "do not cross the street at a red light" or "do not steal the property of others").

Children are exposed to these external controls since birth. Their behavior is almost completely controlled by external agents (for example, parents); over time, this control gradually becomes internalized (Bandura, 1986; Freud, 1935/1960; Mischel, 1986). Theorists assert that the first signs of self-control appear in the second year of life, after infants have realized that they are separate and autonomous beings. They learn that their behavior has consequences. In the second and third years, children begin to judge things according to what Freud called the *reality principle.* Children, in this period, internalize logical control and know how to avoid negative consequences and gain positive ones. In doing so, children learn to sacrifice immediate gratification and to make compromises. These behaviors represent the activity of the ego that emerges in this period as an internal representation of external logical control.

Between the fourth and sixth years, a new sort of control emerges that relies on morals and values. This is the *superego,* which begins to judge the child's behavior according to the values and morals that the child has already internalized. Only in this stage are feelings of guilt and sympathy displayed. These feelings differ from shame, which is displayed already, according to Erikson, in the second and third years. Unlike shame, which is still related to others' behavior, guilt is the exclusive product of internal judgment of the superego.

In an individualistic society, when people reach adulthood, they are expected to be fully developed and to have transformed the logical and moral control of external agents (family and school) into internal ones (ego, superego, or self). Therefore, external agents cease to be an authority that enforces rules and become supervisory agents, if they do not diminish completely. In adulthood, the only external authority that remains in effect is the authority of the law (Figure 4.3).

Although humanistic theorists do not elaborate on developmental issues, they believe that the control of children should be internal starting in early childhood. They assume that a person is born with an intrinsic ability to judge and evaluate his or her behavior, to differentiate between good and evil, and to control his or her actions. They believe that the person has free will and is able to be his or her own master. This is the property of the *self;* therefore,

FIGURE 4.3. Internalization of External Control: Formal Laws, Moral Control, and Logical Control

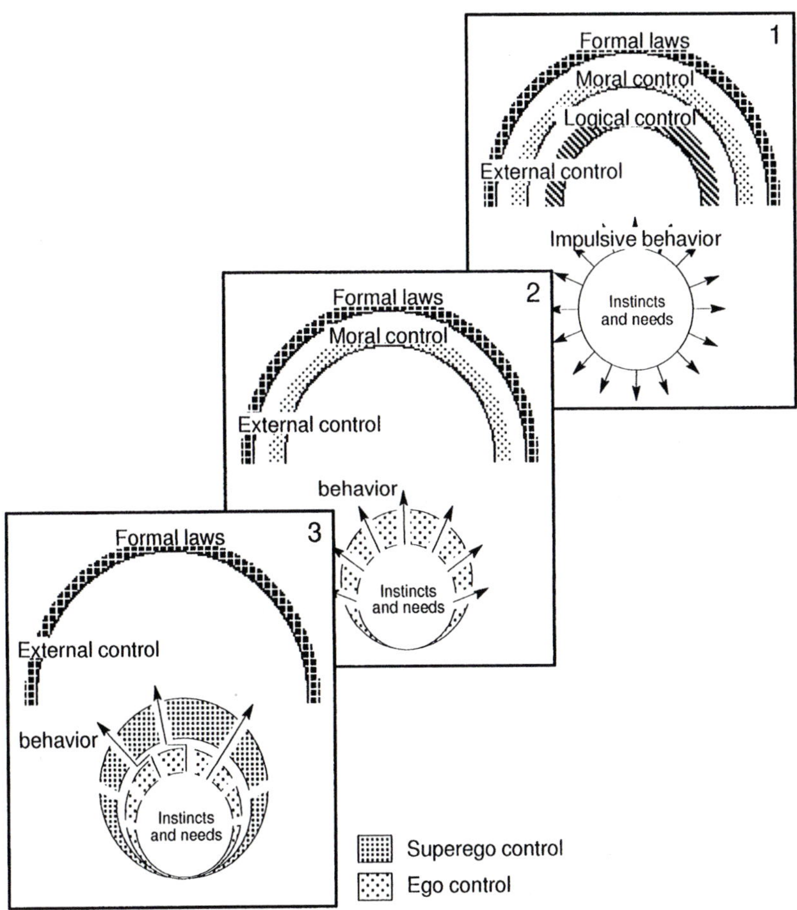

external direction or control may hurt the intrinsic property of self-control and cause incongruence of the self (Liebert and Spiegler, 1994; Monte, 1995).

Despite the differences between psychoanalysts and humanists, both agree that the control of adult behavior is a matter of the self or other internal agents like the ego or superego that may produce guilt feelings when the person abandons his or her values and morals. Both theorists consider these internal personality constructs independent from external agents.

In Chapters 2 and 3, we learned about the educational and cultural environments in which Arab children develop. In Chapter 3, we learned that moralization and punishment used in socialization do not succeed in developing internal independent superegos (or personal value systems) to independently control the child's actions. External strict control remains in effect for Arab adults. Figure 4.4 shows the difference between the agents of control of Arabs compared to those of Western people.

In summary, self-control among Arabs is not an independent personality construct. The ego functions as a controller, but it is specific to control rather than problem solving and functions only in understanding and following authority in Arab society. Serious difficulties are encountered by the ego when facing new situations in which one needs to make personal evaluations and decisions. The superego, on the other hand, does not become differentiated from the social values of Arabic society. Therefore, external control by

FIGURE 4.4. External Control of Arabs versus Self-Control of Western People

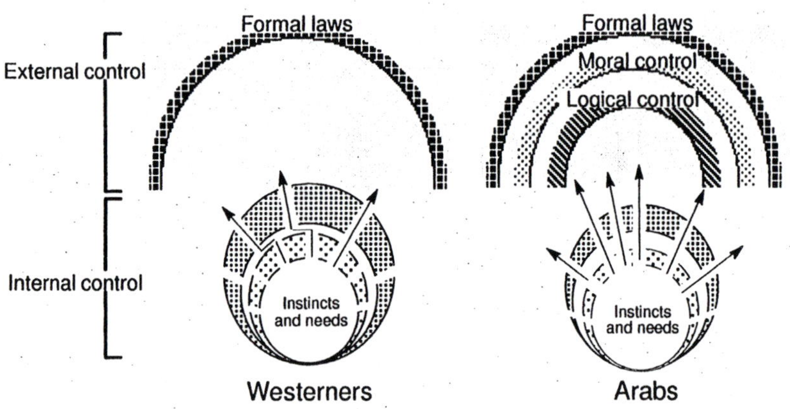

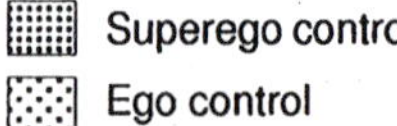

family and society remains dominant over Arab behavior in childhood as well as adulthood.

Before describing the Arab personality, I would like to remind readers that Arabs are spread along a continuum of acculturation (see Chapter 2). Among them, there are Westernized, bicultural, and traditional groups. The characteristics of the personality discussed will be more accurate among traditional Arabs. In the other two groups, some traces of these characteristics are found in conjunction with other individualistic characteristics.

Authoritarian collectivism restricts Arab women's development much more than men's. Moralization and punishments are more rigid; women are observed and controlled to an extent that leaves no space for personal freedom or choice. In many cases, they are physically restrained. As a result, lack of individuation and internal self-control, as well as the other personality characteristics that will be discussed later, are more accurate for Arabic women than men, who may have some degree of individuated personality.

PERSONALITY STRUCTURE AND DYNAMICS

Based on personality constructs, Western theories describe normal and abnormal personality. Although all the theories are based on observation in the West, they claim universality across cultures. To what extent do these criteria of abnormality apply to Arabs? In this section, I will describe the personality structure of Arabs compared with the Western personality as described by Western personality theories applying Western personality constructs.

Collective Personality

All theories of personality, except behavioral theories, define certain internal personality constructs that explain behavior. They propose that, during the course of development, familial and cultural factors influence the development of these constructs; then, in adulthood, they become part of the individual's personality operating independently from, and sometimes contrary to, the social environment.

For psychoanalysis, the *id, ego,* and *superego*, and the dynamics between these constructs explain normal and abnormal behavior. The environment influences behavior only through these internal constructs. In transactional analysis, the constructs *child, adult,* and *parent* explain behavior (Berne, 1961). Humanistic approaches are similar, claiming that the quality of the *self* explains behavior. External reinforcements or punishments operate only through the self, which explains individual differences that appear in response to the same external circumstances. Cognitive psychology, too, believes that inner cognitive constructs control the response rather than external events (Liebert and Spiegler, 1994; Monte, 1995) (Figure 4.5).

As a result of the lack of an individuated personality among Arabs (see Figure 4.2), all of the internal personality constructs mentioned by Western theorists remain enmeshed in the collective

FIGURE 4.5. Collective Arab Personality versus Individuated Western Personality

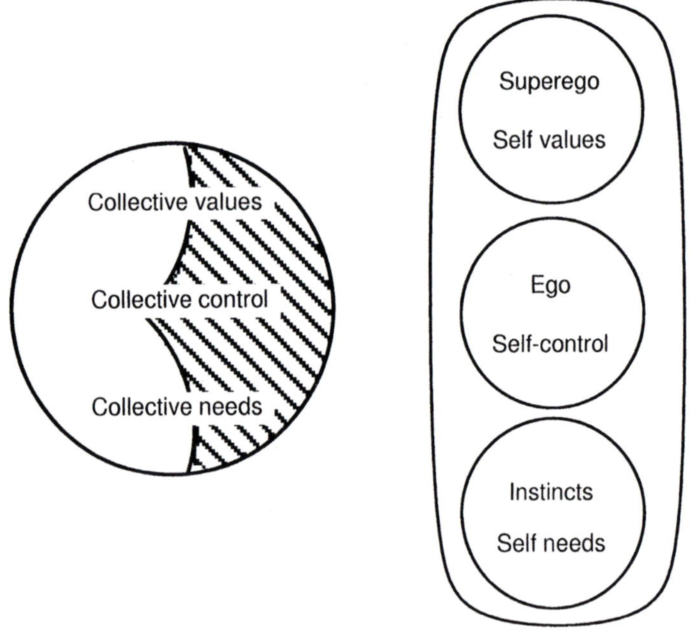

personality. The id, ego, and superego are collective rather than personal. When Arabs talk about their experiences they tend to say *we* rather than *I*. Even when *I* is used, it refers to the whole family. Traditional Arabs express an apology when they say *I am* or *me*. They say *a'aooth bellah men qaul ana,* which means, God help me to avoid saying I am.

Individual differences within the Arab community are narrower than those in Western society. Differences in Arab society are related to social roles rather than personal differences. Fathers are different from sons, grandsons are different from younger sons, men are different from women. Within the same role, people are much the same and follow collective norms and values.

Analysis of voting trends in political elections among Arabs in Israel shows that families tend to be united in their political attitudes. This is obvious in elections for local councils in small villages. A whole family, old and young, male and female, unite around one party or leader (Al-Haj, 1989). To adhere to the family is the proper attitude regardless of the rightness of the political attitude they follow.

The Arab ego is culturally specified, which is very efficient in helping the individual adapt to Arabic culture and cope with problems as part of the collective. Difficulties may occur in coping outside of that known context. For instance, Arab students face some difficulties when they have cross-cultural meetings with Western students. In Palestinian-Jewish student meetings in Israel, Palestinians show an ability to describe their attitudes and values, but they have difficulties in argumentative and reasoning conversations. When Arabs encounter Western culture for which they are not prepared, they may have some difficulties adapting when they discover that the answers and directives that they had are no longer appropriate, and they need to make personal judgments and decisions.

External Sources of Anxiety and Repression

Freud and other psychodynamic theorists differentiate among three kinds of anxiety that cause repression of needs and drives.

1. *Objective anxiety:* The fear that is caused by an external danger or an objective threat.

2. *Neurotic anxiety:* A kind of anxiety caused by the ego, which understands the negative consequences that may happen if the drives are fulfilled. Anxiety comes as a result of internal conflict between the ego, which realizes the external demands and consequences, and the id, which is impulse-driven.
3. *Moral anxiety:* An internal anxiety caused by the superego, which makes a person experience guilt feelings when the id is expressed.

According to this approach, the source of moral anxiety is internal. Therefore, internal means, such as *defense mechanisms,* are able to contain anxiety. These are psychological manipulations that the ego conducts to hide parts of the conflicts in the unconscious.

Because Arab behavior is controlled by others, and because the internal constructs (ego, self, and superego) are undifferentiated and remain collective constructs, the source of repression for Arabs is still external. Losing the vital economic, social, and emotional support of the family and the society, as well as punitive reactions of the social environment, are the main threats that make Arabic persons contain their drives and needs. Of course, the collective ego, that knows exactly what the social consequences are, is partly behind this anxiety, but because external observation and control continue throughout life, the threat of the ego almost never operates without an actual objective threat from society. Therefore, the typical anxiety among Arabs is a combination of objective anxiety and neurotic anxiety. It is an objective-ego anxiety.

Moral anxiety does exist, but it remains secondary to objective-ego anxiety. Many theorists claim that society cultivates shame rather than guilt and obedience from fear rather than from love, conviction, or respect, resulting in defective superego development (Sharabi, 1977). Therefore, when Arabs behave inappropriately, they experience more shame, which stems from the attitudes of others, than guilt, which stems from the superego (Bazzoui, 1970; Gorkin, Masalha, and Yatziv, 1985; Sharabi, 1975). A similar observation has been reported among other South/Eastern (or non-Western) societies (Hofestede, 1991; Walker, Trimboli, and Trimboli, 1995). This issue is not so simple. On one hand, because the superego of Arabs is not individuated and because external control is continuous and strict, social reaction will be the primary focus; therefore, shame will override guilt. On the other hand, situations that may evoke guilt or shame are different in the two cultures (Barakat, 1993). Because the superego is a collective construct in Arab society, guilt and empathy feelings may be noticed among Arabs much more than among Westerners. Arabs react deeply to personal or national tragedies of others and enlist themselves to help. They help any person in their community that experiences a tragedy. They reacted deeply to the Palestinian, Iraqi, and Bosnian tragedies and do not understand how the human rights values that Western countries claim accord with the policy of these countries in the Third World. Arabs find it difficult to understand how humans care for pets in the West but are careless about the homeless people in the West or poverty in Africa.

In certain personal issues, such as relations with family members, especially mothers, Arabs feel deep feelings of commitment. They feel deep guilt if they betray their parents or siblings or neglect them in difficult times. Relationships with the land and homeland are charged with authentic guilt feelings too. Many Arabs are ready to sacrifice themselves for their homeland. On the other hand, in many other areas of life, shame overrides guilt. For instance, when one behaves inappropriately toward the opposite sex, shame rather than guilt is the dominant feeling.

Humanistic and existentialist theorists, such as Carl Rogers, Ronald Laing, and Erich Fromm, note that the main anxiety that the Westerner experiences is in the relationship between the self and others. Rogers (1961) thought that an *incongruence* between the self and experience, or an alienation from the self, causes anxiety. Laing (1959) describes an anxiety of being *engulfed* in relationships with others and losing the self. Fromm (1941) describes the anxiety and *aloneness* that Western people experience after they have turned to individualism. According to Fromm, Western people gain personal integration and self-strength, but they lose the security they had in the collective society.

Individualism that enables the development of the self is a precondition to the anxieties about which Rogers, Laing, and Fromm talked. People raised in a collective society who do not develop an individuated self will not experience the *incongruence* with, or an *alienation* from, the self, or feelings of being *engulfed* in relations with others. They still experience the security that the collective society provides. Their anxiety is related to a possibility of losing that security. They are afraid to be rejected by or isolated from their social environment. For this, they are ready to sacrifice their personal needs, wishes, and rights.

In summary, Arabs' anxiety is a combination of what Freud called objective anxiety and neurotic anxiety. It is an objective-ego anxiety rather than moral anxiety or guilt. Guilt feelings are experienced in a collective way. As a community, Arabs empathize deeply with others' tragedies and offer their assistance. Betrayal of parents, siblings, homeland, or abandoning of children evoke deep guilt feelings among Arabs. Their main source of anxiety is related to the possible loss of familial and social support, rather than being engulfed in relationships with others or being alienated from the self.

External Sources of Happiness

In the era of individualism, Western people enjoy the happiness of self-expression and self-actualization (Fromm, 1941; Maslow, 1970; Rogers, 1961, 1965). In collective societies, such as Arab society, people lack this kind of happiness. Approval of others, especially the family, is the source of happiness in Arab society. Because others' attitudes depend on fulfilling expected roles, it becomes another source of happiness. If they get good grades at school, Arab students run to show them to their parents. This is very normal in early childhood among all societies, but among Arabs this dependency on parents' appreciation continues as the child matures. They do not develop internal satisfaction for successful actions, or become immune to a parent's disapproval. On the other hand, Arab parents are very happy when they can sacrifice themselves for their children. Success of their children is a major source of happiness even at the expense of their own needs. Because Arab parents invest all of their lives for their children, many of them are shocked and become depressed when they find that their investment was in vain. It seems that the most disastrous event for Arab parents is the failure to raise successful, compliant children. The importance of children in Arab families extends from the emotional needs of the parents; children are an asset that make their parents proud in the community. Successful children mean more capacity for economic production, more power in cases of conflict with others, more safety in case of social and economic problems, more insurance when parents become old, and most important, successful children mean more pride in the family.

Accomplishments of an Arab bring happiness to the extent that they receive appreciation from others rather than self-satisfaction. Arabs' happiness in weddings, building a new house, or graduation from college is highly related to others' appreciation. Therefore, these issues occupy a huge amount of their communications with others.

In summary, happiness, as well as depression, among Arabs is related to others' attitudes and reactions. A person's actions are designed to maintain others' positive attitudes rather than serving the person's own needs. Actually, the appreciation of others is the most basic need, overriding the other personal needs that Maslow mentioned. This is because of the sociocultural system in Arab society that makes almost all needs dependent on others.

Interpersonal Coping Rather Than Intrapsychic Defense Mechanisms

Since we have learned that the source of repression is external in Arab society, and that the primary conflict for an Arab is interpersonal rather than intrapsychic, we can learn the techniques they use to cope with conflicts.

When the primary conflict is intrapsychic, as it is for Westerners, intrapsychic defense mechanisms that manipulate the inner personality constructs are the main technique to handle these conflicts. When the source of repression is mainly external, social and interpersonal techniques are the answer.

One unconscious collective defense (identification with the oppressor) and three conscious techniques (*mosayara, istig'aba,* and *fahlawia)*, are the main techniques that help a person adapt to the authoritarian collectivist Arab society.

Identification with the Oppressor

Anna Freud (1936/1966) described a psychological defense mechanism in which a person identifies with an aggressor to withstand inevitable or unbeatable aggression. This defense helps a victim coexist with the aggressor by providing an illusion of power and helps a victim find a meaning for the aggression. Freire (1970/1995, 1992/1994) described a similar mechanism in a collective context when he analyzed the psychology of peasants in Brazil. Freire asserted that:

> during the initial stage of their struggle the oppressed find, in the oppressor, their model of "manhood." . . . They prefer gregariousness to authentic comradeship; they prefer the security of conformity with their state of unfreedom to the creative communion produced by freedom and even the very pursuit of freedom. . . . They are at one and the same time themselves and the oppressor whose consciousness they have internalized. The conflict lies in the choices between being wholly themselves or being divided; between ejecting the oppressor within or not ejecting them; between human solidarity or alienation; between following prescriptions or having choices; between being spectators or actors; between acting or having the illusion of acting through the action of the oppressors; between speaking out or being silent, castrated in their power to create and recreate, in their power to transform the world. . . . How can the oppressed, as divided inauthentic beings, participate in developing the pedagogy of their liberation? Only as they discover themselves to be "hosts" of the oppressor can they contribute to the midwifery of their liberating pedagogy. . . . Liberation is thus a childbirth, and a painful one. (1970/1995, pp. 28, 30-31)

Because of the long collective experience of Arabs with authoritarianism, the psychology of the oppressed that Freire asserted applies to them. On the political level, Arabs are familiar with undemocratic, oppressive regimes. They prefer having some peace and security in conformist attitudes rather than to struggle for their rights. Arab leaders easily find supporters among the oppressed sections of the society. Many Arabs adopt the image that their leaders draw for them, and blame themselves for their misery. During the first three decades since the establishment of the state of Israel, the vast majority of Palestinians, who were shocked by their

national disaster, supported mainstream political parties that were responsible for their tragedy. Only in the mid-1970s did they regain a sense of power and start to abandon these parties. As a result of intensive and continuous dehumanization of Arabs by Israeli and Western propaganda, some Arabs, especially Westernized groups, adopted negative attitudes toward their nation and became convinced that Arabs are really terrorists, dirty and inhuman, while Western people are civilized and humane. This self-hatred is the result of the process of identification with the oppressor.

On the social level, the lower classes feel shameful and inferior when they encounter middle- or upper-class Arabs. They adopt the view of the upper classes toward the values and the norms of the lower class. Concerning social oppression of individuals, especially women, the vast majority adopt the authoritarian oppressive norms and values from which they themselves suffer. Arab women, the most oppressed group, adopt the most traditional attitudes toward their daughters and the most rejecting attitudes toward other women who begin to move toward personal freedom.

Arabic women justify violence against women (Shq'er, 1996). Despite the discrimination against women in politics, Arabic women continue to vote for traditional male political leaders who are partly responsible for that discrimination (Abu Baker, in press). They do so not after they have freely considered their choices, but because they are afraid and unable to face the oppressor.

To realize the vital role of identification with the oppressor, we need to imagine how Arab people, especially women, can maintain an awareness of rebellion side by side with continuous oppression. This is a very tough and incongruent situation that motivates people to achieve a cognitive consistency to ease distress even at the cost of giving up actual courses of action to change the situation (Festinger, 1957).

Mosayara

Mosayara means to get along with others' attitudes, wishes, and expectations through hiding one's real feelings, thoughts, and attitudes (Dwairy, 1992a, 1992b, 1992c; Griefat and Katriel, 1989; Sharabi, 1975). It is to behave in a way that pleases others and helps one get along with them. Arabs consider *mosayara* a positive, mature, diplomatic behavior. In their study, Griefat and Katriel (1989) cited attitudes of some Arab respondents showing how *mosayara* is common and deeply rooted in the Arabic culture: "*Mosayara* is in the blood of every Arab person"; "You drink it with your mother's milk"; "It is in the air, you breathe it in" (p. 121).

We must recall that, in an authoritarian society, individuals have only one choice, to conform. This choice inevitably causes a suppression and repression of an individual's needs and attitudes; otherwise, they will be punished. Therefore, *mosayara* is a reasonable social means to avoid confrontation and maintain good relationships between people even if it is only on the surface. It is the way to keep the equilibrium of the collective social structure.

Mosayara is more than a behavior, it is a lifestyle in which a person tends to bend to conform to the expectations of the other. In this lifestyle, one avoids the word *no*. Instead, Arabs have developed a variety of terms that mean no without saying no. *In shaa' Allah* means "if God wants," *in Allah besmah* means "if God allows me"; they remove the responsibility for noncompliance from the self and put it on God. Phrases such as *bisier kh'er* mean "just good will happen," *menshoof* means "we will see," and *bah'awel* means "I will try." All leave an open option for later manipulation. On the other hand, sometimes a shaky "yes" means "no." A real "yes" should be insistent. In other times, "no" may not mean "no." This happens usually when a person tends to agree but is expected to refuse; for instance, when X is offered a refreshment (or hospitality, help, etc.) by Y, X is expected to refuse and allow Y to withdraw. If Y is serious, he or she is expected to place some pressure on X to help differentiate between a real offer and a *mosayara* offer. Obviously, it is confusing. It is very important to learn the nonverbal cultural codes and expectations and to be able to understand the verbal codes. Many Arabs consider the standard offer of hospitality of Western people as indifference or carelessness. On the other hand, a Western person may be bothered by the insistent hospitality of Arabs, even after he or she has said "no."

Although *mosayara* makes people avoid self-expression and makes them do things that contradict their real desires, it does not seem to cause any discomfort. On the contrary, it is the comfortable way to communicate. People are aware of the incongruence between their wishes and their behaviors, but they still believe deeply, by virtue of unconscious identification with the oppressor, that it is the best way to live.

As the director of the Psychological Services Center in Nazareth, Israel, I initiated, in the early 1990s, an Assertive Training Program. We expected some difficulties from teachers and parents who are not ready yet to accept assertive behavior by the students. To minimize the chance of sabotaging the program, we thought it would be wise to prepare teachers and parents for it. We conducted three group meetings using interpersonal situations, for which we discussed different reactions: aggressive, assertive, or regressive. The vast majority of the teachers and parents tended prefer the regressive ways, in which one applies variations of *mosayara.* When they started to role-play assertive options, they displayed tremendous emotional discomfort and distress. Many of them expressed their opinions about assertive behavior, saying that it is arrogant, rude, impolite, and insulting. Some of them employed an Arab proverb that says *kh'alliha fi al k'alb tijrah' wla ben elnas tefdah,* which means "let it hurt in the heart, rather than making a public scandal." It was obvious that the main motivation for *mosayara* is the fear of losing social relations.

This is the educational climate in which Arab children grow and the general culture in which adults are immersed. The question is, what happens to the needs, feelings, and thoughts that are suppressed? How do Arab people handle these restraints? The answer is through *istig'aba.*

Istig'aba

The common meaning of *istig'aba* is to express one's ideas in the absence (*g'eiab*) of others who have something to do with the topic. The *istig'aba* is not limited to verbal behavior. Private actions that one does away from the "eyes of the society" to avoid isolation or punishment are called *istig'aba* too. It is the way to discharge forbidden needs or wishes without losing social approval and vital social support.

Mosayara and *istig'aba* are two complementary social means that maintain the authoritarian structure (by *mosayara*) and, at the same time, allow personal expression (by *istig'aba*). They make

Arab behavior inconsistent, changing from one social setting to another. If personality is, by definition, relatively stable and consistent across situation and time, *mosayara* and *istig'aba* make the variability of Arab behavior much greater.

Although *mosayara* is highly appreciated, *istig'aba* is not. People usually deny using *istig'aba.* When they talk or act in the absence of others, they reframe it or cover it in different language, such as, "I did not tell him that because I did not want to insult him" or "I did it privately because I did not want my father to worry" or "We are not gossiping, we are just discussing social issues."

Fahlawia

The character type *fahlawia* was identified by Hamid Ammar (1964) among Egyptian Arabs, and has been applied by Sadiq Jalal El-Athem (1969) to analyze the personal cultural factors that contributed to the military defeat of Egypt in the 1967 war with Israel. The *fahlawia* personality includes a combination of coping means and is distinguished by six characteristics:

1. *Mosayara* and extreme flexibility to meet situational expectations and achieve easy, smooth adaptations. It is considered a smart, sophisticated, and seasoned behavior rather than weak one.
2. A sense of humor to ease stress and avoid direct confrontation. In terms of Anna Freud, it may be considered a kind of reaction formation. Indeed, in the Arab world, Egyptian Arabs are considered gifted with a sense of humor more than any other Arab nation.
3. Verbal exaggeration of self-achievement by denying one's shortcomings. This is the way to compensate for inferiority feelings even at the cost of denying the truth. This characteristic reflects the importance of others' opinions and appreciation.
4. Projection of responsibility onto others or external factors. This is similar to an external locus of control. In an authoritarian society, things are not determined and controlled by a person; therefore, experience teaches people to be helpless and that external agents (authority or God) are responsible for

one's actions. Hence, it is not a psychoanalytical projection but a natural product of objective experience.

5. Difficulties in long-term planning and looking for shortcuts to accomplish immediate goals. Because authoritarianism offers answers to any problem and limits individual experience, Arabs lack experience of systematic long-term planning. They find it difficult to sustain long-term plans, although they may show high enthusiasm in the beginning, followed by withdrawal.
6. Preference for individual work rather than group work. This trait has been mentioned by El-Athem in the military context, and it seems to appear in very specific situations. Arabs may find it difficult to work in a team that has decision-making systems different from the authoritarian way to which they are accustomed. Typically, Arabs tend to share with others and find it hard to be away from them.

These characteristics describe Egyptian Arabs in certain contexts and periods. Many of these characteristics, but not all of them, may apply to all Arabs, such as *mosayara,* verbal exaggeration of the self at the expense of acknowledging and dealing with shortcomings, external locus of control, and difficulties in systematic long-term planning.

Two Distinct Layers of Personality

Personality theories propose that individuals possess stable, consistent traits across situations and time. They describe the personality in various terms or with hypothetical constructs. These internal constructs help to describe individual differences and, presumably, can predict an individual's behavior. As we noticed before, Arab behavior is influenced and predicted by external situational factors much more than by internal constructs that are unindividuated. Therefore, in a conformist submissive society, norms and social roles, more than personality, predict individual behavior.

Two distinct layers of Arab personality structure can be identified that will help clarify the variability in individual behavior: a social layer and a private layer.

Social Layer of Personality

The public personality communicates with others according to social rules and values. It is skillful in social roles and expectations. Its function is to maintain social support and avoid confrontations. It identifies with the authoritarian collectivist norms (the oppressor) and applies *mosayara* and *fahlawia* to accomplish its goal (Figure 4.6). It is the personality that is active in work, social relationships, and familial and parental duties. It is governed by the collective ego and superego.

Private Layer of Personality

The private personality is activated away from social control. Its function is to express what was not allowed to be expressed in

FIGURE 4.6. Two Layers of the Arabic Personality: Social and Private

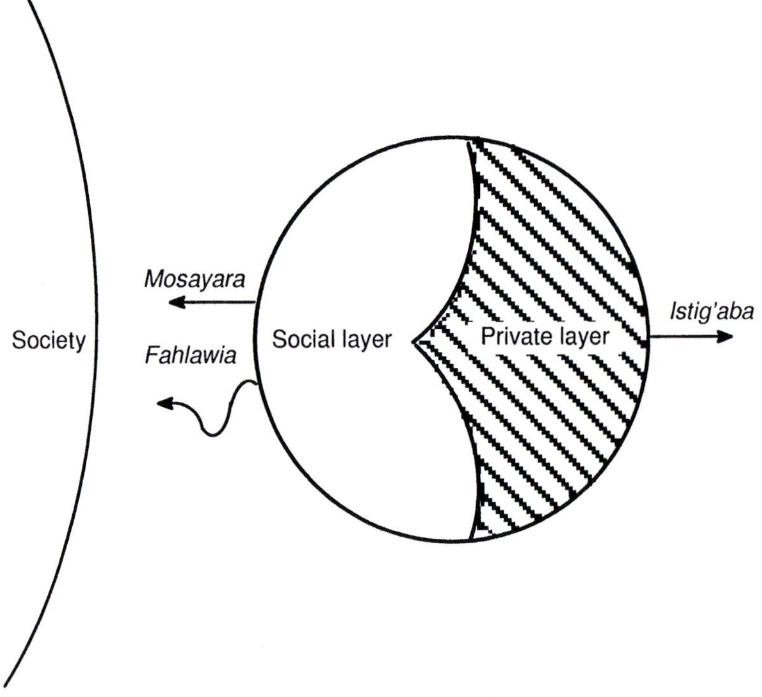

public social relationships. It allows forbidden sexual, selfish, and aggressive drives to function without being punished. It is the personality connected with inner personal drives, (id) and it uses *istig'aba* to fulfill them.

These two personalities accomplish together what seems an impossible mission. They enable the expression of forbidden drives without provoking the social authority and structure that provides vital support. This mission becomes possible through alternation of the two personalities. A person who has visitors may fulfill social expectations and be polite, smiling, generous, and unsparing (*mosayara* and *fahlawia*) and, after the visitors leave, may express discomfort about them. Indeed, this discrepancy between public behavior and private behavior is not exclusive to Arabs, but because Arabs avoid any assertive expression almost completely and adhere to *mosayara* and *fahlawia*, this discrepancy becomes extreme. A big discrepancy is found in the behaviors of parents, teachers, and social and political leaders. In public they may have one attitude; they even may preach for justice and equality between people, and after an hour or so when they are at home, they may use very oppressive punitive behaviors toward their wives and children. Some progressive social leaders may preach for women's liberation and democratic education; however, they may still have very traditional attitudes in their private lives. Many teachers who lecture morals and values to their children may commit immoral acts when they are away from social control.

One should not confuse these two personalities with what is known in clinical psychology as multiple personality disorder, or MPD (or dissociative identity disorder, according to DSM-IV [American Psychiatric Association, 1994]). In MPD patients, one personality is unaware of the existence of other personalities, and there is lack of communication between them. Sometimes they may even fight each other. The patient suffers from amnesic gaps. Unlike MPD, despite the alteration, Arabs are not dissociated; the person is still aware of the activity of each personality layer. There are no internal fights; on the contrary, there is a sort of cooperation and division of responsibilities between the two layers.

The activity of the two layers may explain the contradiction in the reports of parents about methods of socialization, presented in

Chapter 3. The same parents who reported verbal supportive methods reported punitive methods when they were asked, "What would you do if your child disregarded your directions?" Students reported a similar discrepancy in the behavior of teachers (see Chapter 3). They reported high levels of verbal supportive behavior and, at the same time, high levels of punitive aggressive behavior. It seems that the same person alternates between politeness and aggressiveness toward the same person. The socialization methods are predicted by contextual factors much more than personality factors.

Sexual behavior among Arabs is another example of the activity of the two layers of personality. In public and social contexts, Arabs strongly condemn sexual relationships outside marriage. They all deny any behavior that violates the strict limits society has created. They report that they protect females in the family from any sexual harassment. They state that they are ready to physically fight anybody who harms what is called "the honor of the family." Does that mean that Arabs contain their sexual drives more than other nations?

Field research that was conducted among eighty-six male and ninety-eight female Arab students, age eleven to twelve years old, revealed that 22 percent of male and 10 percent of female students anonymously reported sexual abuse that included "undressing and touching with the genitals and other sexual organs, that was accompanied with pain feelings" (Dwairy, 1997b). In 40.1 percent of the cases, the abuse was recurrent. In 43.4 to 57.1 percent of the cases, the abuser was one of the family members. The vast majority of the subjects did not dare report the abuse to any adult because they were afraid of punishment. Obviously, the reported rate of sexual abuse among Arab children is not different from that in many Western societies (Finkelhor et al., 1990). This means that Arabs, similar to others, commit sexual crimes despite the conservative face they show. They are similar to others in sexual behavior, but they are extremely different in their public attitudes toward sex. Again, we may associate the public sexual attitudes with the social layer of personality and the actual sexual behavior with the private layer.

Table 4.2 summarizes the main differences between the Arabic and the Western personalities. These differences could be applied to many other South/Eastern societies.

TABLE 4.2. A Comparison of Western and South/Eastern Personalities

	Westerners	Arabs and South/Easterners
Individuation	individuated self	unindividuated self
Personality	more independent	more collective
Main source of control	more self-control ego and superego control	more social-control family and community control
Main conflict and main source of repression and anxiety	more intrapsychic	more social/interpersonal
Main source of happiness	self-actualization	social approval
Coping	more defense mechanisms	more social and cultural skills
Prediction of behavior	behavior predicted more by personality	behavior predicted more by norms
Consistency of personality	more consistent across situations	more contextual

SUMMARY

Because the survival of Arabs depends on social support, interdependence, rather than dependence, characterizes the relationship between the individual and the family. Personality structures such as ego, superego, and self are not individuated and remain collective and dependent on the family. The source of repression, as well as happiness, is external, related to social approval. Because the main conflict is interpersonal rather than intrapsychic, social coping measures, rather than defense mechanisms, are applied to cope with conflicts and stresses in Arabic society. Identification with the oppressor, *mosayara, istig'aba,* and *fahlawia* are the main coping methods in Arabic society. Norms and social context predict behavior much more than personality. Arabic personality contains two layers: social and private. The social layer uses *mosayara* and *fah-*

lawia to deal with social life. The private layer uses *istig'aba* to discharge forbidden needs and emotions. Despite the difference in behavior from one context to another, these two layers are crucial to maintain the authoritarian lifestyle and, at the same time, allow personal expression.

Chapter 5

Epidemiology of Psychological Disorders in the Arabic Societies

Epidemiological studies have identified differences in both morbidity and diagnostic features of psychological disorders among Arabs compared to Westerners (Dwairy, in press a). This chapter will present the main findings concerning the prevalence and the characteristics of each disorder in the Arab world.

PSYCHIATRIC MORBIDITY

General Morbidity

Based on the Clinical Interview Schedule (CIS) (Goldberg et al., 1970), the prevalence of psychiatric morbidity among consumers of primary health care in United Arab Emirates was 27.6 percent (El-Rufaie and Absood, 1993). A high prevalence was also reported in Saudi Arabia (26 percent) (El-Rufaie, Albar, and Dabal, 1988), and among women in Dubai (22.7 percent) (Ghubash, Hamdi, and Bibbington, 1992; Ghubash and Bibbington, 1994). This rate is higher than that found in the West and in four developing countries: Colombia, India, Sudan, and the Philippines, which were between 10.6 percent and 17.7 percent (average 13.9 percent) (Harding et al., 1980).

Based on Eysenck's scales, Egyptian students had higher neuroticism scores and lower extroversion scores than American and British students. Egyptian students were more anxious, worried, overresponsive, and depressed (Ibrahim, 1979). Libyan students scored significantly higher on social anxiety and shyness scales than comparable cultural groups (Ibrahim and Ibrahim, 1993).

Contributing Factors

Several factors have been considered to contribute to the high morbidity in Arab countries.

Social Oppression

Social oppression, especially of women, has been a major issue. In Egypt, anxiety over and the predisposition to develop neurotic disorders under stress have been attributed to social constraints imposed on Arabic individuals (Ibrahim, 1979). Conflicts between traditional collectivistic authoritarian values and individualistic liberal ones contribute heavily to the distress of Arabs. According to El-Islam (1979, 1982), intergenerational conflicts precipitated 50 percent of suicide attempts, 20 percent of neuroses, and 17 percent of schizophrenic illnesses among young Arab patients. Among the Palestinian clients of this author's clinic, 65.7 percent reported client-family conflict. Of those, 18.1 percent of the clients exhibited that conflict right in the beginning of therapy, while 47.6 percent brought the conflict in during the course of therapy. In only 34.3 percent of the cases, this familial conflict did not emerge at all in therapy (Dwairy, 1997b).

Social Change

Fast social change in Saudi Arabia and the Arab Gulf states is one major contributing factor. The people there have passed through tremendous cultural change since the discovery of oil in 1937. They moved from a traditional, almost tribal system to an urban system. In contrast with the tribal way of life that existed in Dubai before the discovery of oil, today 95.3 percent of the population are living an urban lifestyle. They are exposed to foreign cultures that were brought to the country by expatriates from Western and other Arab countries who became the majority of the population in Dubai. Ghubash and his colleagues (1992, 1994) examined the relationship between social attitude, behavior, and morbidity among women in Dubai and found that psychiatric morbidity increased when the attitude score and the behavior score departed considerably from each other. Morbidity was particularly high in women who harbor traditional beliefs but are less conventional in behavior. In Saudi Arabia, a positive correlation was found between the concern about sociocultural changes and depression. Those who were upset by social transformation and perceived change as negative were more inclined to become depressed (Ibrahim and Al-Nafie, 1991).

Family Transformation

The transformation from traditional extended families to urban nuclear families seems to be wrapped in stressful experiences. In a newly urbanized area in Sudan, 40.3 percent of young adults, twenty-two to thirty-five years old, had at least one psychiatric symptom, and 16.6 percent received clinical diagnoses (Rahim and Cederblad, 1989). Children of Sudanese nuclear families had more conduct, emotional, and sleep problems and were more likely to be overly dependent than those who were still living in extended families. These differences may be attributed to the educational and supportive role of the extended family or to the stressful life events that accompany the process of acculturation or urbanization (Al-Awad and Sonuga-Barke, 1992). Schizophrenic Arabs living in extended families, compared to those living in nuclear families, tended to present earlier for treatment, had less sinister illness manifestation, and were found to be less prone to deterioration into affectively blunted withdrawn states (El-Islam, 1979). Boucebci (1985) observed that childhood psychosis tends to be rare in the traditional extended family with a large number of children in Algeria (cited in Al-Issa, 1989, pp. 244). Pakistani Muslim children who live in extended families in Britain exhibit significantly fewer behavioral problems than those who live in nuclear families, but living in extended families was associated with more distress for Pakistani mothers (Shah and Sonuga-Barke, 1995). In Dubai, Ghubash and his colleagues (1992, 1994) found no association between type of family and psychiatric morbidity. This may be because nuclear families in Dubai still live in fairly close association with other family members.

In many areas in Arab countries, people live in difficult socioeconomic situations that contribute to their distress. In a longitudinal study conducted in a village in Sudan, it was found that life situations such as unemployment, marital conflicts, and loneliness explain 67 percent of the variance in adult Sudanis' mental health. Childhood problems predicted only 17 percent of the variance (Cederblad and Rahim, 1989). In another study, Rahim and Cederblad (1989) found that the person most likely to develop a behavioral disorder in Sudan was a child who belongs to a family that has recently immigrated from a rural to an urban area and has a low income and low living standards as well as an overcrowded home.

Morbidity Among Women

Women and children were found to be more vulnerable and at higher risk of psychiatric illness. Studies indicate higher morbidity among women in the United Arab Emirates (31.9 percent women versus 20.3 percent men) (El-Rufaie and Absood, 1993). Higher morbidity among females was reported in other developing countries too (Harding et al., 1980). Arab women reported more symptoms of anxiety and depression than men (Ibrahim, 1991) and scored higher in neuroticism (Abdel-Khalek and Eysenck, 1983). Although the general morbidity in Saudi Arabia was higher among men than women (El-Rufaie et al., 1988), more women, with a ratio of 1.6 to 1, were represented among hospitalized patients of some hospitals in Saudi Arabia (El-Rufaie and Mediny, 1991). In other hospitals of the same country, men outnumbered women (El-Sayed et al., 1986). The general information we have today suggests the existence of covert morbidity among Arabic women that is not represented in medical facilities. Several cultural factors may explain this phenomenon: (1) in Saudi culture, women are totally dependent on men to bring them to the hospital; (2) many of the psychiatric symptoms in women, such as anxiety and depression, are looked on as being part of feminine behavior and thus not requiring medical attention; (3) women may be more encouraged to seek traditional healers than men; (4) in Eastern societies, women have a culturally defined attitude of acceptance toward discomfort and pain; and (5) Arab families attempt to hide psychiatric illness in females and manage at home. Unmarried, widowed, separated, polygamously married, and childless women were at high risk for somatic symptoms and schizophrenia in Saudi Arabia (Chaleby, 1986; El-Islam, 1982) and for psychiatric morbidity in general in Dubai (Ghubash, Hamdi, and Bibbington, 1992).

Morbidity Among Children

Children are also a higher-risk group. Children represent 65 percent of outpatient visits in Saudi Arabia; almost 35 percent of them showed psychiatric disturbances that warranted intensive care (Ibrahim and Ibrahim, 1993; Tuma, 1989). This high number of children in outpatient clinics may be partly attributed to the stigma for adults, especially females, who approach mental clinics, which makes the referral of children much easier.

Among the clients of the author's clinic, male children greatly outnumber females. Several factors contribute to these differences: (1) girls' problems, such as anxiety and depression, tend to be more emotional than behavioral, and these problems may not be considered to need therapy; (2) girls receive less attention and care than boys in the Arabic family, and their problems may be denied; and (3) the social stigma is greater for girls than boys, which may make parents avoid making a referral to psychotherapy unless the problem becomes unbearable.

War Zones

In many areas in the Arab world, people are living in stressful circumstances because of poverty, cultural transformation, or wars. Under these circumstances, children are the most vulnerable group. In areas where war conditions have existed for decades, such as Palestine, Lebanon, Iraq, Kuwait, and Sudan, research has shown a high prevalence of psychological disorders, especially among children.

In the occupied territories of Palestine (the West Bank and Gaza Strip), 40 percent of the casualties among Palestinians have been under the age of fifteen years. The vast majority of Palestinian children have been shot, detained, arrested, beaten, or tear-gassed (Raundalen and Melton, 1994). Psychological disorders have been correlated with the number and level of traumatic events to which

Palestinian children have been exposed. During the Palestinian *Intifada* (uprising) since 1987, problems of depression, fear, sleep disturbances, and fighting with others have been reported to have increased by 15 to 26 percent compared to the pre-*Intifada* occupation period, in which the level of psychological disorders was already high (Baker, 1990).

In Lebanon, 20 to 30 percent of children exhibited one or more behavioral problems of hyperactivity, overdependence, aggression, depression, or social misbehavior (Chimienti and Abu-Nasr, 1992-1993; Nassar, 1991). Following the Israeli invasion of Lebanon in 1982, the prevalence of psychosomatic symptoms among Lebanese children was as high as 58 percent (Rayhida, Shaya, and Armenian, 1986). In southern Sudan, 40 percent of the children have lost at least one of their parents because of war. Many children have fled from the war and become street children, choosing life on their own instead of probable death with their parents (Raundalen and Melton, 1994). In Iraq, most children live under the threat of death because of military actions or starvation. They still remember the mass death during the Gulf War. After seeing many dead bodies as a result of shelling, one twelve-year-old Iraqi girl said, expressing her fear, "My home is my horror" (Raundalen and Melton, 1994). Taking into account that the vast majority of traumatized Arab children are not likely to get any professional therapy, they are expected to suffer from a variety of psychological disorders as adults and also as parents who are supposed to raise a new generation.

DISTRIBUTION OF THE DISORDERS

The prevalence as well as the manifestation of psychological disorders are different in Arab society than in the West (Dwairy, in press a).

Somatoform Disorders

Researchers who study Arab society have reported a high prevalence of somatization (Al-Issa and Al-Issa, 1969; Gorkin, Masalha, and Yatziv, 1985; Isaui, 1994; Racy, 1980, 1985; West, 1987). Somatoform disorders are highly prevalent, and the physical aspects of depression and anxiety are very salient and overshadow the emotional aspects. Distress in general is expressed by somatic complaints related to the heart, shoulders, and back, or fatigue that involves practically the whole body (El-Islam, 1982; Racy, 1980). Somatic expression of distress has been noted also among various South/Easterners (or non-Westerners): Chinese, Puerto Ricans, and Greeks (McGoldrick, Pearce, and Giordano, 1982).

Conversion disorder (hysteria) prevalence has decreased in the last few decades in Western countries. It constitutes only 1 to 3 percent of outpatient referrals to mental health clinics (American Psychiatric Association, 1994, pp. 455). In the Arab countries, it is still high in outpatients as well as inpatients. Conversion disorders constitute 8 percent of the inpatients in Saudi Arabia (El-Sayed et al., 1986), 10.9 percent in Egypt (Okasha, 1968), and 10 percent in Sudan (Hafeiz, 1980).

Somatic problems in the South/Eastern cultures are accompanied by much misunderstanding in the West because they are perceived according to the dualistic Western conceptualization of human (mind-body) problems. The DSM-IV (American Psychiatric Association, 1994) defines somatoform disorders as "the presence of physical symptoms and suggests a general medical condition but which are not fully explained by a general medical condition, by direct effect of a substance, or by another mental disorder" (p. 445). This definition assumes psychological causes of physical manifestations. Therefore, somatoform disorders are considered to be a somatization of psychological problems.

Ancient and Renaissance medical approaches in Europe were holistic. Physical problems, as well as psychological ones, were considered mind-body problems that were inflicted by evil spirits. When Cartesian dualism became the dominant philosophical conceptualization of human problems, a clear distinction between psychological and physical disorders became evident. Along with this development, the self had emerged as an independent entity in the West. As a result of the attention given to the psychological aspects of human problems in the West, such as emotions, thoughts, and behaviors, these psychological aspects became distinct in the conceptualization of the problems of human beings. Since then problems such as stress, depression, and anxiety are considered psychological and assumed to be related to psychological constructs (such as the self or ego) or to psychological processes (such as conflict or repression) and almost detached from the body. This historical-cultural development in the West contributed to "psychologization of the mind-body." Consistent with the process that distinguished between somatic and psychological processes and to the emergence of the self and other psychological functions as independent entities, physical aspects of human distress seemed to be unusual because distress is supposed to be displayed by psychological symptoms such as anxiety or depression. Since the emergence of this distinction, physical manifestations of distress have been considered the somatization of psychological problems.

Two main cultural characteristics should be kept in mind to understand the manifestation of distress in South/Eastern societies: (1) in most of these societies, a distinct individuated self still has not completely emerged yet as has happened in the West; therefore, the body more than the self constitutes the individual's identity; (2) most people are still preoccupied with fulfilling their basic biological needs rather than higher psychological needs, such as self-actualization. Well-being in these societies is measured by physical rather than psychological means. Considering these two facts, an assumption of psychological manifestation of problems, as in the West, might not be valid for South/Eastern cultures. Distress in these societies cannot be manifested psychologically as long as the self and other psychological functions are still not legitimized and distinctively individuated. Human distress in these societies cannot be psychologized as it is in the West. Therefore, reports about somatization in South/Eastern societies, in fact, indicate the *depsychologization* of human problems rather than somatization.

There is yet another cultural factor that helps to explain the high prevalence of somatoform disorders. As an authoritarian society, the Arab community assumes that people are able to control their minds (thoughts, emotions, and behavior) but not their bodies. Therefore, psychological deviation is not tolerated and sometimes is punished, while physical problems evoke sympathy, attention, and care. People who live in this culture do not consider psychological problems to be the ones that require treatment by others but as ones that should be tolerated. A depressed woman or anxious man will be blamed rather than offered help or care for their inability to handle emotions. It is believed that people have no control over their bodies; therefore, every physical complaint evokes attention, if not overattention, and care from all of the family. A sign of distress will make the family free the symptomatic person from the many duties that are assumed to be causing that distress. Of course, people living in this climate will not bring their psychological complaints to the attention of others and may became detached from their own emotions. When distressed, they present their physical complaints and become immersed in them.

Anxiety Disorders

Anxiety disorders usually are not taken seriously by Arabs. When they occur, they are treated by cultural prescriptions suggested by elders or healers. Only in severe cases are people who suffer from anxiety referred to psychiatric institutes. Only 8.2 percent of the admissions to Ain Shams psychiatric hospital in Egypt were for anxiety disorders (Okasha, 1993). Female Palestinian clients who entered this author's clinic presented with more anxiety complaints than males. Emotional complaints are considered a sign of weakness, which is not legitimate for Arabic men. Therefore, Palestinian men tend to manifest somatic complaints, especially pain, that may suggest to others an overload of responsibilities that they carry, which will evoke sympathy (Dwairy, 1997b).

In a strict Arabic society, such as Saudi Arabia, a high prevalence of social phobia has been noticed (Chaleby, 1987). It constituted 13 percent of the neurotic disorders in the clinical population (compared to 2 percent in the Western literature). Chaleby found the disorder to be most prevalent among young, unmarried males with relatively high educational and occupational levels. He attributed this problem to the overt criticism, limited privacy, and exaggerated importance of appearance and good first impressions in Saudi Arabia. According to Chaleby, the relatively low incidence of social phobia among Saudi women is due to the fact that they are "protected" from exposure to anxiety-inducing social situations, to which men are exposed. Their social relationships are exclusive to women's gatherings that have fewer social rituals than male social meetings.

Okasha and his colleagues (1994) reported that the clinical picture of obsessive-compulsive disorder (OCD) in Arabic patients is colored by Islamic religious elements. According to him, the Islamic religion orders people to do several duties each day that may seem like obsessive rituals. They are required to pray five times a day according to a strict timetable. Each prayer is preceded with ritualistic cleaning processes (*El Woodooa'* or ablution), which includes the washing of several parts of the body in a specific order, each three times. The ablution is annulled by any form of excretion or ejaculation and, for radical religious people, by any contact with the opposite sex, even as slight as a handshake. If this happens, the Muslim should repeat the whole process of ablution. Muslims are educated to acquire these behaviors at an early age, which legitimizes ritualistic behavior and obsessive ways of thinking. Okasha and his colleges found that the most commonly occurring obsessions (60 percent) among OCD patients had religious and contamination content. The most commonly occurring compulsions were repeating rituals (68 percent) and cleaning and washing (63 percent). In contradiction to one of the criteria (criteria B) of OCD in the DSM-IV, Okasha and his colleagues reported that the majority of the OCD cases in Egypt did not recognize the absurdity of their symptoms (Okasha et al., 1994).

Al-Issa (1989) reported that OCD in Algeria appears as *waswas,* which is associated with the Muslim ritual of ablution and prayer. When a person, typically male, suffers from *waswas,* he finds it hard to terminate the ablutions because he is afraid that he is not yet clean enough to carry out his prayer in the lawful manner. He may repeat the introductory invocations and the raising of the arms more times than required. His thinking is confused, and he feels that he is not yet fully focused on God. At the end of the prayer, he becomes preoccupied with doubts about whether he might perhaps have forgotten some words of the prayer, so he will start all over again from the beginning. *Waswas* is not perceived as an illness that should be treated, but it is considered instead as a temptation by the devil intended to distract the person from his prayer (Al-Issa, 1989). Religious rituals are usually applied to undo the devil's influence.

Many psychiatric conditions in the Arabic society are believed to be caused by a trauma, *raa'bi* or *fija'* (a fright as a result of sudden threat) (Swagman, 1989). This explanation is usually applied when the onset of the condition is associated with a traumatic event.

Raa'bi or *fija'* are not applied exclusively to anxiety disorders but to a variety of psychiatric conditions such as depression, dissociation, and psychotic reactions.

Depression

While depression is considered a mood disorder characterized by sadness and anhedonia, Bazzoui (1970) reported milder mood changes among depressive patients in Iraq than in similar cases in the West. Physical symptoms and hysterical behavior were the most outstanding features of depression, found in 65.5 percent of the cases. Mood changes were found in only 34 percent of depressed cases, and only 37 percent of manic cases displayed an elated mood. Guilt feelings and worthlessness were almost absent (only 13.8 percent) among depressed patients. Fear of breaking the rules or shaming themselves and their families were dominant, much more than feelings of individual responsibility and guilt. Suicidal thoughts and attempts were rare. Paranoid ideas, projection of responsibility, aggression, and "noisiness" were not unusual among depressed cases (27.6 percent) and prevalent among hypomanic cases (47.5 percent) in Iraq. Interestingly, about one quarter of the depressed population exhibited a desire to run out of their homes into the wilderness, but the impulse was acted out only in a few cases. Bazzoui suggests that a diagnosis of depression could be made for Arab patients even when miserable feelings are absent, and diagnosis of mania could be made without the presence of elated mood. Bazzoui claims that the development of personal responsibility and superego, as well as the ability to feel guilt, must exist before a person experiences depressive feelings or feelings of worthlessness; otherwise, depression may be manifested in a physiopathological sense only (Bazzoui, 1970; Bazzoui and Al-Issa, 1966). In Sudan, Baasher (1962) reported similar characteristics of depression among Sudanese patients and noticed that the fear of breaking the rules or shaming themselves and their families was more dominant among these patients than feelings of individual responsibility and guilt. Budman, Lipson, and Meleis (1992) reported that adolescent Arabs in the United States show more shame than guilt; therefore, they consider shame to be a clinical symptom of depression for Arabic clients. Al-Issa (1989) reported a similar clinical picture of depression in Algeria, which was dominated by the prevalence of somatic symptoms. Mood disturbance was either minor or not verbalized at all by the patient. Self-depreciation and guilt feelings were rarely observed in depressive patients. Suicide rates are low in Algeria, and are the lowest during the Muslim fasting month of Ramadan, suggesting that religion has a preventive effect. One of the most frequent subtypes of depression in Algeria is called delusional depression, which is characterized by persecution themes, bewitchment, and possession and poisoning; sometimes this is accompanied by aggressive behavior. The diagnosis of delusional depression is often confused with *bouffées délirantes*, or schizophrenia, but the first tends to respond to antidepressants rather than neuroleptics (Al-Issa, 1989).

Because somatic components of depression usually overshadow the psychological components, it seems that the prevalence of depression in Arabic society is relatively low compared to the high prevalence of depression in the West. In 1970, Bazzoui reported that only 1.3 percent of the patients admitted to psychiatric hospitals in Iraq (1,120 admissions) were depressive, and 2.9 percent were manic patients (Bazzoui, 1970). The prevalence of depression, in its Western DSM-IV shape, is still low in rural traditional areas. Among the Palestinian clients of this author's clinic, 60 percent complained of anxiety or anxiety-related disorders such as phobia, somatoform disorders, and obsessive-compulsive disorders, compared to 32.6 percent who complained of depression (Dwairy, 1997b).

Gradually, the clinical picture of depression in the urbanized Arab is approaching that of the West. In urbanized regions, symptoms of distress seem to progress gradually from body to mind, and somatoform manifestations of distress have come to be expressed in more psychic terms (Racy, 1977; West, 1987). Among Saudi university students, it has been reported that there there was a much higher prevalence of depressive and other related symptoms such as self-blame (64 percent), inability to concentrate well (54 percent), shyness (53 percent), shivering and shaking when a student is irritated by someone (42 percent), and problems related to school and study (33 percent) (Ibrahim and Al-Nafie, 1991). In Dubai, an epidemiological study has reported that the prevalence of depression was higher (13.7 percent) than anxiety (7 percent) or mania and psychotic disorders (1.9 percent). In addition, depressed mood was presented in two-thirds of the anxiety cases, and autonomic (somatic) signs of anxiety were present in over half the cases of depression (Ghubash and Bibbington, 1994; Ghubash, Hamdi, and Bibbington, 1992). The most common diagnoses encountered in the United Arab Emirates have been neurotic depression (55 percent of the cases), anxiety-depressive disorders (13.3 percent), and anxiety disorders (11.7 percent) (El-Rufaie and Absood, 1993). In Egypt, Okasha (1993) reviewed the diagnoses of 800 patients admitted to the psychiatric center in Ain Shams in 1991, and this study revealed that 18.3 percent of them had mood disorders.

Because of the qualitative differences in the manifestation of depression among Arabs, researchers have used diagnostic criteria that are not uniform; therefore, it is still difficult to reach a definite answer concerning the prevalence of depression. The data that have been accumulated so far suggest a high prevalence of "mood depression" in urban Arab communities and high "somatic depression" in rural traditional communities.

Psychotic Disorders

In Okasha's report about psychiatric patients in Egypt, only 16.1 percent of the patients were schizophrenics (Okasha, 1993). The manifestation and the course of the common psychosis are different from that reported in the West. The most frequent diagnosis among psychotic patients in Egypt was psychogenic or brief reactive psychosis. In 68 percent of the acute psychotic cases, the onset was in less than five days. A stressor preceded the onset in 74 percent of the cases and correlated positively with favorable outcome at a one-year follow-up. During this same follow-up period, 64 percent of the cases had full remission. Surprisingly, the social and clinical outcome of the cases had no correlation with family history of psychiatric illness (Okasha et al., 1993). These results agree with other studies that have shown similar feature differences among other South/Eastern cultures (Cooper, Jablensky, and Sartorius, 1990). These results verify the presence of a diagnostic category for acute psychosis that is mostly precipitated by stress, has an acute or abrupt onset, and, in a majority of cases, shows a rapid recovery and maintenance of well-being after a one-year follow-up period. Symptoms presenting with these psychoses are rather polymorphic, including schizophrenic (e.g., delusions and hallucinations), affective (e.g., depression and delayed sleep), and neurotic symptoms (e.g., worry and excitement).

Recently, three psychiatrists from Tunisia, Morocco, and Algeria edited the *Manual of Psychiatry for the North African Practitioner* (Douki, Moussaoui, and Kocha, 1987, cited in Al-Issa, 1989). They reported some unique psychotic categories in North African Arabs, such as "psychosis of passion," which includes erotomania (the delusion that one is loved by someone else) and delusions of jealousy and revenge. *Bouffées délirantes* is another syndrome that is characterized by a

> sudden onset with vivid hallucinations, delusions, clouding of consciousness, and rapid mood swings. Themes of delusions are related to religion (prophetic inspiration, divine revelation, messianic conviction, end of the world, and resurrection), sexuality, jealousy, poisoning, bewitchment, and persecution. Some of the stressful life events related to the syndrome are sudden death, migration, forced marriage, sexual abuse, and incest. A frequent type of *bouffées délirantes* is nuptial psychosis which happens the day after marriage as a result of the stresses inherent in arranged marriages and is experienced by the bride. In general, patients with *bouffées délirantes* tend to be mostly females between the ages of 20 and 30. (Al-Issa, 1989, p. 242)

Side by side with reactive psychosis, endogenous schizophrenia was also observed in the Arab countries. Chaleby (1988) observed a trend of clustering schizophrenia in families in Saudi Arabia. This trend was found in consanguineous marriages, which are encouraged by Bedouin customs. He found that children of the consanguineous marriage of schizophrenics are at risk for schizophrenia, which supports the hypothesis of a genetic origin of this disorder.

Still another cultural factor causes confusion when comparing psychosis in Arabic and Western societies. It is misleading to evaluate psychosis in Arabic society according to Western conceptualization. Psychotic disorders, as defined in the West, have to do with reality testing. The more a person lives in an imaginative subjective world, the more he or she is detached from objective reality. Many South/Eastern cultures, including the Arabic culture, have concepts of reality different from those used in the West (Al-Issa, 1995). People in these societies have daily imaginative experiences that are considered real. They get guidance from visions and dreams in a way that affects their lives. Crucial life decisions are sometimes made according to this guidance. Sometimes, pathological hallucinations are explained according to religious beliefs that family members of the Prophet Mohammed appeared to direct or advise the person. Trance states are thought to be healing events, as when the *Zar* ceremony is held (El-Islam, 1982). *Sufism* (a branch of Islam) considers objective reality the unreal one. For them, the *real* reality can be reached only through meditating (or trance states), which brings the *Sufi* closer to God.

In Arabic society, there are delusional cultural beliefs that the devil, sorcery, and the evil eye cause mental illness. Unacceptable wishes, feelings, and acts are projected onto the devil and manifest as *wiswas* or *jinni* (Genie) possession. *Wiswas* is a rumination involving aggressive or sexual impulses that are attributed to the devil; this enables people to avoid responsibility and feelings of guilt. *Jinni* possession states permit acting out forbidden drives and claiming to be unaware of and not responsible for these acts (El-Islam, 1982). Judging these cultural behaviors by Western concepts may mislead the naive observer and make him or her pathologize them. On the other hand, understanding these cultural beliefs should not make the psychologist normalize psychotic cases. A thin line differentiates between pathological delusions and cultural ones. A rigid delusion involving personification of the devil or *jinni* as a persecutory figure is pathological or alien to the culture, whereas thinking about the devil or *jinni* as supernatural agents is considered to be culturally normal (El-Islam, 1982). The amount of behavior explained by the *jinni* is another indicator of pathology. The more behaviors attributed to the *jinni* rather than the self or social factors, the more the likelihood of pathology.

Along with the aforementioned cultural way of thinking, Arabic clients tend to describe their complaints in metaphoric rather than objective ways. They may say "my heart is burning in fire," "my heart is dead," or "I feel ants running inside my body." These descriptions may sound psychotic to the naive Western psychologist. In fact, Arabic language in general has been held to express emotivity at the expense of rationality. Therefore, Arabic patients tend to exaggerate their verbal reports of distress, which may mislead the practitioner who is unfamiliar with the Arabic culture into a diagnosis of hysterical neurosis (El-Islam, 1982), or psychosis.

Concepts of reality, cultural beliefs, and metaphoric descriptions should be taken into consideration during the diagnosis of Arabic and other South/Eastern clients.

Personality Disorders

As a result of authoritarian collectivistic methods of socialization, Arabs may seem, to a naive Western practitioner, to have "dependent personality disorder"; they need the help and support of others to survive, and are afraid to lose it; therefore, they avoid expressing disagreement with others (*mosayara*) and are ready to do anything to maintain a relationship. They do not feel responsible for their problems and project responsibility onto others. Technically speaking, these cultural features meet the criteria for dependent personality disorder. But when we take the sociocultural background of Arabs into consideration, we realize that these features are very adaptive and reasonable.

Because adults in the West no longer depend on their families for survival, dependency, such as a fear of opposing the parents' wishes or an inability to make personal decisions, is considered a sort of transference from childhood or a sign of a dependent personality. Therapists who encounter such cases help patients realize that they are no longer dependent and are able to make their own decisions independently. Such a therapeutic attitude would be far from realistic for many Arab clients because they are objectively still dependent on their families.

Concerning borderline personality disorder, Gorkin, Masalha, and Yatziv (1985) reported different characteristics of borderline Arabic clients than of Western clients. They are less schizoid and rarely have the feeling of detachment and emptiness. When they act out sexual or antisocial drives, it seems to be accompanied by feelings of enormous passion.

Eating Disorders

Food plays a central role in the lives of Arab families. Love, care, and respect are expressed by providing food or invitations to meals (Meleis, 1981). They associate plumpness with attractiveness and health (Timimi, 1995). Eating disorders (anorexia and bulimia) are considered rare or absent in Arabic society (Al-Issa, 1966; El-Sarrag, 1968). During this author's work for sixteen years in the Palestinian community in Israel, he encountered very few cases of anorexia or bulimia. In the last decade, there is an indication of eating disorders among the acculturated Arabs. Nasser (1986) found 12 percent of female Arab undergraduate students attending London universities to be bulimic but found no bulimia or anorexia cases among matched female Arab students in Cairo, Egypt.

Sexual Disorders

Sexual behavior and dysfunction has rarely been studied in Arabic societies. Regarding the strict restrictions on sexual behavior, especially among women, it is reasonable to assume a high prevalence of problems related to guilt, anxiety, and inhibition. Clinical impressions suggest a high prevalence of vaginismus among Arabic women, which is usually not treated. When it happens in the early days of marriage, it is considered normal. The bride is encouraged by her family to keep withstanding that pain. If she continues to be reluctant, divorce is the main option. Because Arabic society in general does not claim absolute equality between genders, many problems of sexual inhibition that the DSM-IV defines as disorders are not considered disorders when they occur in Arabic women. Among these problems are hypoactive sexual desire disorder, female sexual arousal disorder, and female orgasmic disorder. Arabic women are assumed not to have sexual desires and are expected to function as wives who meet their husbands' sexual needs. In some Arabic societies, females are circumcised to prevent sexual gratification.

On the other hand, premature ejaculation is rarely considered a disorder for Arabic males. For some of them, it may be considered a symbol of high sexual potency or masculinity. Erectile problems are the main issues that worry Arabic men. Erectile problems of men and vaginismus problems of women are the main sexual problems that receive attention in the Arab society. Typically, family members are involved in helping to solve these problems (see case number six in Chapter 10). They may suggest traditional prescriptions or a referral to traditional healers. Some of them may be referred for medical help. Okasha and Demerdash (1975) reported on 68 male Arabs (Kuwaitis, Palestinians, and Egyptians) who suffered erectile disorders and premature ejaculation. Many of them had accompanying somatic complaints, mostly backache; this may be because of the traditional belief that the back is the source of semen. About half of the patients reported a past history of homosexuality. When asked about their own evaluation of their disorder, most of them attributed it to undersized or diseased genitalia. Few of them blamed supernatural causes or masturbation. Based on their psychoanalytical approach, Gorkin, Masalha, and Yatziv (1985) claimed that a large number of Arab cases demonstrate obvious oedipal complexes and attributed impotence to castration anxiety and fears of sexual temptation by females.

The cultural attitude of Arab society toward sexuality explains various sexual dysfunctions, many of which are the result of the impact of the wedding night. It is sometimes nerve-racking for the couple to find their whole extended families at the doorstep of the bedroom awaiting the consummation of the marriage. If the bride fails to prove her virginity, she will bring on herself the family's violent revenge, particularly by the men (Bazzoui and Al-Issa, 1966). Not surprisingly, many men have found themselves unable to achieve erection under these circumstances. Fortunately, these customs have ceased in urban areas, but the intervention and the pushing of the family toward conception still exist in various ways.

Because relationships between male and female Arab children are restricted, sexual games that usually take place during the course of sexual development involve homosexual behavior and masturbation. Homosexuality may occur in Arabic society either as a sexual game or as exploitation of younger boys by older boys or men (Al-Issa and Al-Issa, 1969; Parhad, 1965). Unlike the West, homosexual behavior in Arabic society is usually situational and is not necessarily associated with sexual identity. Despite the high prevalence, homosexuality and masturbation are condemned and denied in the Arab society. Almost nothing is known about homosexual behavior or masturbation among Arabic women.

Unfamiliarity with the cultural style of communication among Arabs may mislead the Western observer. Physical expression of warmth and friendship is practiced within the same gender and almost prohibited between genders. When Arabs meet after a long absence, men hug and kiss each other, and women do the same with women. It is not uncommon to see, in public, two male friends holding hands or one putting his hand on the shoulder of the other. Brides, in many areas, hold women's parties in which women dance with other women. All of these socially accepted behaviors are the result of the strict segregation between genders rather than an indication of homosexuality.

Sexual experiences in Arab societies are accompanied with much anxiety. In the author's Palestinian clinic, more women (18 percent) than men (7 percent) expressed anxiety related to sexual behavior. These differences may be attributed to the higher sexual oppression of women or to the difficulty for Arab men to admit their fear concerning sexual behavior. This is because fearfulness of men, especially about sexual issues, is not accepted in the Arab society.

Sexual Abuse

Sexual abuse in Arabic society is not less than that in the West. In research conducted by the centers for psychological services among eleven-year-old Palestinian children in Israel, 22 percent of male and 10 percent of female children indicated that they had been sexually abused. The abuse included undressing, touching genitals, and feeling pain. Considering the difficulty of admitting sexual behavior, especially for girls, it is reasonable to assume higher rates of abuse. Of the abused children, 40.1 percent were victimized more than once. About half of the abuse was perpetrated by a family member (Dwairy, 1997b). When an abused Arabic child disclosed the abuse, the claim was usually denied and the child blamed or punished. Therefore, the vast majority of abuse is not reported to any adult and does not get any treatment.

Dissociative Disorders

In light of the causal relationship between sexual abuse and dissociation (Putnam, 1989), dissociative disorders are expected to be as common among Arabs as they are in the West. To my knowledge, there are no empirical reports about the prevalence of dissociative disorders in Arab countries. Clinical impressions suggest that dissociation between the self and the body (e.g., somatoform disorder) is the most common among Arabs, rather than dissociation of the self. Multiple personality disorder seems to be very rare or nonexistent in Arab society. Considering that the "self" among Arabs does not individuate completely and does not exist as an independent entity (see Chapter 4), it is reasonable to assume that a split of the self is not feasible. Therefore, multiple personality disorder does not occur.

In addition, Arabs believe that mental disorder is caused by possession. *Zar* is a term used to refer to several mental illnesses. It is a class of spirits that is believed typically to possess women. Treatment of these illnesses is done by means of a *zar* ceremony in which a trance state is induced by a healer who works to convince the *zar* spirit to leave the body (Al-Sabaie, 1989). During the course of the illness, as well as during the *zar* ceremony, the patient experiences dissociative states in which he or she expresses forbidden aggressive or sexual acts, believing that these are the responsibility of the spirit not his or her own acts.

Substance Abuse

The use of cannabis (kif, hashish) is tolerated in traditional North African Arabic societies. The drug users are typically normal married adults who are no different in their values and moral principles from the rest of society. The traditional picture has recently changed, as intake of drugs has become more compulsive despite repressive legislation (Al-Issa, 1989). Epidemiological reports in the Arab countries have consistently reported a very low prevalence of alcoholism (Al- Sabaie, 1989; Rahim and Cederblad, 1989). Islamic religion is the major preventing factor. According to Islamic law, alcohol and drug consumption are absolutely prohibited. Therefore, alcoholism is almost absent in traditional communities in the Arab world. In many Arab countries, such as Saudi Arabia, there is strict legislation against substance use. Smuggling or trafficking of drugs in Saudi Arabia risks invoking the death penalty. Alcohol use and abuse in the Arab world is found only among a small portion of Arabs, typically urbanized, artists, or middle-upper class.

PSYCHOMETRIC CHARACTERISTICS OF ARABS

Few studies have addressed psychometric aspects among Arabs. Ibrahim (1977, 1979, 1982) found some psychometric features among Egyptians. He found Egyptian students to be more dogmatic than Western students (Ibrahim, 1977) and less extroverted than the Americans and British (Ibrahim, 1979). He found that cultural features such as oversensitivity, superstition, and concern for socially sanctioned behavior and social desirability were more important personality factors among Egyptians than neuroticism, psychoticism, and extroversion, which are more common cultural features in the West (Ibrahim, 1982). The latter three factors apply in Arab societies as well, however (Farrag, 1987). El-Zahhar and Hocevar (1991) tested several aspects of anxiety among Egyptian high school students and found higher emotionality, trait anxiety, test anxiety, worry, and arousability than in students in the United States and Brazil. Similar results have been reported for Jordanian and Saudi Arabian students. While the average test anxiety level in the world is approximately 40 points on the Test Anxiety Inventory (TAI), with an average standard deviation of about 10, the average test anxiety level for high school students in Arabic countries is approximately 50 points (Ahlawat, 1989; El-Zahhar and Hocevar, 1991).

Based on clinical experience and field research, the author has found the following psychometric characteristics of Palestinian performance on some well-known (Western-developed) psychological tests (Dwairy, in press a).

WISC-R

Compared to Jewish and American students, Arab elementary school students in Israel had significantly lower IQ scores. The gap increases with age, suggesting a main socioeducational effect. The most common difficulties were on the similarities and comprehension subtests. The only subtest on which Arab students outperformed Jewish students was information. These differences may be at least partially explained by the culturally alien test items given to Arab students. In addition, these scores reflect the Arabic educational climate that encourages rote learning, helps to store information, and discourages analytical thinking and the decision-making process, which are needed on the similarities and comprehension subtests.

Bender-Gestalt and Draw-a-Person

In both tests, performance of Arab students is similar to that of Americans until age seven; after that, the Arab scores show a comparative decline. At age ten to eleven, the performance of Arabs is equivalent to that of eight-year-old American children. This lag may be explained by the lack of encouragement for graphic activity by Arab parents and educators. Graphic experience is limited in Arab homes and schools compared to American ones.

The relative retardation of Arabs on the WISC-R and the other graphic tests should never be interpreted as an absolute retardation because these tests are oriented toward Western testing skills that are important for successful adaptation in Western societies. These skills are not necessarily needed in traditional Arab society. In these societies, knowing the norms and behaving accordingly, knowing how to heal illnesses without modern medical services, predicting the weather based on environmental signs without a TV forecast, knowing the herbs that may nourish or heal and how to differentiate them from poisonous ones, surviving in the desert climate without any modern facilities, and tracking the traces in the desert are some of the vital skills. Of course, if an intelligent Western person is tested in these skills, the results will not indicate his or her intelligence. The same occurs when South/Easterners are tested by Western tests.

Rorschach

The performance of fifty Arab students, age sixteen, was compared to a similar age group of Western students (reported by Levitt and Truumaa, 1972). Only slight differences were found. Arab students showed lower R (17.2 versus 20.8), higher W (35 versus 21.9), lower P (4.5 versus 5.3), and higher shading scores.

All other scores were equivalent. The results here too should not be interpreted according to Western norms. Therefore, they do not indicate any pathological sign, rather cultural characteristics.

SUMMARY

Several sociocultural factors contribute to higher psychiatric morbidity in the Arab countries than in Western or other developing countries. Among these factors are the social oppression caused by the authoritarian social system and the cultural confusion caused by the rapid transition in some countries from traditional to urban lifestyles. The manifestation of disorders among Arabs differs qualitatively from that described in the DSM-IV. Differences in the level of individuation between Arabs and Westerners make considerable difference in the characteristics of the disorders. Social stresses, more than intrapsychic conflicts, precipitate the onset of the disorder (e.g., psychotic disorders). The manifestation of distress is physical more than psychological (e.g., depression). Despite the high prevalence of abuse, dissociation occurs mainly between the self and the body, rather than within the self. Many problems that are considered disorders in the West are considered normal in Arab society (e.g., some sexual disorders). Some disorders are rare or do not exist in Arab society (e.g., eating disorders and multiple personality disorder). Psychometric differences have been observed in the performance of Palestinians on some well-known (Western-developed) psychological tests. Unfamiliarity with the cultural features of Arabs may cause misdiagnosis by clinicians (e.g., dependent personality disorder and delusional disorder). It seems crucial to reexamine the diagnostic criteria of psychological disorders within the context of the South/Eastern societies.

Chapter 6

Arab Cultural Attitudes Toward Mental Health

TRADITIONAL ARAB THEORY OF PSYCHOPATHOLOGY

The Arabic word for madness, *junoon,* is derived from the word *jinni,* which means evil spirit (Al-Issa, 1989; Bazzoui, 1970; Timimi, 1995). It has been thought that *junoon* happens when an evil spirit possesses a person. Arabs do not attribute psychopathology to intrapsychic causes; rather, they attribute illness to external natural factors such as germs, nerves, food, poisoning, or supernatural factors such as the evil eye, sorcery, spirits, or possession (Budman, Lipson, and Meleis, 1992; Dwairy, 1997b; Meleis, 1981; Timimi, 1995). Many mental illnesses are attributed to sorcery or the evil eye, which may be motivated by envy, jealousy, or even admiration of an enemy or friend. Ill wishes are believed to be transferred to another person through witchcraft or directly through the eye. Knot magic is another form of magical control Arabs believe in. For instance, a male sexual dysfunction may be regarded as being caused by a jealous woman who wants to destroy a marriage, thus knotting the husband (Bazzoui and Al-Issa, 1966).

Many psychological disorders are attributed to a traumatic event: *raa'bi* (an extreme fright as a result of sudden threat) or *fija'* as it is called in Yemen (Swagman, 1989). This explanation is applied to a variety of disorders when the onset can be associated with a traumatic event. Mental illness can be attributed to many external factors. Lack of eating or sleeping, moving to a new house, buying a new dress, having a new neighbor, having a new in-law in the family, and many other changes in life could be identified as the cause of the illness.

The Islamic influence on Arab psychology is revealed in the idea that life, as well as the future, is "in the hands of *Allah*" (God). In the authoritarian way of living, almost everything is determined by an external authority, which leaves small room for a person to feel a sense of responsibility for his or her own destiny. In complete opposition to this external locus of control is the Arab attitude concerning behavioral control. Naturally, a person is assumed to have full self-control; therefore, unacceptable behavior is punished. When people display unacceptable behavior in the course of psychopathology, they are thought to have lost self-control, which is attributed to external factors. In this case, they are no longer considered responsible and give up the respect and dignity that usually derive from the ability to behave according to social norms and values. Hence, a stigma is attached to a mentally ill Arab.

To avoid the stigma, a person who is still able to withstand the distress, such as in emotional or neurotic disorders, tends to avoid verbal and behavioral display; rather, it is displayed in physical symptoms over which the person is naturally assumed to have no control. This is another factor that contributes to the high frequency of physical symptoms of depression and anxiety among Arabs (Al-Issa and Al-Issa, 1969; Racy, 1980, 1985). For additional factors see the section on somatoform disorders in Chapter 5.

Unlike Westerners, Arabs tend not to pathologize behavior. Only extreme cases are considered to be *junoon,* while other manifestations of emotional distress are considered normal. For instance, anxiety and depression among women may be considered part of their femininity. Fatigue or physical pain among men may be considered the result of heavy duty or work. Individuals with mild mental disorders or mild retardation are considered *faq'ir* (mentally deprived) and almost absorbed in the community. In many rural Arab communities, the mentally retarded are viewed with a mixture of reverence and awe. They can have simple and useful occupations (El-Islam, 1982). Ruminations and cleanliness rituals are sometimes considered a part of the cultural and religious attitude that conservative Muslims hold toward cleanliness. They usually perform cleanliness rituals before each prayer and after touching a member of the opposite sex (e.g., by shaking hands) (Okasha, 1977).

Arabs, in general, tolerate mental and emotional disturbance to a considerable degree as long as it is not expressed in undue violence, shameful behavior, or uncontrollable overactivity. The emotional component of a patient's symptoms is seldom enough to bring him or her to therapy; it is the behavior that is decisive in seeking treatment. Sometimes, even hallucinations are explained according to religious beliefs that family members of the Prophet Muhammad may appear to give some directives or advice (Bazzoui and Al-Issa, 1966).

Once a person is recognized as mentally ill, he or she is excused for any deviant behavior. People who display physical complaints are excused from doing their duties and are overloaded with sympathy, care, and support from the whole family. For a distressed person who has not been listened to previously, this change becomes a huge secondary gain for the illness and reinforces the complaints.

Because Arabs do not believe that personal, familial, or interpersonal conflicts are associated with psychopathology, they do not seek help through psychotherapy. Treatment is sought either through a physician who treats the body or by healers who work to neutralize the effect of the *jinni.* These referrals are considered to be less stigmatic than a referral to a psychiatrist. To undo the effects of the *jinni,* sorcery, or the evil eye, some rituals may be performed. Examples are antisorcery and antienvy rituals including the use of incantation and amulets containing verses of the *Qura'an,* fumigation with incense, visits to the tombs of religious sheikhs, and purification rituals that involve drinking or washing in water that has been washed off *Qura'anic* verses written on a plate (Dwairy, in press a; El-Islam, 1982).

Another common ritual is the *zar* ceremony. Originally, *zar* was a term for a variety of illnesses usually suffered by women, as well as a class of spirits who are believed to cause these illnesses through possession (Dwairy, in press a). Treatment procedures include diagnosis of the illness as being caused by *zar* possession and the identification of the particular *zar* involved by means of a dialogue between the healer and the patient while both are in a dissociated state (Al-Sabaie, 1989). In this group ceremony, all participants experience states of trance under the influence of drumming, chanting, and dancing, during which they express worries and wishes that are otherwise socially prohibited. Each song is directed by the *zar* healer to a particular spirit which, if present in the body of a member of the audience, will speak through him or her. It is to the spirit that strange wishes are attributed. Such wishes must be answered by sacrifices, for example, to placate the spirit and to persuade it to leave the possessed body. Birds, rams, and lambs are often slaughtered as sacrifices, and parts of them are then eaten by the person to be exorcized. Blue beads or figures involving the number five, such as hand symbols, are frequently used to protect people from the evil eye, sorcery, and *jinni* (El-Islam, 1982). According to El-Islam, native healers fit the general cultural tendency toward projection rather than personal responsibility. They seem to enforce the mechanism of projection that psychodynamic psychiatry usually tries to undo.

In the authoritarian Arab society, drives and feelings are kept unexpressed. The *zar* ceremony actually offers an accepted outlet for these unexpressed drives without imposing any personal responsibility. When the *zar* is held on a recurrent basis in the community, it becomes the solution the culture offers to keep the social homeostasis. This solution both maintains the authoritarian system and allows relief of the drives in a culturally accepted way.

Exorcism has been applied by some religious healers in many Arab countries. In Lebanon, exorcism was used by European preachers and priests. In the Lebanese mountains, there was a cave that was known for casting out evil spirits. Katchadourian (1980) described the traditional way of exorcism as it was done in that cave at the end of the nineteenth century.

The entrance to the cave was guarded by two large rocks, arched over and surmounted by a cross. The person being led to the cave was watched for signs of fear as he or she approached the arch. If the person became apprehensive at the sight of the cross or refused to proceed further, this was taken as additional evidence of possession.

The attempt at cure took place within the large cave where water dripping from the walls formed stalactites, which were broken up and sold as amulets by the monks. Along the walls of the cave, there were stone blocks on which the person was seated and his or her neck was secured to the wall by a heavy collar and chain. The initial treatment consisted of merely letting the afflicted person remain in the cave for three days. On the third night, the patron saint was expected to appear, cast out the demon, and restore the person to reason. If the subject survived the wait but did not recover, the monks then resorted to more forceful methods. The person was to face the priest who beat him or her on the head with a heavy boot while reading the text of exorcism: "Get thee away from this person, accused devil, and enter into the Red Sea and leave the temple of God. I force thee in the name of the Father, the Son, and the Holy Ghost to go to the everlasting fire." In cases when the patient died while in the cave, the monks told his or her family that Saint Anthony had loosened his chain and had taken him or her straight to heaven, which entitled the monastery to a donation (Katchadourian, 1980, pp. 547-548).

Today, exorcism is applied mainly by Muslim religious healers. During exorcism, the healer converses with the evil spirit through the patient. He may appeal to or threaten the evil spirit by repeating a religious magical formula, burning incense, and offering a sacrifice of a black cock. The healer may simply beat the patient with a stick as a last resort to expel the evil spirit from the body (Al-Issa, 1989).

When the psychiatric condition is believed to be a traumatic reaction, such as the *raa'bi* or *fija'*, several ways have been used to undo the effect of the trauma. Beside rituals, a counterbalancing shock may be applied. Swagman reported a *fija'* case that had been treated in this way:

> A 30-year-old woman witnessed her husband's Toyota Landcruiser begin to roll towards a sheer drop with her son in the back seat. The vehicle stopped just before reaching the edge, but the woman was so frightened that she became weak and dizzy. She rested for a while and seemed to recover from the shock, but later that evening, she had very disturbed sleep. The next day, she began to complain of dizziness and dropped plates and bowls while preparing the noonday meal. She began to complain that she was suffering from fija', and, after some discussion among her family, it was decided that her fright had brought on her illness. Later that evening, she was suddenly grabbed from behind by her husband, and while she was held down, her brother applied a glowing hot iron to the back of her

> neck. After she stopped sobbing and wailing and began to recover from the second counterbalancing shock, she went to bed and rested. The next day, she had to contend with a severe burn but was no longer suffering from the symptom of fija'. (Swagman, 1989, p. 384)

In another treatment of *raa'bi* or *fija'*, the subject may be directed to drink water from a special metallic bowl engraved with religious verses called *Taset el raa'bi* (the bowl of *raa'bi*-fright). It is believed that this act will undo the effect of the trauma.

In addition to the aforementioned traditional treatments, marriage is often regarded as "the cure" for Arab patients. Schizoid, retarded, and depressed individuals may be forced into marriage by family elders on the assumption that marriage will take them out of their seclusion and improve their health, an assumption that is often disproved when they experience psychotic episodes soon after marriage (El-Islam and El-Deeb, 1968).

HELP-SEEKING BEHAVIOR

Generally speaking, Arabs tolerate psychological distress for a long time before seeking help (Dwairy, in press a; Okasha et al., 1994). Influenced by the Bedouin appreciation of courage, some Arab communities, such as the Saudis, dictate that pain is to be accepted with indifference (Story, 1985). Only when pain or distress becomes unbearable is psychotherapy sought. Among the Palestinian clients who sought help in the author's clinic in Nazareth, Israel, 44.2 percent came to therapy after years of hesitating, and another 44.2 percent came after months. Only 11 percent of the clients came after a couple of weeks, and 0.6 percent came without any delay (Dwairy, 1997b).

Arabs believe that physicians, native healers, religious figures, or family members are the proper alleviators of illness and distress. A psychiatrist or psychologist is a last resort (Okasha et al., 1994; Timimi, 1995). Traditional and religious healers play a major role in primary psychiatric care. Most of the psychiatric conditions are dealt with by local and, usually, religious healers (Timimi, 1995). An estimated 60 percent of outpatients at the university clinic of

Cairo, which serves mostly low-status socioeconomic patients, had sought treatment from traditional healers before coming to a psychiatrist (Okasha, 1993; Okasha, Kamel, and Hassan, 1968). When Arabs engage in psychotherapy after they have been involved with traditional healing or medical doctors, they question the relationship between personal information and their health. When they encounter comprehensive assessments about childhood, personal, and familial life, they feel invaded and sometimes become uncommunicative. Typically, they minimize the personal and familial problems, absolve the family from responsibility for the illness, and focus on the complaints from which they suffer.

Arab families discourage long-term hospitalization or institutionalization for their family members. They feel the right and responsibility to be the caretakers of their unfortunate members. Okasha (1993) reported that caring for an elderly demented person outside of the family is considered shameful; Egyptians, therefore, prefer to assimilate chronic mental patients within the community. The parents of retarded or hyperactive children also feel a primary responsibility for them rather than relinquishing them to institutionalized care (Okasha, 1993). Similar attitudes seem to exist in Qatar (El-Islam, 1982).

During hospitalization, Arab families do not discontinue their supportive role; on the contrary, family members and friends volunteer to attend to the patient. Groups of them stay with the patient for hours in the hospital, comforting him or her, bringing food from home, and offering their help. This cultural way of support seems unusual for the Western practitioner and may be considered intrusive. Meleis and La Fever (1984) reported that nurses and doctors in the United States often label Arab family members as "anxious" and "intrusive," consider Arab patients to be "unpopular" or "chronic," and give them less time and personalized attention.

Males are currently seeking psychotherapy more than females. Among the clients of the author's clinic, 65.3 percent were males. Similarly, more males (69 percent) than females (31 percent) were represented in outpatient clinics in Cairo. Women treat their health needs only after their children's and husbands' needs have been fulfilled (Okasha et al., 1994). It seems that women may be more vulnerable to the stigma of psychotherapy. The family does its best to hide and manage psychological disorders of females within the home. They may even consider some disorders such as anxiety and phobias normal. Males, on the other hand, are less vulnerable to the stigma and are not hidden at home. It is more difficult for men, who are the providers, to be substituted for; therefore, when distressed they are referred to therapy faster than women. It seems that psychiatric assistance is expedited for women only in severe cases when the decision is finally made by the family. Therefore, women were represented in the referrals to hospitals more than men. The ratio of women to men among Saudi psychiatric hospitals was 1.6:1 (El-Rufaie and Mediny, 1991).

Arab clients typically are focused on their complaints and are less aware of their mood and emotions. They find it difficult to talk about emotions or their personal lives. Initially, they present very beautiful, supportive family relationships (see cases in Chapter 10), and describe their complaints in somatic terms, using metaphoric expressions such as "my heart feels like a dark room" (Bazzoui, 1970; Timimi, 1995). Based on the belief that life, as well as the future, is "in the hands of *Allah*," clients do not assume responsibility for their pathological actions (West, 1987). They place the responsibility for change on the therapist. They often appear silent and expect the therapist to do all of the work. Their answers are frequently vague and nonspecific because they question the relevance of personal information to their health (Meleis, 1981; Meleis and La Fever, 1984). The concept of working to improve the self is generally nonexistent in Arab cultures (West, 1987).

Typically, Arab patients assume that medication by intrusive methods (injections, rather than pills) is most effective (Meleis and La Fever, 1984). They do not believe that talk therapy is worth paying for unless it is in the form of direct advice. This has to do with the cultural value of talk, which is a way to please others and meet their expectations or a way of communication to make social expectations clear rather than a precise description of a person's actual experiences. Authoritarian society, a lack of "psychological mindedness," and other-directed culture affect the therapeutic relationship. Arabs are unfamiliar with insight-oriented therapy. Long-term and nondirective therapy may confuse and frustrate the patient who is used to being in a well-defined environment (Dwairy and Van Sickle, 1996; Gorkin, Masalha, and Yatziv, 1985; West, 1987).

Despite the above, psychotherapists and psychiatrists are considered authorities deserving respect in Arab societies. Influenced by sexist attitudes, however, Arab clients prefer and respect male rather than female therapists. Female therapists experience greater difficulties. In the personal experience of this author when he interacted with clients along with a female psychologist, they would frequently refer to the female colleague as a nurse and this author as a doctor.

Racy (1980) reported that Saudi Arabian women preferred a male therapist. They could not understand how a female therapist could be both an expert and a woman. He also described, in detail, the behavior of a typical female Saudi patient. He reported that she will come to the clinic veiled and accompanied by a male member or several members of the family. She will limp in and lean on the arms of a male relative. Dropping heavily into a chair, she may remain quiet and veiled until spoken to. Her demeanor reflects passivity to an extreme. Initially, she may say nothing and refer any questions to the accompanying relative. Shoulders are frequently shrugged, and "I don't know" is a common answer. She will answer only when pressed. Interpersonal and psychological difficulties are usually denied, and the therapist is assured that all is well and everyone is happy. Anger is transformed into sadness, disappointment, and/or self-blame, particularly when the object of the anger is present. The patient may express her problem in somatic terms that prevent her from attending to her household duties and force her to spend much time resting. She does not assume responsibility for her illness nor does she accuse anyone else. She expects to be examined and prescribed a medication. Injections and large colored pills are preferred (Racy, 1980).

In other Arab countries, especially in urban populations, client behavior may be much different than in the Saudi example. Racy (1977) reported that, among urbanized Arabs, the behavior of depressed patients is approaching similarity to that in the West. In places where mental health services exist, more clients take personal responsibility and initiate mental health treatment. The existence of the services helps to develop the awareness of psychotherapy. In 1980, when this author opened the first clinic in the Palestinian community in Israel, parents who brought in their mentally retarded children or other severe cases were the majority of the referrals. Gradually, other cases with problems such as anxiety, somatoform disorders, and depression started to come in. And more clients started to approach the clinic by themselves without their families. More clients claimed responsibility for their referral as well as for the therapy. Among the clinic's clients during the last five years, 29.6 percent came without informing their families, and 12.9 percent came in spite of family opposition. The rest of the clients were accompanied by family members or at least by the ones who had been informed of the decision to seek treatment (Dwairy, 1997b). Not all the personal referrals to therapy indicate individuation. Many such clients did so to avoid the stigma associated with therapy or to bypass the opposition of their families. Typically, males were able to do this much more easily than females. Among the clients of the author's clinic, only 9 percent who approached therapy without the knowledge of their families were females (compared to 18.7 percent males).

The level of education was a major factor in predicting referrals to the author's clinic, especially among females. The percentage of clients who had finished high school (72.7 percent) was twice their percentage in the community. The parents' education was a significant factor in children's referrals as well. The percentage of young clients' parents who had finished high school (40 percent) was higher than their percentage in the community (32 percent). Unfortunately, the parents' education was a contributing factor with their male children in psychotherapy but was not significant in allowing female children to engage in therapy. The percentage of female children who were referred by educated parents was still very low (about a fifth as many as for males) and resembled those referrals made by parents with little education.

In addition, more single clients approached this author's clinic. Although Arab singles in the Palestinian community constitute 19.8 percent of the population, their percentage at the clinic was 42.9. This suggests that bachelorhood in the Arab community is associated with many stresses related to crucial decisions in life. Firstborns constituted 59.3 percent of the male clients and 27 percent of the female clients in this clinic. This has to do with the unique responsibility and high expectation that is assigned to the Arab firstborn in general and males in particular.

Generally speaking, it is difficult to maintain professional relationships and boundaries with Arab clients. They often prefer to discuss problems in a social visit to their homes rather than in a formal session at the clinic. They may come late to the session, appear on the wrong date, or they may invite the therapist to the family home for a visit or for a meal with the family. The therapist's negative response to such behavior is likely to be found insulting. Arabs expect the relationship with the therapist to be continuous rather than task-oriented (Timimi, 1995).

Arabs typically expect an instant cure. Lack of an early success coupled with skepticism about psychotherapy leads to drop-outs or to doctor shopping. Many clinicians have reported the difficulties of Arab clients in long-term therapy; little information has been reported about the attrition rate. In the author's clinic, only 15 percent of clients remained in therapy for more than ten sessions, and 49 percent dropped out after they achieved initial relief during the first five to ten sessions. The remainder of clients were referred to other kinds of treatment (hospitals or psychiatrists) after the intake session or after reaching an impasse (Dwairy, 1997b).

The denial of the role of emotions in physical health is common, not only for patients, but for physicians as well. That somatic symptoms could have a psychological origin is beyond the imagination of the average Arab patient and beyond the knowledge of many medical practitioners. Both physicians and patients are somatically oriented. When doctors fail to locate disease in the body, they typically make the diagnosis of "general physical weakness" and prescribe vitamins and rest (El-Islam, 1982).

HEALTH SERVICES DELIVERY SYSTEM

The first mental hospitals in the world were built in Arab countries: first in Baghdad, Iraq in A.D. 705, and later in Cairo (A.D. 800) and Damascus (A.D. 1270) (Okasha, 1993). Although Arabs were the first to develop psychiatric institutions, their psychiatric problems today are often referred either to native (usually religious) healers

(Timimi, 1995), or to medical doctors due to the somatic manifestations of their distress. When they do receive services from psychiatrists, they are provided with medications or other medical treatments rather than psychotherapy (Gorkin, Masalha, and Yatziv, 1985; Ibrahim and Ibrahim, 1993; West, 1987). Psychiatric treatment, then, typically occurs in one of two settings: a traditional mental hospital or an outpatient setting. Private psychiatric clinics are also an option for some. A few private corporations, universities, and religious organizations own and operate some health services that also provide psychiatric services (Ibrahim and Ibrahim, 1993); however, in most of these institutions psychotherapy per se is not represented. Variations of counseling, behavior therapy, and family therapy are sometimes employed.

Obviously, the mental health system in the Arab world reaches a very small portion of the population that needs psychological attention. Marital counseling, parental counseling, vocational guidance, crisis intervention, crisis support groups, school psychology, and other mental health services are rare or absent in most Arab countries. Psychologists who are trained in any form of psychotherapy are rare, making the need for research on mental health, in general, and training programs, in particular, imperative (Ibrahim and Ibrahim, 1993).

In general, little information is available about mental health services in Arab countries. Okasha (1993) reported in detail about the mental health system in Egypt, which is considered one of the most developed Arab countries. According to this report, only 450 psychiatrists served 57,000,000 citizens of Egypt (1 per 127,000 citizens). There are about 8,000 psychiatric beds (1 bed per 7,000 people), 5,750 of them in Cairo. Only 250 clinical psychologists were reported to be practicing in Egypt with hundreds of general psychologists working in fields unrelated to mental health services. There are many social workers practicing in psychiatric facilities, but they are not trained in psychiatric social work.

Out of twenty-four governerates (like counties) of Egypt, nineteen have some kind of psychiatric clinic and outpatient unit, while five have no psychiatric services. Community care, in the form of hostels, day centers, and rehabilitation centers, is only available in Egypt's big cities. In the rural areas, community care is implemented without health care workers. Chronic and mild psychiatric patients are "rehabilitated" by cultivating and planting fields under the supervision of family members. The programs for community care in big cities take the form of outpatient clinics, hostels for the elderly, institutions for the mentally retarded, and centers for drug abuse and programs of education in mental health and psychiatry. For thirty-five years this system has offered a master's and doctoral program in psychiatry (Okasha, 1993).

In Saudi Arabia, with a population of about ten million, only two of the four medical schools have full psychiatric services in their participating hospitals. Medical students in these two hospitals receive their psychiatric training in two to three weekly sessions during their fifth and sixth years. There is no specialty training program for psychiatry in the whole country. Health services, including medications, are provided free. All but the private hospitals are fully funded by the Saudi government. The majority of psychiatric wards are locked, and physical methods of restraint are frequently used. Psychiatric treatment is typically medication-oriented, and psychotherapy is brief and supportive. Occupational therapy is available at some centers, but, for the most part, patients spend their time listening to music or playing cards. Patients are usually discharged to the care of their relatives. Because of strong family bonds, day hospitals are very rare and halfway houses are not necessary. Child psychiatry services are poorly developed. In all of Saudi Arabia, there are only two or three child psychiatrists. Children's problems are usually ignored. Only severe child illnesses are recognized and treated with special education. Because of the rigid boundaries in the Saudi family, family or group dynamic therapy tends to be extremely difficult (Al-Sabaie, 1989).

In Algeria, there were 250 psychiatrists serving about twenty million citizens in 1985. About half of them are not Algerians but are from Eastern Europe, with no knowledge of the native language. In 1987, there were ten mental hospitals. Besides that, there are also outpatient clinics in the main general hospitals. Still no trained clinical psychologists exist in the country. There is a department of social-clinical psychology in the Institute of Psychology and Education Science at the University of Algiers, but its program is similar to educational psychology (Al-Issa, 1989).

In Lebanon, state hospitals were never developed; instead, the government subsidizes a number of beds in three main mental hospitals that are run by private sectarian leadership. One of the mental hospitals is under British leadership with a British orientation. A second has a French orientation. The third hospital is Islamic. In the last two decades, an increasing number of Lebanese psychiatrists have been trained in the United States, thus introducing a new orientation to the practice of psychiatry in the country (Katchadourian, 1980).

Fortunately, some Arab countries are witnessing the nascent growth and dissemination of information to practitioners about the psychological and social contributors to illness. The psychiatric center in Ain Shams, for example, emphasizes a biopsychosocial approach to outpatient care. In addition, they are encouraging intensive psychiatric outpatient programs in all general hospitals (Okasha, 1993).

The Palestinians in the Gaza Strip and the West Bank, as well as inside Israel, have made significant progress in developing mental health services during the last few years. In the Gaza strip (an area with 800,000 citizens), one psychiatric hospital and one community mental health program direct three local clinics. Programs utilize a multidisciplinary approach that employs psychiatrists, psychologists, social workers, nurses, and other specialists. In the West Bank (1,500,000 citizens), there is one large psychiatric hospital (320 beds) and three related local clinics. In 1995, the Palestinian Authority initiated professional development courses for physicians to increase their awareness of mental health issues. In addition, a mental health plan was initiated to meet the needs of schools and families adversely affected by the twenty-nine years of Israeli occupation (Palestinian Authority Report, 1994-1995). For the Palestinians who live in Israel (800,000 citizens), there has been significant progress in the psychological services provided to schools. At least twenty-four centers for psychological services are now providing mental health services to the Palestinian Arab schools in Israel (Israeli Ministry of Education Report, 1994).

Despite limited mental health services and the lack of information about psychotherapy, the number of Arabs seeking psychotherapy has been steadily increasing (Dwairy, 1997b; Gorkin, Masalha, and Yatziv, 1985; Okasha, 1993).

SUMMARY

Arabs, in general, attribute psychopathology to external natural factors such as germs, nerves, food, poisoning, and traumatic events, or to supernatural factors such as the evil eye, sorcery, spirits, or possession. Arabs tend to tolerate mental and emotional disturbances as long as they are not expressed in undue violence, shameful behavior, or uncontrollable overactivity. In general, they tend not to pathologize abnormal behaviors. Only extreme cases are considered *junoon*. Arabs do not seek help in psychotherapy. They do not believe that talking about problems helps. Also, referral to psychotherapy carries a stigma. Instead, they seek help from physicians or traditional healers who apply antisorcery and antienvy rituals. *Zar* and exorcism are other rituals used for healing.

When a family member suffers from psychopathology, all of the family is enlisted to help. They do not encourage hospitalization, rather preferring to offer help within the family. Even during unavoidable hospitalization, they stay with the patient for hours in the hospital. Traditional Arab clients typically focus on their complaints and are less aware of their mood. They are not open to talk about personal or familial issues. They are passive and do not take responsibility within the treatment. They come to therapy to seek advice or medication. The mental health system is undeveloped in most of the Arab world. Basic services are found mainly in the big cities.

Chapter 7

Difficulties of Western Psychotherapy in a Traditional Arabic Society and Other South/Eastern Societies

Marwan Dwairy
Jane Jagelman

The development of psychology in general, and psychotherapy in particular, has occurred as a part of the emergence of the individual. Both developed during the course of sociopolitical changes in Western Europe and the United States in the last few centuries. Central to the sociopolitical developments are the changes in the individual-family relationship as well as the individual-state one. The individual-family relationship has moved from a state of interdependence to one of independence. This change became possible after the modern Western state became responsible for the welfare of the citizens, which subsequently made familial support less vital. These changes have made the emergence of the individual as an independent entity possible.

Psychology began as an attempt to understand the nature of the *newborn* (the individual), and psychotherapy suggested methods of intervention to make changes in the individual and in his or her functioning in Western society. The definition of normality and the goals of psychotherapy have been influenced by Western social norms of individualism. Traditional insight-oriented psychotherapy is founded on Western political thought, which promotes the concepts of individualism, egalitarianism, self-efficacy, and self-actualization. Many of the theorists who have been revered as authorities in developmental psychology believe that individuation and subsequent separation from the family of origin is an essential process in the normal development of a child (Erikson, 1963; Mahler, 1968; Mahler, Bergman, and Pine, 1975). Also, the failure to do so is viewed not only as an incomplete development, but as a form of pathology. The form of psychotherapy most commonly practiced in Western cultures such as the United States and Western Europe is focused on these concepts of the individual and the process of individuation.

With the emergence of the individual, the self and other psychological entities not only became distinct from the collective identity but also became distinct from the body. This dualistic perspective dominated the Western theory of mental as well as physical health.

Western cultural values inherent in this form of psychological treatment are in direct opposition to the values espoused in a traditional Arabic culture. Arabic society does not subscribe to the same beliefs about individuation and self-efficacy (Dwairy, 1997a; Dwairy and Van Sickle, 1996). People in this culture adopt a collective identity in which the individual is seen as secondary to the group. The individual gains his or her identity through group membership. Children, as well as adults, are expected to remain in an interdependent relationship with their parents and conform to this group identity. Society pressures individuals to conform to prescribed values as a way to maintain the group collectivism. Attempts to individuate or separate from this group identity are discouraged and can also be viewed as deviant behavior that may warrant punishment (Dwairy, 1992a, 1992b, 1992c).

Therefore, Western psychotherapy contains elements of theory and technique that make it unsuitable for work with a traditional client. This chapter will outline the ways in which a Western approach to psychotherapy can cause difficulties in the treatment of such clients. The following chapter will then provide a suggested model of psychotherapy that is more appropriate for working with clients from a traditional culture seeking psychological treatment. In this chapter we will break down the problems with Western psychotherapy into two major categories: unsuitable theory and goals, and unsuitable techniques.

UNSUITABLE THEORY AND GOALS

Western theories of personality describe the nature of the individual in terms of inner psychological constructs (e.g., id, ego, superego, unconscious, and self) and intrapsychic processes (such as conflicts, thoughts, and emotions). According to these theories, normal and abnormal behavior can be explained and predicted in terms of intrapsychic constructs and processes. Social-cultural factors, as well as physical ones, are minor components of these theories. Psychotherapy, accordingly, provides methods or tactics that aim to make changes in the intrapsychic dynamic of the individual (Corsini and Wedding, 1989; Liebert and Speigler, 1994; Monte, 1995). Inherent in this perspective is a dualism between psychological and biological processes. Psychological distresses are expected to be manifested in psychological symptoms such as anxiety or depression, whereas physical symptoms are typically attributed to physical malfunctioning.

South/Eastern (or non-Western) societies, such as the Arabic one, still adopt a holistic perspective on people's problems. They do not psychologize the individual's distresses but continue to attribute them to mind-body problems, or to external natural and supernatural events. Therefore, South/Eastern clients expect to be helped by certain external changes in the natural or supernatural realms, or by medications; they do not expect relief to come from intrapsychic interventions such as psychotherapy.

Western psychotherapy assumes that intrapsychic conflicts or repression are the major problems that warrant intervention. These assumptions are accurate so long as the client is individuated psychologically from the family and conducts his or her life according to the personal authority accorded the individual. Behavior of South/Eastern clients who are still enmeshed in the familial identity is still controlled by external authorities rather than internal ones. For these clients, social norms and external pressures predict behavior much more than intrapsychic constructs or processes. Intrapsychic repressions caused by the self or the superego are minor issues compared to the external repressions experienced in a collective culture.

Regardless of theoretical orientation, psychotherapy in general aims to reveal repressed content and promote increased self-awareness that serves to augment the process of self-actualization (Pedersen et al., 1989; Sue and Sue, 1990). The goal of psychotherapy then is to promote self-awareness in order for the client to become more cognizant of personal wishes, feelings, and needs that are often repressed. Through the course of therapy, it is expected that a client will not only gain awareness of these repressed needs, but also begin to find ways for those needs to be expressed and met outside of therapy. The different schools of thought describe this process in various manners, but all promote individualistic values as a means of reducing the psychological distress experienced by the client.

Psychodynamic psychotherapy contends that in order to reduce psychological symptoms and distress, clients must become aware of their internal conflicts that are unconscious and have been repressed (Freud, 1949). These conflicts frequently arise because of unacceptable impulses that are often aggressive or sexual in nature. During psychotherapy, the analyst interprets behavior and symbols as a way to reveal these repressed wishes. Subsequently, clients are expected to become aware of and to express these angry or sexual feelings through the assistance of the therapist's interpretations. Only through a new self-awareness of these repressed feelings and wishes will clients experience any relief from their symptoms (Freud, 1949). Typically, psychodynamic therapy reveals impulses prohibited in Arab society. The expression of these impulses can cause new conflicts between the individual and the family.

In the humanistic or client-centered style of psychotherapy, the therapist provides an unconditional positive support for clients and an empathic and genuine environment in order for clients to feel comfortable enough to explore their internal states. This allows clients to get in touch with their authentic selves. In this humanistic environment, the client will be able to discover his or her "true self" and begin to shed the "false self" (Raskin and Rogers, 1989; Rogers, 1961, 1965). Therapy will help clients experience their "true selves," which were discarded to conform to the social environment. This process of awareness of the "true self" leads to self-actualization (Liebert and Speigler, 1994; Raskin and Rogers, 1989).

Another approach to psychotherapy that is not insight oriented and therefore may appear to be without Western cultural biases is behavior therapy (Ellis, 1974, 1989; Skinner, 1953, 1974). This approach focuses on individual symptoms as the result of interactions between clients and their environment. Although this therapy does not promote insight and self-awareness, nor does it have a model for normality and pathology, it is still founded on Western beliefs and values about the way individuals should interact with their environment. A common tool used in behavior therapy is assertiveness training, which helps clients gain a sense of self-efficacy over their environment (Cotler and Guerra, 1976; Ellis, 1986). This tool promotes the notions of individualism and self-efficacy and, therefore, contradicts the Arabic cultural expectation to be submissive. When treating behavioral problems among children, therapists may apply behavioral management techniques that are consistent with the needs of the children as well as the needs of the parents. This intervention actually challenges the hierarchical structure of the Arabic family.

Cognitive therapy, such as rational emotive therapy (RET), attempts to accomplish emotional and behavioral change by altering the way the client perceives events. In RET, the therapist actually enforces new ways of thinking that are more scientific and logical, instead of ways acquired in the course of development.

The inner thoughts of clients who come from collective societies represent the collective cultural way of thinking. They are enriched with traditional values and norms. Therefore, replacing those thoughts with scientific or logical ones may cause mental alienation from the client's culture and will cause new adaptation problems.

When treating children and families, Western psychotherapy commonly attempts to establish a new balance between the parents and the children. It is customary for family therapists to provide each family member with equal respect and treat their opinions and wishes with equal importance (Foley, 1989; Haley, 1967; Minuchin, 1974; Satir, 1967). This democratic approach, in which all family members are accepted and valued equally, is inherently threatening to the hierarchical structure of Arabic culture. In this culture, all family members are not considered equal and respect is unidirectional toward the authority figure in the family. Attempts to impose these liberal attitudes on traditional families will be met with strong resistance from the parents, especially the father.

The overriding consensus of all schools of Western psychotherapy is the belief in the individual and the promotion of self-efficacy, self-expression, and self-actualization. The obvious result of using Western psychotherapeutic approaches with Arabic clients is that they will become more focused on their personal needs and desires than on maintaining attention to the needs of the group.

The resulting effect is that therapy engenders external conflicts with which clients are not prepared to cope. Rather than alleviating internal, intrapsychic conflicts, this treatment approach will likely result in a great deal of societal and familial conflict for clients (Dwairy and Van Sickle, 1996). Gaining awareness of personal wishes that cannot be met in their society will only lead to greater frustration, helplessness, and anger, which will not help reduce psychological problems. This awareness will likely only add to the difficulties. This environmental conflict is iatrogenic in that the problems originated from the treatment itself.

Accomplishing the intended goal of psychotherapy will typically antagonize the family and the society, because it threatens the social order. Family members may attempt to sabotage any changes, and sometimes they may terminate therapy. The following example will serve to illustrate this point.

I treated a twenty-year-old Palestinian Arab male who suffered from stuttering. His symptoms were related to anger he felt toward his father and brother, with whom he worked in the family carpentry business. The client reported that he felt belittled and exploited by his father, who, according to the client, showed preference for the brother. The family attended a single therapy session in which the father stated that his son's stuttering was "shameful," and he showed little compassion for his son's difficulties.

During treatment, the client made significant progress and became more independent and eventually began to work outside of the family business; however, this progress was ultimately undermined by his family. The father's response to his son's decision to work outside of the family business was to ask whether his son was crazy. When the son attempted to explain his decision and that he had spent a lot of time discussing this during therapy, his father responded with, "What therapy is this? We sent you to the doctor to help you talk, not to have you abandon your family!"

In this case, when the client's anger and hatred of his father and family were uncovered, a number of familial conflicts emerged. However, pressure from the family proved to be much more formidable than the client's need for autonomy. As a result, the client returned to the family business, which again exacerbated his stuttering. In this case, treatment actually caused harm rather than healing. The conflict between the client and his family worsened as a result of his failed bid for independence.

Given the lack of individuation, a traditional client will lack the ego strength needed to stand up to and survive the familial and social reactions to the changes that will be initiated in therapy. This will leave the client vulnerable to harm from external conflict, and the client will not be in a position to battle and overcome the severe reactions from external forces when he or she begins to seek independence and express personal needs. The client will be without the support of the family that is crucial to traditional culture when coping with external pressures. Instead, the family will be the source of the external pressure.

This approach to psychotherapy, then, can be quite harmful for an Arabic client within a traditional culture. In summary, Western therapy addresses the wrong conflict for traditional clients (intrapsychic instead of social conflict), turns minor internal conflicts to unsolvable external ones, and may leave the client with severe helplessness.

UNSUITABLE TECHNIQUES

Self-Disclosure

Western psychotherapy technique relies on the client sharing with the therapist information related to the client's internal states, life circumstances, interpersonal relationships, and emotions. These intimate details are readily discussed and evaluated by both the client and the therapist. Psychotherapy is founded on the practice of client self-disclosure.

This technique is founded on the Western democratic belief that self-expression is a basic right of all people and that it is a part of everyday life. Self-expression is a way for people to express opinions, needs, and rights that are unique to them as individuals. However, in a traditional culture, self-expression is discouraged (Everett, Proctor, and Cortmell, 1983; Gulick, 1976; Laval, Gomez, and Ruiz, 1983).

Within the framework of Arab culture, the extent of self-expression that is permitted, particularly of emotions, is limited to the family context. In fact, the culture has developed its own jargon that pertains to speaking without the consideration of social consequences. *Lesnak hosanak in sonto sanak* means "Your tongue is like your horse; if you watch over it, it will watch over you." *Alshakua lag'air allah mathalla* means "Complaining to anyone other than God is a disgrace." *Alhetan btismaa* means "The walls can hear." All of these sayings serve to warn Arabic people about the dangers of self-expression.

Arabs are quite concerned with the reputation of their family. They tend to avoid revealing problems in the family as a way to save the face of the family. Typically they view their families in a very positive way. Disclosing familial conflict is considered a form of betrayal of the family. Encouraging Arabic clients to do so may cause feelings of guilt or early termination of therapy. Therefore, revealing personal information, especially to a stranger, is highly discouraged with the culture, and it would be inappropriate for a therapist to expect an Arabic client to participate in this type of interchange.

Verbal Communication

The main technique implemented in Western psychotherapy is conversation. Western psychotherapy is founded on the conviction that the active participation of two parties to discuss the client's personal difficulties will result in symptom relief and that the client will, subsequently, be healed.

An Arabic client will likely find this technique worthless and confusing. Since verbal communication is not used for self-expression in traditional cultures, these clients will probably not see the benefits of talking as a means to a cure (Dwairy and Van Sickle, 1996). Verbal exchange is a way to give directives to others or to express those feelings that are acceptable but not necessarily authentic. South/Eastern cultures often seek other methods of healing, such as medications or herbs, to treat problems. When talk therapy is sought it is expected to be directive, such as giving advice or a prescription.

Self-Exploration

Self-exploration is a tool in psychotherapy through which insight is gained. Therapists anticipate that their clients will engage in self-exploration to gain further self-understanding and awareness. Inherent in the notion of self-exploration is independent thinking. The ability of individuals to explore within themselves is commonly called *psychological mindedness*.

Arab societies do not subscribe to the value of independent thinking or self-exploration. Rather, the emphasis is placed on obedience and rote learning. As a result, individuals within this culture learn to ignore their own thoughts and focus, instead, on external directives. Sometimes, self-exploration is considered the cause of headaches, and thus may be determined to pose problems for a traditional client. According to Western theory, however, primary to the client's problem is the lack of attention that an individual in a traditional culture gives to internal personal experiences. The solution, for these clients, may not necessarily come from a course of self-exploration. Second, the traditional client is not likely to understand or make any connections between symptoms and conflicts (Kinzie, 1985; Nisio and Bilmer, 1987). In terms of Western psychotherapy, this client would not be considered psychologically minded. This cultural difference would make it difficult for an Arabic client to understand the reasons for such a discussion as well as for that client to participate in the process.

Affective Material

It is common for psychotherapists to ask their clients how they feel about something. As discussed previously, it is an essential technique of psychotherapy to address topics related to the client's feelings and emotions. However, Arabic clients will be unable to engage in such communication.

Arabic culture has conditioned its members to avoid such material within themselves. Generally speaking, Arabic clients have no awareness of their own emotions; therefore, they find it difficult to answer questions about them in therapy. This difficulty should not be viewed as resistance to talking about feelings, but as evidence of the cultural forces that serve to distance people from their feelings.

Emotional expression in Arabic culture is only allowed when it is confined to the family context.

Arabic clients who have been conditioned throughout their lives to avoid their emotions will have no prior knowledge or experience of how to communicate this information to the therapist. If a therapist were to ask Arabic clients how they felt about something, the clients would likely respond, "I felt nothing" or "I felt as I normally do." These responses indicate the amount of separation Arabs have from their emotions.

Central to psychodynamic psychotherapy is the interpretation of transference. Therapists are expected to address the emotions that clients display toward them. This process helps illuminate what aspects of their past relationships the clients are reenacting in the therapy. Humanistic therapists are also expected to address personal feelings between the therapist and the client. Therapists are supposed to be genuine in therapy and to express what they experience in relation to their clients.

For an Arabic client, discussion related to emotions experienced in the therapeutic relationship is likely to be perceived as threatening and uncomfortable. This is especially so if the therapist is of the opposite sex. Within a traditional culture, this type of conversation is typically considered to cross the boundaries of the professional relationship between therapist and client and may cause the client to suspect malignant intentions on the part of the therapist.

In addition, discussing sexual development, sexual fantasies, and sexual experiences is central in many Western psychotherapies. Interpreting symptoms in terms of repressed sexual conflict is a significant component of psychodynamic approaches to psychotherapy. This type of open communication can often be threatening and embarrassing to an Arabic client who considers sex a taboo subject that should never be talked about in a formal professional setting. Misunderstanding by the client is expected, and can result in premature termination of treatment.

Nondirective Therapeutic Setting

Many forms of Western psychotherapy approach sessions in a nondirective and ambiguous way. It is expected that the client will take the lead and direct the therapist to material that is important. To allow the transference and unconscious material to emerge in the therapeutic relationship, psychoanalysts minimize their participation in the session and allow clients free association with their own thoughts. In projective psychological tests such as the Rorschach Inkblot Test or the Thematic Apperception Test (TAT), clients are exposed to ambiguous stimuli; these techniques are expected to promote access to unconscious material. Nondirective Rogerian therapy leaves clients in an open space. The intent is to let clients experience unconditional acceptance. The session is available for them to discuss those issues that are most relevant. Although behavioral therapy is more directive, therapists still expect clients to be active participants in planning and goal-setting.

As is common in many South/Eastern cultures, Arabic clients come to treatment seeking advice or guidance. Within their highly structured culture, Arabic clients will find a nondirective approach confusing, uncomfortable, and threatening. They will expect the therapist to tell them what to do; when this does not happen they will likely feel disappointed in the treatment. Nondirective approaches may be perceived as an indifferent attitude on the part of the therapist. Instead of helping clients reduce their anxiety, a nondirective form of therapy with an Arabic client will increase the client's anxiety and sense of helplessness. Again, this can result in early termination.

Concept of Time

Western psychotherapy has traditionally been based on a fifty-minute hour in which the client arrives on time and is seen promptly. The therapy session is usually for a scheduled time that is constant from week to week. Time schedules for therapy are part of Western culture, which emphasizes doing and working according to a timetable.

South/Eastern cultures do not have the same concept of time as Western cultures. Most South/Eastern societies adopt a *being* rather than a *doing* lifestyle. For many of them, social relationships are more important than achievement and competition. Many Arabs experience seeking services, whether from medical centers or government agencies, as a time of waiting and delays. Also, most will rely on public transportation to attend appointments; as is common in many cultures, public transportation does not always follow a timely schedule, which can result in late arrivals. For these reasons, Arabic clients are not expected to adhere to the time schedule of therapy. A therapist who maintains a rigid time frame will be seen as uncaring and unreasonable.

CULTURAL COUNTERTRANSFERENCE AND MISUNDERSTANDINGS

Cultural Countertransference

Western psychotherapists receive training in how to conduct psychotherapy; however, only a few receive training on working with cross-cultural clients. The majority of therapists develop faith in their approaches to psychotherapy because they are successful with Western clients. However, when these approaches are used with South/Eastern clients, the therapists are likely to experience a high number of treatment failures. Since they have faith in the treatment approach, these therapists are inclined to, at least unconsciously, begin to blame the clients. Therapists working in Arabic societies are likely to experience countertransferential feelings of disappointment, impotence, helplessness, and anger. Therefore, therapists must endeavor to learn about the culture and understand these clients within a cross-cultural context. It is important for therapists to be flexible in their approaches and utilize what is most appropriate for the client and the culture (this topic will be addressed in the next chapter).

Misunderstanding the Client's Behavior

If the therapist is not familiar with Arabic culture, there is apt to be a number of misunderstandings between the client and the therapist. A client may fail to express his or her innermost feelings because this behavior has been ingrained for many years. Direct eye contact is expected in Western society as a sign of attention and respect. However, this practice is considered disrespectful; quite the opposite, Arabic clients will avoid eye contact as a means of showing respect. If the client does not arrive on time for sessions, it can be the result of the different concepts of time in Western and traditional cultures. These are all likely to be interpreted by Western therapists as resistance to treatment when, in fact, they are merely cultural differences that need to be understood.

Arabic clients tend to act in therapy according to the cultural tradition of *mosayara,* which means to conceal one's true feelings to please others. The result is that clients will often avoid any expression of anger or disappointment and will attempt to fulfill the therapist's expectations. The client might report therapeutic progress when no such progress has been made. The consequence of this is inaccurate reporting about the client's true experiences and circumstances. It is not unreasonable for a Western therapist to attribute these behaviors to the individual's personality rather than the culture.

Misunderstanding the Therapist's Behavior

Another form of misunderstanding is confusion about the therapist's behavior. In Western psychotherapy, therapists avoid interacting with their clients outside of therapy and do not get involved in client's lives. Therapists also attempt to maintain emotional distance from their clients. If the Arabic client is able to develop enough trust in therapy to disclose, he or she is likely to interpret the therapist's reactions to this material as indifferent and unemotional. This misunderstanding can do a great deal of damage to the development of trust that is essential in treatment.

There are common phrases used in psychotherapy that can cause misunderstandings for traditional clients. Questions that include the word "why" are frequently interpreted as argumentative or as comments that disagree with the client. Also, comments such as "I understand you" may threaten some clients, who will think that their malevolent intentions have been uncovered. This illustrates that misunderstandings can go both ways. It is not merely that the therapist might misunderstand the client, but the client might misinterpret statements or behaviors of the therapist. The therapeutic encounter is an encounter between two cultures. It is helpful for therapists to learn about Arab culture and understand the nuances that are specific to traditional cultures as well as their own.

SUMMARY

This chapter has described many factors of Western psychotherapy that can create difficulties in the treatment of Arabic clients. Western psychotherapy promotes attitudes and beliefs about the individual that are inconsistent with traditional values. These therapies approach psychological problems as intrapsychic in origin and not related to external conflicts; therefore, these approaches have goals that are not appropriate for Arabic clients. The techniques typically implemented in psychotherapy pose problems with Arabic clients because all are discouraged in Arab culture. Based on cultural beliefs about healing and cures, it is easy to understand how Arabic clients are likely to misinterpret the function of verbal exchange in psychotherapy; these clients will expect the therapist to be directive and to offer advice for a cure. Also, Arabic clients do not live their lives according to Western notions of time, which can cause confusion if a Western time frame is expected by therapists. Finally, cultural differences between therapist and client can result in misunderstandings about each other's intentions and motivations.

It is important for therapists to keep in mind that failure to participate in the expected way (i.e., according to Western values) by a South/Eastern client should not be interpreted as merely resistance. It is often the case that the treatment approach being used does not take into account the differences between Western and Arabic cultures. Maintaining a rigid stance about the curative benefits of Western psychotherapy with traditional clients will likely result in increased treatment failures and increased frustrations for both the clients and the therapist.

The following chapter will propose a model for working with traditional clients that is more compatible with the cultural beliefs and values of Arab society.

Chapter 8

Applying Psychotherapy with South/Eastern Clients

Marwan Dwairy
Jane Jagelman

Generally speaking, when psychotherapy is to be used with Arabic clients, the clinician faces two options at opposite ends of a continuum: either (1) insight therapy that has the intent to reveal repressed needs and emotions and generate new intrapsychic order, including psychoanalysis, psychodynamic, humanistic, and gestalt therapy; or (2) behavioral therapy that avoids digging deep in repressed needs and helps the client accomplish behavioral change and gain relief from symptoms.

For the therapist to know whether a client may be helped by insight-oriented psychotherapy, a pretreatment evaluation must be completed. The following section will describe the assessment needed before using insight therapy. In addition, some other recommendations, based on the experience of clinicians in South/Eastern cultures, are presented.

PRETREATMENT EVALUATION FOR INSIGHT THERAPY

The therapy of choice for Arabic clients should not be based on the therapist's theoretical preference, but on the client's characteristics. Prior to deciding what treatment modality might be appropriate for any particular client, three areas of the client's functioning must be evaluated: the client's ego strength, the client's cultural self-identity, and the strictness of the client's family (Dwairy, 1997a; Dwairy and Van Sickle, 1996).

Ego Strength

Ego strength is a fundamental prerequisite to undertaking any form of therapy that might uncover repressed issues of the client. In a traditional culture, uncovering these repressed needs will leave the client in conflict between individual wants and societal demands. This type of conflict can result in removal of financial, emotional, and social support by the family as well as rejection and punishment. In addition, this conflict may upset the emotional balance and cause anxiety and guilt. A client who is lacking adequate ego functioning will be unable to sustain such conflict with the family and will likely deteriorate and develop more symptoms as a result of treatment. The task becomes extremely difficult when a client needs to function independently against the family, which is the source of support.

In evaluating a client's ego functioning, the therapist should assess the client's emotional stability, impulsivity, level of frustration tolerance, reality testing, and basic mental status. Any aspect of the client's personality that might indicate an inadequate ego should be evaluated sufficiently. If the client has a weak ego, therapy that involves the awareness of repressed needs is not recommended.

Cultural Self-Identity

As mentioned in Chapter 2, Arabs have different levels of acculturation; therefore, their cultural identity varies between authoritarian collectivism and liberal individualism. Three subgroups may be identified here: traditional, bicultural, and Westernized. The cultural identity of the client will reveal his or her value system. This evaluation predicts whether the client's own superego (or value system) will resist any change toward individuation and self-actualization. This will indicate how willing the client is to introduce changes in behavior and lifestyle and thus oppose traditional values. This type of evaluation will suggest which form of therapy will be more readily accepted by the client: insight-oriented

Western psychotherapy or a concrete, behavioral, and directive approach.

Regardless of the client's cultural identity, however, the therapist must always maintain a respectful and accepting attitude toward the client's values and should not attempt to alter them. Clients who endorse a traditional Arabic cultural identity and believe in a hierarchical family structure and group collectivism will reject Western ideals and values that are more liberal and influenced by individualism and self-efficacy. Western psychotherapy is unlikely to promote any significant change in functioning for these clients. Any attempts by the therapist to introduce liberal concepts or to discover repressed needs will be met with resistance and may cause premature termination of the therapy.

Those clients who are more liberal in their thinking and social values may be more receptive to Western psychotherapeutic interventions. These clients have an assimilated or bicultural identity. As a result of more liberal thinking, these clients are typically more willing to consider making changes in their lives that will promote personal needs and wants. Western psychotherapy might be appropriate for these clients, especially if they possess ego strength that allows them to make changes in their social environment.

Family Cultural Identity

Many clients may have interdependent relationships with their families. It is understandable that families will affect the course of any psychotherapy, and therefore they are an essential part of any assessment. The cultural identity of the family will likely indicate the family's strictness and reaction to changes in the client during the course of therapy. Understanding the cultural identity of the family will help the therapist predict external resistance to change (Dwairy 1997a). In traditional families, it is reasonable to expect that the family will reject any changes toward self-actualization even if the client's value system tends to accept these changes. A strict, traditional family will likely interfere with any type of therapy that encourages the client to express forbidden needs or conflicts with the hierarchical structure of the family. Not only will the client experience conflict within the family, but therapy will probably end in premature termination by the family. However, a family that endorses more liberal values might be able to endure a course of therapy and allow the client to continue self-exploration and accomplish a transformation in personality and behavior.

Gender of the client is also an important mediating factor in evaluating the expected reactions of the client's family. If the client is female, it is likely that the family will react in a far more authoritarian and oppressive manner (Dwairy, 1997a). Behavior that is outside traditional values is considered much more serious for a woman. It is threatening to the family and can disgrace them. Reactions can range from mild emotional neglect and silence to the withdrawal of economic support or confinement within the family home to physical punishment that can result, in extreme cases, in the death of the woman.

A client who has a strict, traditional family is not well suited for a course in insight-oriented psychotherapy, especially if the client is also lacking adequate ego strength to withstand confrontation. It is probable that the client will be unable to endure such a response from the family. As a result, it would be better that any therapy that might initiate such conflict be avoided with this sort of family structure, particularly with female clients.

Ego strength, the client's cultural self-identity, and the strictness of the client's family all must be evaluated in the preliminary stages of any therapeutic process. The therapist must have adequate knowledge about how these three areas of the client's functioning will affect the course of treatment. If the client presents with adequate ego functioning, a bicultural or assimilated cultural self-identity, and a more liberal family, then the client is probably an appropriate candidate for Western therapeutic approaches such as psychodynamic psychotherapy or humanistic therapy. However, if any of those conditions do not exist, then the therapist should not attempt any interventions that might evoke repressed needs and create conflict between the client's or the family's cultural values and therapy. The therapist should be cautious about the negative effects that Western psychotherapy can have on a traditional client and should avoid uncovering issues that are unlikely to be satisfied in the client's environment. For these clients who are considered inappropriate for insight-oriented treatment, the alternative can be a concrete behavioral intervention within a biopsychosocial model, which will be discussed in the next chapter.

Psychotherapy Is Not a Cultural Battlefield

Regardless of the therapy applied, successful therapy is that which helps the client to find solutions and to function and adapt in a better way within *his* or *her* culture. Clients come to us to get help with their problems, not to be turned into soldiers in sociocultural battles to serve our causes. Who knows better than we, as psychologists, that there is no absolute right way to live? We need to be aware of the countertransference that involves egalitarian individualistic values that we have absorbed either from being Western or from the psychological literature that typically preaches of self-expression, or both. Missing this point may turn the psychotherapy to serving the values of the therapist regardless of its effect on the client. Therefore, we should start any therapy with an accepting and nonjudgmental attitude about the client's culture. The culture is a given and fixed factor in a client's background as well as in personality (Dwairy and Van Sickle, 1996).

In every culture, there are oppressions and punishments. The differences are in the way they happen. In the West, as mentioned in Chapter 2, the state has its institutions of justice to judge misconduct and to impose punishments that may include fines, loss of property, restrictions, prison, or, in some states, the death penalty. In these societies, all the citizens agree to give the state this authority and consider it the pathway to social justice. South/Eastern societies adopt different perspectives on justice that are no less fair. In these societies, familial authority still has absolute responsibility and power over the members. It shares the application of social justice with the state. The state typically maintains the economic and political rulings, and the family fills the role of judge and police concerning personal and social behavior. The authority of the family, rather than the juries or the judge, makes judgments and sentences. The family and the community, rather than the police, enforce the sentence. Putting it this way, it is difficult to make a decision about which is a more accurate way to judge and punish, the father and the family or the juries and the police. Evaluating this system through

Western lenses may make us call it abusive. This justice system is different from that in Western societies.

Not all multicultural therapists adopt an attitude of cultural understanding. One such model is Multicultural Counseling and Therapy (MCT) as outlined by Ivey (1995), who calls it "psychotherapy as liberation." The basis of this therapy is for the individual to begin to identify the societal oppression in his or her life and become active in the fight against it.

The goal of MCT is for clients to use the new knowledge about themselves and the impact of their environment to facilitate changes in the oppressive parts of society. It is not sufficient for clients to merely understand how their environment contributes to their distress; they must also actively pursue ways to make a difference. To develop an understanding of the oppressive nature of society and to do nothing, MCT claims, will likely result in a self-defeating experience and feelings of helplessness. MCT aims to show clients that they need not be victims of oppressive conditions in their environment and that they can and should attempt to make changes. It seems meaningful to reiterate that this approach is not recommended for clients who lack the ego strength to pursue such a goal, who endorse a strict, traditional identity, and who have families who are also highly traditional. The selection of clients for MCT should include consideration of the likelihood of success in making changes in the clients' contexts.

Here are two cases that may help to illustrate how ego strength, cultural identity, and strictness of the family can determine the outcome of psychotherapy.

Case 1: Ahmad

The first case is an eighteen-year-old male, Ahmad, who was brought to psychotherapy by his father. The client was experiencing constant anxiety and obsessive thoughts that had prevented him from sleeping and functioning for two weeks. He reported being obsessively preoccupied with a physical fight that he had had with a friend from school two years previously. His father was concerned because he had made arrangements for Ahmad to study medicine in Italy in a month.

Ahmad was the oldest son of a middle-class Arabic family in Israel. He had four younger brothers and three sisters. Ahmad's father was a well-educated poet and a leader of a progressive political party. As a leader of the party, Ahmad's father had written many articles calling for social change. Ahmad's mother was a housewife.

At the beginning of treatment, Ahmad expressed feelings of admiration and gratitude toward his father and was especially grateful that his father supported him when he experienced the anxiety and obsessional thoughts. As treatment progressed, he began to recall times when his father had been oppressive and punitive. He reported that his father scoffed at his interests in soccer, sports, and social activities. Ahmad's father wanted his son to be "the best" and constantly pushed him to excel academically.

Ahmad's family had decided that it would be good for him to become a doctor, and they attempted to engage him in this goal "for his own benefit." For Ahmad, however, this career direction was oppressive because it was not what he wished to do. A combination of traditional moralization and socially sanctioned oppression prevented Ahmad from confronting his family and expressing his lack of interest in becoming a doctor. As a result, he came to therapy with a lot of repressed anger aimed, in particular, at his father.

Prior to treatment, Ahmad identified with his father and denied his own needs. He was unaware of his anger and opposition to his father's plans. Therapy helped Ahmad gain insight into his struggle and his own real needs and to discover his anger.

By the end of a long course of psychodynamic therapy, Ahmad realized that his obsessive thoughts about the fight with his friend symbolized displaced feelings of aggression that he held toward his father who, at the time of the fight, found that it was reason for Ahmad to relinquish soccer and focus on school. The displacement was underscored by the manner in which the obsession was represented: replaying a fight against a soccer opponent on the soccer field of the school. Ahmad gained more awareness of his own needs and interests during treatment. He eventually chose to oppose his father and not attend medical school. Instead, he got a job as a traveling merchant; Ahmad sold shoes in the surrounding villages. He began to play soccer again and used his own money to support his interests.

Ahmad's family expressed feelings of humiliation about his job and his decision not to attend medical school. His relationship with his family, especially his father, became tense and conflicted. Ahmad, however, possessed the strength to oppose his family and pursue his own goals. The father was able, with much difficulty, to absorb the change.

In a follow-up session two years later, Ahmad was free of any symptoms. He had succeeded in opening up his own shoe store and had attained economic independence from his family. He also had plans to get married and was playing on the village soccer team. With regard to his family, Ahmad reported, "My mother is proud of my occupational success. My father is dissatisfied with my vocational choice, but he doesn't dare express his opinions. I don't particularly care what he thinks. He keeps a distance." (For a full report about the case, see Chapter 10, Case 2).

Case 2: Bushra

Bushra, a thirty-one-year-old female, was the wife of a carpenter and the mother of two sons and a daughter. She was the daughter of an Arab Christian family that she described as "supportive." She stated that her marriage had been generally successful although she had experienced symptoms of agoraphobia for several years. During treatment, it became apparent that Bushra's family had actually rejected her and was not the "supportive" family that she had described.

During high school, Bushra had been attracted to a male teacher who had shown a special interest in her. He encouraged her to read nationalistic books and poetry. This relationship was forced to end when her father arranged her marriage to her current husband, the carpenter. She had repressed her romantic feelings toward her teacher as well as her anger toward her father and husband. Instead, she presented an idealized picture of her marital and familial situations.

Following several years of marriage, Bushra experienced her first agoraphobic attack on Land's Day, which is a national holiday observed by Arab Palestinians residing in Israel. Land's Day is associated with the revolution against oppression. This holiday appeared to have triggered repressed feelings in Bushra related to her former teacher, who had instilled in her his own nationalism.

During psychotherapy, Bushra became aware of her anger toward her father and her husband, since they had prevented her from marrying her "true love." Although Bushra experienced relief from the agoraphobia, she was faced with a new irreconcilable conflict. She realized that she would never have the relationship that she wanted, and she became disgusted by sexual intercourse with her husband. This rejection caused him to become more aggressive. She expressed her anger at her family passively by not visiting them. Her family subsequently perceived her as acting in a stubborn manner and blamed her for her husband's aggressions. When Bushra confronted them, they discredited her feelings and told her that she was an "arrogant daughter." No one in Bushra's family provided any support or understanding for her situation. Because Arabic Christian society forbids divorce, Bushra's need for love would go unfulfilled. The personal insight that Bushra gained in therapy, therefore, only served to increase her isolation and alienation.

Bushra's impasse was partly the result of an overly rigid personal value system. Divorce was morally unacceptable to her. She felt that she could not be fully devoted to her children if she pursued a relationship outside of her marriage. Even her romantic dreams produced anxiety attacks. Her marked vulnerability and lack of emotional stability rendered her unable to withstand a confrontation with her husband and family, even if she was willing to make attempts to actualize her repressed feelings. In addition, the strict value system espoused by her family would not allow her to deviate from behaving in the socially expected manner. Arabic society usually reacts with strong disfavor toward a woman who asks for a divorce. The woman who does so is considered immoral and would be subject to the rejection of her family. (For a full report about the case, see Chapter 10, Case 1).

In the cases of Ahmad and Bushra, therapy brought awareness of forbidden needs and emotions that had been previously repressed because they conflicted with the will and values of the family and society. For Bushra, awareness of her repressed needs was iatrogenic because there was no possibility that these needs would ever be met in her society. Unlike Ahmad, who had greater ego strength, a flexible value system, and a more bicultural family identity, Bushra lacked the ego strength and emotional stability to withstand the resulting inevitable external conflicts with her family. And most important, Bushra's own superego was too rigid and demanding to allow any expression of the needs that were revealed in therapy.

Ego strength, cultural identity, and strictness of the family are not all-or-none variables and not always in full concordance. Clinical decisions should be made for each case. In the case of Bushra, even if the family was more flexible, her own ego and superego would not have allowed the change. Other cases illustrating how these three factors determine the outcome of therapy will be presented in Chapter 10.

THERAPEUTIC RECOMMENDATIONS FOR TRADITIONAL CLIENTS

When the ego strength, cultural identity, and strictness of the family do not indicate that insight-oriented therapy should be applied, the following are some recommendations from therapists who have worked with other South/Eastern cultures, such as Hispanics, Asians, African Americans, and Native Americans (Paniagua, 1994; Pedersen, 1986; Pedersen et al., 1989; Pedersen and Ivey, 1993; Sue and Sue, 1990). Although Arab society is different from other South/Eastern cultures, it shares some of the same characteristics. A major commonality among South/Eastern cultural groups is an authoritarian social structure characterized by interdependence and affiliation. As a result, much that has been learned from other cultural groups such as Hispanics and Asians is also applicable to Arabic culture.

Table 8.1 summarizes the factors that should be evaluated before treatment, and recommendations based on clinician experience in South/Eastern cultures.

Short-Term, Directive, and Goal-Oriented Psychotherapy

When revealing repressed needs through insight-oriented therapy is not recommended, behavioral therapy may be the treatment of choice. A notion commonly held by cross-cultural therapists is that traditional clients expect that treatment will be directive, time-limited,

TABLE 8.1. Guidelines for Psychotherapy with South/Eastern Clients

Psychotherapy	
Behavioral—	—Psychoanalysis
Ego strength	
Weak ego—	—Strong Ego
Client's cultural identity	
Traditional—	—Westernized
Strictness of the family	
Strict—	—Liberal
Clinician experience in South/Eastern cultures	
Short-term, directive, and goal-oriented	
Systematic eclecticism	
Culture-centered therapy	
Outreach treatment	
Orientation to psychotherapy	

and involve discussion of the presenting problem only (Atkinson, Morten, and Sue, 1989; Kinzie, 1985; Ruiz and Ruiz, 1983). South/Eastern clients often anticipate that therapists will offer guidance and solutions to the presenting problems, and they will be unprepared for the discussion of personal details that often occurs during Western psychotherapy. Given this expectation, therapists should maintain a directive stance and take an active role in treatment, perhaps much more active than would be expected with a Western client. This directive role is especially important during the early phases of treatment and may be eventually transformed into a more nondirective position depending on the individual client (Gorkin, Masalha, and Yatziv, 1985).

Traditional clients often envision that therapy will be for a predetermined period of time, enough time to receive the advice of the therapist about the presenting problem. A short-term and goal-oriented approach to therapy is most suitable for traditional clients. Therapists should limit the discussion to information pertaining to the presenting problems or symptoms, with minimum elaboration on childhood and other intimate issues. Behavioral interventions, since they are concrete and confined to the client's symptoms, are consistent with a traditional cultural perspective.

Systematic Eclecticism

Therapists should serve the clients' needs for adaptation in their culture, rather than serving a theory that therapists adopt. Theoretical flexibility and mobility among theories are important conditions for successful therapy (Budman, Lipson, and Meleis, 1992). Therapists must carefully select their interventions and techniques with an eye toward cultural sensitivity and understanding. They should not limit themselves to a specific theory or approach but should use an eclectic approach that is both systematic and culturally meaningful. For some clients, it is possible to combine techniques from different approaches such as Rogerian empathy, behavioral systematic desensitization, and interpretation of some unconscious issues. Many times psychotherapy with traditional clients may include vocational and career counseling (West, 1987).

Avoid Culture-Free Therapy

Many therapists who hold humanistic attitudes try to ease the tension with South/Eastern clients by undermining the cultural differences and emphasizing the universal human qualities of both therapist and client. For a South/Eastern client for whom the culture occupies a large portion of his or her personality, this culture-free approach will be experienced as if the therapist is rejecting the client and the client's cultural background. Instead, therapists should encourage clients to bring into therapy the cultural parts of their personality and background. The therapist should have a genuine intent to listen and learn about the cultural background of the client. This may help the therapist understand the problems within the culture and give the client a feeling of acceptance and respect.

Outreach Treatment

The fifty-minute hour in which the client comes to the therapist's office is a Western notion that is likely to be uncomfortable for South/Eastern (Pedersen, Fukuyama, and Heath, 1989) and Arab clients. These clients would prefer to be in their natural environment rather than a clinical setting (Atkinson, Morten, and Sue, 1989). When possible, it can be beneficial for a therapist to perform outreach services. This can take the form of relinquishing the traditional treatment structure and becoming more flexible to fit into the traditional culture. By conducting treatment sessions in a client's own environment, the therapist is communicating a level of respect and interest in the client and the client's culture. In addition, outreach treatment will expose the therapist to cultural information about the client's life that could not have been discovered in the clinic.

Orientation to Psychotherapy

Since psychotherapy is a foreign practice to many people in a traditional culture, an orientation to psychotherapy can go a long way to facilitate the process (Acosta, Yamamoto, and Evans, 1982; Lambert and Lambert, 1984). This orientation should consist of expressing the expectation that clients will talk about their problems and take an active role in their treatment. This introduction serves to alleviate much resistance and anxiety that Arab clients might have about the process of psychotherapy. It can also serve to clear up any of the typical misunderstandings that occur when clients first enter psychotherapy. Because Arab patients have many misunderstandings about psychotherapy, West (1987) suggests that issues of trust, the therapist-client relationship, and the status differential need to be discussed openly in early stages of therapy.

SUMMARY

The goal of this chapter was to provide guidelines for therapists in the treatment of Arabic clients. We have discussed approaches that are alternatives to insight-oriented therapy and may be better suited to work with Arabic people. Before deciding which approach is appropriate, therapists must evaluate the levels of ego strength, cultural self-identity, and cultural identity of the family. No decisions about treatment should be made before these areas have been considered. The case examples illustrated why these factors need to be assessed to avoid any negative consequences of psychotherapy. The client's culture should be part of the therapeutic encounter.

With traditional clients for whom culture occupies a significant part of their identities, culture-free therapy will be perceived as a rejection. In addition, based on the experience of clinicians with South/Eastern clients, systematic eclecticism, short-term and goal-oriented therapy, outreach therapy, and orientation to psychotherapy are recommended alternatives to insight therapy. The following chapter will describe a comprehensive model of treatment that is well suited to South/Eastern and Arabic clients. The model is based on a biopsychosocial approach to treating psychological disorders.

Chapter 9

Biopsychosocial Model for Psychotherapy with South/Eastern Clients

Sociocultural changes in the West that led to the emergence of individualism affected the whole perspective on health, in general, and mental health, specifically. With the emergence of the individual as an entity independent from the family and the community, the mind, self, and psychological processes such as thoughts and feelings became almost completely distinct from the body. The consequence is that psychological problems or symptoms such as anxiety and depression are considered to be related exclusively to psychological constructs (e.g., ego, superego, unconscious, or self) and processes (e.g., conflict, repression, or thoughts) and are almost disconnected from the body and from social life. Psychological distress manifested through physical symptoms is considered odd and a somatization of psychological problems.

Western society gradually moved away from the holistic approach and treats the mind and the body as separate parts that require different treatment. Along with these changes, Western culture adopted a scientific perspective according to which natural and social phenomena are reduced to a group of factors or variables that are measurable. Objectivity became a hallmark of the scientific approach. Western societies have valued objectivity and undermined subjective experience. Imagination became appreciated for creative work and art exclusively. When imagination occupies a significant part of the individual's daily experience, psychopathology is suspected.

South/Eastern societies view people's distress and mental health issues in a holistic manner. They do not make clear-cut distinctions between individual and family, mind and body, objective and subjective experiences. South/Eastern people are likely to value physical health and moral character more than emotional health. Anxiety and depression are not considered psychological disorders and are not attributed to psychological constructs or processes, but to a miserable life, physical illness, or supernatural powers. Distress is considered to be holistic too. Unlike the West, they do not psychologize their distress; instead they focus on the physical manifestations. This is why many studies have reported a high rate of somatization among South/Eastern societies (Al-Issa and Al-Issa, 1969; Chien and Yamamato, 1982; Kirmayer, 1984; Racy, 1980, 1985; West, 1987). Behind this evaluation is the Western assumption that psychological distress is supposed to be manifested psychologically, which does not hold true in holistic societies. Within a holistic culture, people are less psychologically minded than in Western culture; therefore, distress is not supposed to be expressed in psychological symptoms as long as the people are not fully individuated, and the self still not differentiated from the collective as well as from the body. Furthermore, it would seem more accurate to say that the West has *psychologized* human distress than to claim that other societies *somaticize* them.

The concept of reality in South/Eastern societies contradicts that in the West. Many South/Eastern societies consider imagination a part of their normal daily life. They do not pathologize hallucinations and delusions. For many people in these societies, visions and dreams are considered important experiences that convey messages and guidance for their lives. Crucial decisions are affected by visions and dreams. People who are familiar with visions and dreams are considered wise, and others seek their advice. Some South/Eastern cultures consider objective reality to be the false reality. For them, the real reality is reached by means of praying and meditation, which will bring them closer to God (Al-Issa, 1995; Dwairy, in press b).

In a psychologized society in which individuals are independent from their families and experience and express their distress in psychological terms, psychotherapy seems to be a very effective method of treatment. In holistic societies in which the individual's problems are experienced in terms of mind-body rather than psychological distress, psychotherapy seems to be missing the point.

For holistic cultures, holistic therapy is suggested to extend the realm of intervention to include the body as well as the social life. The biopsychosocial approach seems to be appropriate for this goal.

A summary of the differences between Western and South/Eastern systems is presented in Table 9.1.

A BIOPSYCHOSOCIAL MODEL

This model is a substitute for psychotherapy when the client's sociocultural background is holistic. In such societies, psychotherapy that works within the intrapsychic structure and disregards the body and the society is useless at best, if not harmful, as I indicated in Chapter 7. Therefore, a biopsychosocial model that considers the connections among the mind, body, and sociocultural factors is suggested (Donovan, 1988; Gross, 1981; Schwartz, 1982, 1984, 1989; Zucker and Gomberg, 1986).

In Figure 9.1, I present a systemic biopsychosocial model. According to this model, an ongoing interaction between the organism and the sociocultural environment takes place from birth. Affected by past experience as well as the current sociocultural interaction, the mind-body unit is always in a developing and changing state. Basically, the mind-body has four subsystems. Two, personality and genes, are relatively stable and fixed. Two other components represent ongoing processes: psychological and bodily. According to this model, interaction, rather than causality, explains what is going on in any aspect of the system. The interactions are typically ongoing, simultaneous, and multidimensional among the subsystems.

This holistic and systemic model incorporates the real complexity of human existence and represents it with all the richness that it deserves. Human existence is mind and body, past, present, and future, individualistic and sociocultural, and materialistic and spiritual. After realizing this richness, it becomes apparent that the major theories in psychology are neglecting many important factors to focus on only one or two. Every theory has provided proof to illustrate the effect of the factor on which it focuses. Psychoanalysis supplied clinical and empirical evidence to show how studying the unconscious and early childhood enables us to understand behavior.

FIGURE 9.1. Biopsychosocial Model of Health

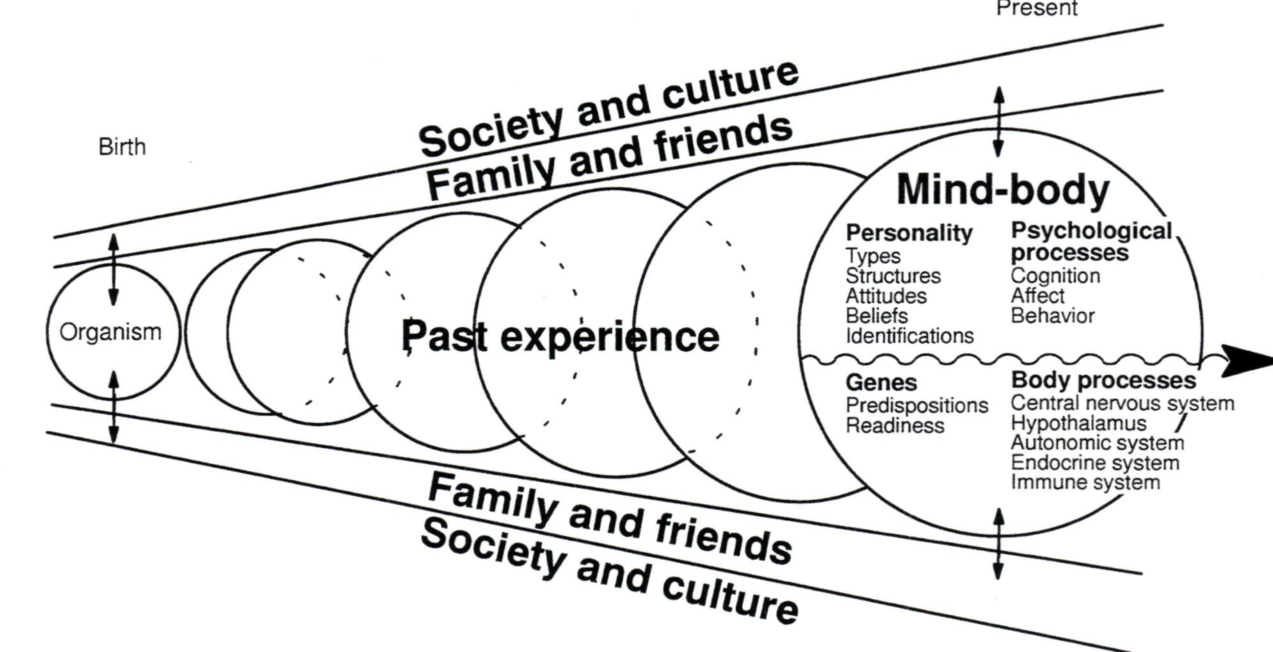

Reprinted from *Clinical Psychology Review*, M. Dwairy, A Biopsychosocial Model of Metaphor Therapy with Holistic Cultures, in press, with kind permission from Elsevier Science Ltd., The Boulevard, Langford Lane, Kidlington OX5 1GB, UK.

The behavioral approach denied the unconscious and gave evidence about the effect of contingencies and reinforcements. Then the cognitive-behavioral approach added the role of inner thoughts and images on behavior. We may add to this the psychiatric approach, which is focused on neurological and other physical factors, and the medical approach, which emphasizes heredity and germs as major contributing factors in health problems. All of these approaches have studied very important factors, but each still focuses on a very small part of human experience. All of them are partly right, but all of them fail to tell the whole rich story of the human being. Ideological dogmatism and fanaticism may be behind this denial. In addition, it seems that the human brain is still unable to handle the complexity of interactions and simultaneous multidimensional processing; therefore, researchers tend to focus on manageable factors, one at a time, and have based their theories on them.

According to the biopsychosocial approach, treatment should not be limited to psychological or physical intervention. Beside psychotherapy and medication, therapists should apply interventions to initiate change in the familial and social contexts within which distress occurs. They should employ cultural and spiritual factors that have healing effects. Imagery and metaphor therapy are highly recommended with South/Eastern clients who experience and describe their problems metaphorically. In the last chapter, we focused on psychological interventions and how to apply psychotherapy with South/Eastern clients. In this chapter, we will discuss familial-social interventions as well as metaphor therapy, all within a biopsychosocial perspective.

Familial Intervention

Because the distress of the individual in South/Eastern societies is an integral part of familial experience, it is unreasonable to assume that therapy can bring relief without an appropriate familial and social intervention. This is crucial because the main source of distress is not intrapsychic but external oppression. Therefore, making intrapsychic changes is not going to bring relief so long as the familial dynamic remains without change.

Therapy with traditional clients should accomplish changes in the role, status, and life of the client in the family. Therefore, an essential intervention that should be included in any treatment that involves traditional clients is the involvement of the client's family in therapy. Even though the family's authority might be a causative factor in the client's symptoms, it is essential for the therapist to seek assistance and support from that authority for therapy to make any progress. Solutions should be sought within the cultural field of the family. Direct confrontation of the family's authority is not recommended and is likely to cause premature termination of treatment (Dwairy and Van Sickle, 1996; Racy, 1980). To avoid any threat to the family, the therapist should help the family understand that only through their permission can anything change in therapy. By encouraging the family to participate and support the psychotherapeutic process, the therapist has the capacity to initiate small changes in the familial life of the client.

To include the family in treatment, the therapist must make a sincere effort to join the authority of the family, typically the father. Change will be impossible without the cooperation and support of this authority figure. While this should be attempted with all clients, it is especially important with females. Therapists should make special efforts to understand the authority of the family from within the Arabic culture and to shut off the Western judgmental attitude toward the Arabic authoritarian lifestyle. By doing this, therapists will realize that actions that seem oppressive are not motivated by evil intentions; rather, they are protective intentions that motivate people in collective societies. The authority figure of the family is also a member of the same hierarchical structure, in which he too is oppressed by social norms and expectations. In the end, he has his pain and suffering as well. Joining the authority figure by discussing his experience (stresses, pain, attitudes, values) will enable the therapist to be empathic and, from the other side, make him more cooperative and ready to allow change.

Is it possible to accomplish therapeutic change without making the familial authority lose his status? The answer is yes. The more he feels safe, the more he will allow change. Change will be acceptable only if it is viewed as help that the authority figure provides rather than a loss of status. Therefore, creating a safe environment for the authority is a necessary precondition for successful therapy with traditional families.

The therapist can slowly point out subtle contradictions in the family's beliefs. Arabic parents are likely to experience conflict over their actions, especially if they have been exposed to Western ideas. Even the most traditional parents will have conflicts over their feelings and parental ideologies. Contradictions will often be found between the parents' stated intentions and the actual results of their actions. Many parents genuinely believe that their way is the most helpful to their children. Instead of revealing the oppressive characteristics of their way, it is important to join the parents in their genuine motivation to help, then to move together to look for alternative ways to help. Other contradictions may exist between the attitudes and behavior of the father in the family and outside the family. Many Arabic fathers adopt progressive democratic perspectives concerning political and social issues but still use an authoritarian style in their families. Identifying these contradictions and joining the father in his progressive parts will make him more committed and ready to apply these parts in his family. This can lead to small changes within the family system that may reduce the conflict both within the parents and between the parents and their children. Contradictions are found in the cultural heritage too. In each traditional culture, one may find some proverbs that are progressive. Proverbs usually possess a special power to convince traditional people. Therapists may employ these progressive proverbs to influence the family.

Involving the family in the treatment process, however, should not be misinterpreted to include Western approaches to family therapy. Such models of family therapy are based on beliefs of egalitarianism and democracy, both of which are incompatible with traditional culture. With Arab clients, the therapist should not expect that all family members will have the opportunity to express their views and opinions equally or that all opinions will be treated with equal respect. In Arab culture, respect is given mainly to those people in authoritarian positions such as the father. Attempts by the therapist to introduce a more egalitarian structure will likely produce great resistance to treatment and often result in early termination; therefore, such approaches should be avoided.

Racy (1980) suggested that therapists should avoid both extremes: the temptation to be so respectful of tradition that one becomes paralyzed, and the tendency to become a social reformer. A combination of warmth, authority, diplomacy, and verbal facility can go far toward establishing an effective alliance.

In addition to familial intervention, therapists should utilize anything in the society that may help the client. In Arabic societies, traditional healing is very common. People believe in it and seek it when they have psychological or physical problems. The efficacy of these methods should not be discounted. The placebo effect plays a significant role in these healings. In fact, the placebo effect plays a significant role with medications as well as psychotherapy. Therapists in South/Eastern societies should not discourage traditional healings. On the contrary, they may learn from these healings, which worked for these people for many centuries before psychotherapy was developed (Dwairy and Van Sickle, 1996; West, 1987).

METAPHOR THERAPY

Unlike Western clients who are psychologically minded, South/Eastern clients present their problems in a metaphoric and graphic language. They may describe their depression as "dark life" and their fear by saying, "my heart fell down." One old woman described her loneliness by saying, "I am the guard of the walls." Arabic clients may say "my mind flew up" to express astonishment combined with anger and fear. Therapists who are not familiar with this language may find it difficult to understand the client's experience and may misinterpret this as psychotic. This language does not fit the psychological and scientific language of Western therapists. Naive therapists will often ask the clients or their families to help translate this metaphoric language to one that the therapist can understand and associate with psychological terminology. Therapists often try to reeducate the client to fit into professional psychological terminology. This is neither the efficient nor the respectful way of handling this situation. Instead, I suggest that the therapist should move to work within the metaphoric realm of the client. Communicating on the metaphoric and imaginative level may be much more efficient with South/Eastern clients. Intervention and change in imagination is not detached from the real problem; rather, it is expected to be reflected in the biological, psychological, and social levels of the client's life.

Biopsychosocial Model of Metaphor Therapy

A metaphor is "the application of a word or phrase to an object or concept which it does not literally denote, in order to suggest a comparison with another object or concept" (Webster's Dictionary, 1983, p. 901). It is an imaginative and creative rather than literal and concrete description, and it represents a subjective personal experience rather than an objective scientific event (Dwairy, in press b). Metaphors and imagination have biological, psychological, and sociocultural correlates.

Biological Correlates

Our bodies react to images as if they are real. We shed tears while we watch dramatic movies, our hearts pound during horror scenes, and we become aroused by sexual fantasies. Images are classically conditioned to their biological associations (Schwartz, 1984). It is well established in literature that images influence the autonomic nervous system, the endocrine system, and the immune system. All of these systems communicate by way of neurotransmitters, hormones, and neuropeptides. Negative images increase the corticosteroids and the catecholamines released in the blood, which will arouse the body and suppress the immune system, while positive images elevate serotonin, which regulates mood. Based on this, guided imagery has been proven to influence psychological disorders and physical problems such as heart disease, cancer, and chronic pain (Kunzendorf and Sheik, 1990; Ornstein and Sobel, 1987; Rossi, 1993).

Psychological Correlates

Psychoanalysis assumes that real wishes can be revealed by analyzing the symbolic meanings of dreams, free association, fantasies, and creative work. Therefore, images are indirect reflections of the real unconscious experience of the client (memories, drives, wishes, and emotions). From the phenomenological perspective of Rogers and Kelly, the subjective world is the real one. Therapists should make an effort to understand that world and help the client accomplish change within it. Psychoanalysis, humanistic therapy, and cognitive-behavioral approaches teach that a real connection exists between imagination (or phenomenological field) and psychological experience. Therefore, all of them include the idea that interventions in the imaginative realm will be reflected in the psychological one.

Sociocultural Correlates

South/Eastern people use many proverbs and culturally bound metaphors that have developed through the collective experience of the society. These proverbs and metaphors encapsulate collective wisdom, ways of thinking, values, and worldview. They are part of everyday language, symbols, and myths. Some languages, such as Arabic, are characterized as metaphoric languages (Barakat, 1993; Hourani, 1991). Within these cultures, metaphors are the means by which people communicate and convey messages on a daily basis. From a psychodynamic perspective, culturally bound metaphors are the language of the internalized objects, which includes the values and ways of thinking of the objects (the parents). From the Jungian perspective, these metaphors represent the collective unconscious of the people. From a cognitive-behavioral perspective, these metaphors constitute the way in which people construct their experiences and accomplish desired consequences within their culture. Therefore, working within the metaphors that the client brings is to work within the worldview of his or her culture and to find solutions that fit that culture.

Figure 9.2 shows the relationships between the imaginative level and the biological, psychological, and sociocultural levels. This model suggests that the change that imagery or metaphor therapy accomplishes is not magical or unrealistic, but is real and is reflected in real life through biological, psychological, and cultural tracks.

Three Examples of Metaphoric Interventions

Ericksonian Hypnotic Interventions

Utilization is one of the central principles of Milton Erickson's hypnosis (Rossi and Ryan, 1992). It means to respond strategically to whatever aspect of the client or the client's culture was brought to therapy. Metaphoric language was used by Erickson for diagnosis

FIGURE 9.2. Biopsychosocial Model of Metaphor Theory

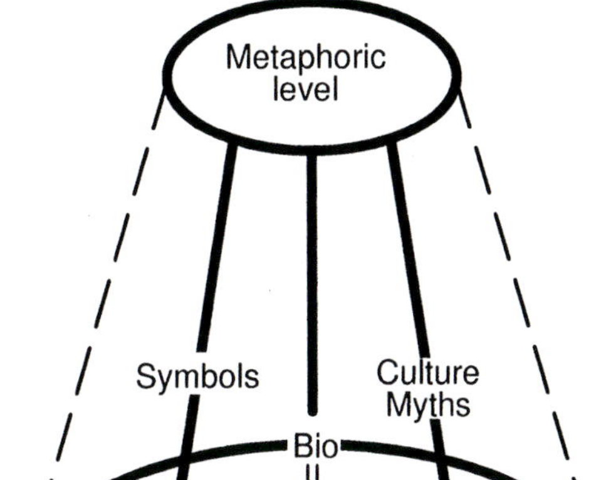

Reprinted from *Clinical Psychology Review*, M. Dwairy, A Biopsychosocial Model of Metaphor Therapy with Holistic Cultures, in press, with kind permission from Elsevier Science Ltd., The Boulevard, Langford Lane, Kidlington OX5 1GB, UK.

as well as therapy. He claimed, for instance, that people who describe their disgust for others in a metaphor such as "I can't stomach them" may have medical problems in their stomachs. People who describe their distress as "a pain in the neck" may have cervical arthritis (Rossi and Ryan, 1992).

Jeffrey Zeig (1995), one of Erickson's students, discussed a client who described his feelings as "a stonelike sensation." Later, Zeig learned that this feeling was related to the client's deceased father, who was a source of reassurance for the client. Zieg used this metaphor and suggested that the client "take something from his yard, perhaps a stone, to the cemetery with him. He could hold the stone against his chest and then place it on the grave site" (pp. 163-164).

Instead of analyzing the metaphor, as a psychoanalyst would, Zeig reassociated the client's internal life and guided his preconscious association to create an effective treatment.

Kopp's Nonhypnotic Metaphor Therapy

Kopp (1995) suggested four phases in metaphor therapy. In the first stage, the therapist should be aware of metaphoric language and identify the metaphors when they are brought in by the client. In the second phase, the therapist asks the client to describe the scene vividly. After the client describes the problem metaphorically, the therapist encourages the client in the third phase to find metaphoric solutions. The therapist may ask, "if you could change the image in a way, how would you change it?" In the fourth phase, the client is asked to apply the metaphoric solutions to the real-life problem.

One of my teenaged clients described his troublesome communication with his parents metaphorically by saying "as if I am talking to a wall." When he was asked to describe the scene, he realized that his way of handling the relationship was not appropriate and said, "I look crazy. People don't talk with walls. Only crazy people may talk to a wall." When he was asked to think what normal people do with walls, he provided several options. "Maybe destroy it," he said, then immediately added, "No, I don't want to destroy my parents." Then, he thought of several things that he might do with a wall, such as opening a window, leaning on it, sitting in its shade away from the sun, and sitting on it and watching things from a higher perspective. When he was asked to apply these ideas to his real relationship with his parents, he was able to see his parents from a new perspective. He realized that his parents may be a wall that he leans on and that protects him from the sun, and they can help him see things from a higher perspective. After this metaphoric discussion, it was clear to him that his former way was crazy and that he does not want to destroy them; rather, he wants only to discuss some problems with them to make a "window" in the barriers that they put in front of him.

Drawing the Problem and the Solution

Bresler (1984) suggested the use of "mind-controlled analgesia" to contain pain. According to this technique, the client is asked to draw three pictures: one of the pain, another of the "pain at its best," and a third that symbolizes a pleasurable experience. Then the client is asked to imagine the first picture, then remove it from his or her mind and imagine instead the second (the pain at its best) and finally the third (the pleasurable state). Patients are typically given prerecorded cassette tapes containing directives to practice several times a day.

This technique actually teaches clients how to contain pain by controlling the metaphoric images in their minds. Reports of patients who used this technique are very promising. The author has applied this technique to other problems such as anxiety and depression. The initial results are also encouraging.

All three techniques presented above allow the therapist to intervene in the metaphoric-imaginative realm. These interventions influence the body, as well as the mind, and allow for changes in the relationships of the client with family and community.

SUMMARY

For clients who experience their distress in a holistic way without differentiation between mind and body, the individual and the family, and objective and subjective realities, psychotherapy should be only part of the therapy. Beside psychotherapy, therapeutic interventions should address the body as well as the social environment of the client. The biopsychosocial model seems to be most appropriate. Within this model, therapists apply the psychotherapy that fits the ego strength, cultural identity, and the strictness of the client's family as described in Chapter 8. In addition, familial intervention is central. This intervention employs the authority figure of the family, by joining with him, to ease oppression and accomplish changes in the familial life of the client. Clients who come from holistic societies experience and describe their problems metaphorically. Therefore, metaphor therapy is suggested to influence the psychological, biological, and social real lives of South/Eastern clients. In addition, medication and spiritual healing may be incorporated with psychotherapy and familial intervention within a holistic biopsychosocial perspective.

TABLE 9.1. Main Philosophical Changes in the West in Comparison to South/ Eastern Societies

Western culture	South/Eastern cultures
1. *Individualism:* The individual emerged as an entity independent from the family.	Collectivism
2. *Dualism:* The self becomes differentiated from others as well as from the body. Dualistic approach to distress.	Holistic perspective toward individual and family as well as toward mind and body.
3. *Psychologization of distress:* Within a dualistic perspective, distress is expressed psychologically through anxiety or depression. Physical manifestations of psychological distress are considered somatization.	Distress is manifested in a holistic way. Physical complaints are part of the manifestation of distress, which is mistakenly considered by Western researchers to be somatization.
4. *Scientific approach:* Clear distinction between objective and subjective reality as well as between reality and imagination.	Imagination, dreams, visions, and trance states are part of life. People consider it the real reality.
5. *Approach to health:* Psychology deals with psychological problems. Medicine deals with physical problems. Tendency toward specialization.	Psychological as well as physical problems are treated within a holistic approach applying rituals, spiritual, herbal, and social-behavioral changes.

Chapter 10

Selected Cases

In this chapter, I will present some cases that represent the types of problems in Arabic society, which can be of some benefit in learning about the process of psychotherapy with Arabs. These cases may help to illustrate how ego strength, cultural identity, and client's family strictness can be applied to therapeutic decision making concerning whether to address repressed needs or to focus on behavioral changes. In terms of Western psychotherapy, all the cases were successful because psychotherapy uncovered unconscious needs or wishes that contributed to the symptoms. But according to my culture-sensitive terms, psychotherapy threw some of the clients (cases 1 and 3) into a defeating familial conflict in which they did not win. If I had the chance to treat these two cases again, I would not have revealed these repressed contents. I would have helped them to contain the symptoms by means of behavioral techniques and interventions with the family to allow for better adjustment within their communities.

CASE 1: BUSHRA

Successful Psychodynamic Therapy Left Her with an Open Wound

Bushra, thirty-one years old, is a Palestinian married woman and a mother to two sons and a daughter. She came to the first session accompanied by her thirty-five-year-old husband. A discrepancy was noticeable between them in their appearance, education, and personality. She appeared older than her age, well-dressed, behaved in a conservative, respectful way, and had a diploma from high school. He had dropped out of high school, worked as a carpenter, was dressed in a work uniform, and looked and behaved as a carefree man in his early twenties.

She complained of anxiety accompanied by a variety of somatic symptoms that are typical for agoraphobia with panic attack, such as dizziness, feelings of suffocation, powerlessness, pain, and increased heart rate. The onset was during the Land's Day* celebration while all the members of her husband's extended family had gathered in her house; suddenly, at noon, she became nervous and yelled at her mother-in-law, then had a panic attack. Since that episode, she had been experiencing anxiety and avoided leaving her house.

At that time, the couple had been married for several years. Both described their marriage as successful although it included some tension between Bushra and her mother-in-law. When Bushra talked about her family, she seemed proud and described her parents as supportive and caring. Although the husband showed support for his wife in seeking therapy, he seemed to ridicule her anxious behavior.

Four stages could be identified during the therapy: resistance, maceration, insight, and open wound.

Resistance Stage: First Nine Sessions

During the first two sessions, I tried to apply cognitive-behavioral techniques. I focused on Bushra's inner thoughts concerning the conflicts with her mother-in-law. In addition, I started on relaxation training to help her control her body tension. She was not able to cooperate in these techniques. She acted out her symptoms and continued to be immersed in her complaints without being able to relax or to focus on a cognitive conversation. All of my attempts to help her contain her tension evoked more tension. She continued to describe tension in her chest, suffocation, dizziness, sweating, and cold hands; she also expressed fear that she would get faint and was worried about her health. She was not able to respond appropriately

---

*Land's Day is a national day for Palestinians, started on March 31, 1976, when Palestinians living in Israel declared a one-day national strike against the confiscation of their lands by the Israeli government. During that day, six Palestinians were killed by the Israeli forces. In addition, tens were injured. Since then, March 31 has been a national day on which Palestinians celebrate their roots in their land.

to any topic other than her complaints. Metaphorically, she described her experience as "burning fire" in her chest. When I paraphrased that metaphor she seemed attentive and continued to elaborate on it.

It seemed to me, at that point, that she still needed these symptoms. I assumed that they were still serving some basic needs. Her vigilant behavior seemed very important to maintain her self-control. It was still not clear what it was over which she was afraid to lose control. In the third session, I decided to stop the cognitive-behavioral techniques and to follow her needs, focusing instead on her description of the symptoms. She continued being immersed in her symptoms and went on with her descriptions until the ninth session.

Maceration Stage: Sessions Ten Through Nineteen

In this stage, she calmed down a bit and seemed able to move her attention away from the symptoms. I asked her if she recalled situations in her past when she felt a kind of "burning fire." She disclosed, for the first time, oppressive experiences during her childhood and adolescence. She described an authoritarian, compulsive father who surrounded her with a lot of restrictions. "Don't make noise; don't go out; don't touch my library," and so forth were part of many daily restrictions he placed on her. She reported that every time he returned home she felt fear. Her mother feared the father, too. While describing her mother, Bushra expressed anger toward her that she had not been able to provide support and warmth to her children.

Bushra was the second daughter among three sisters and a younger brother. The family highly valued academic accomplishment. Bushra's family disapproved of her as a child because she had not been successful in elementary school. In addition, she was considered less beautiful and less attractive than her two sisters. The oldest sister, being the oldest, and the younger brother, as the only male in the family, were the most valuable in the family. Later on, her brother gained more status after he went to law school.

It was in secondary school that Bushra at last found someone who cared for and appreciated her. He was her history teacher in the ninth grade. He was a revolutionist that, unlike other teachers, dared to disclose to his students the Israeli practices against Palestinians and preached for national dignity and the rebellion of Palestinians. He appreciated her interest in knowing more about the Palestinian cause. He brought her extracurricular readings about Palestine's history and national poetry. Bushra vividly recalled his role in the first Land's Day in 1976 in mobilizing the students for the national strike.

Bushra's grades became very good in secondary school. She described that period in her life as a happy time in which she found meaning in what she was doing. Her special relationship with that teacher continued throughout secondary school. Every time she mentioned that relationship during session, she emphasized, "No, it was not love, it was a respectful, special relationship between a student and a teacher." She repeated this distinction every time she talked about it. Knowing the conservative attitudes of her family, she kept this relationship secret from them and was frightened of their response.

At the end of high school, in the twelfth grade, the graduating class usually takes an annual three-day trip. She very much wanted to go on that trip. At that time, her father arranged a marriage for her with one of his relatives, her current husband. When she rejected that proposal, her family suspected that she was having an affair. They threatened to prevent her from going on the trip. Under the pressure of the family and to remove suspicion, she gave up and surrendered to their proposal. Only after that was she allowed to go on the trip.

During that trip, the teacher treated her in a special way. He showed personal care and interest, but she was restrained. During the trip, she became sure that he was seriously willing to offer her marriage. It was important to her to make it clear to me that "nothing had happened between us on that trip." After that session, she called me to make sure that I had not misunderstood that relationship. Obviously, maintaining a modest image was more important than fulfilling her needs. She repeatedly mentioned an Arabic saying, "The man is his name in the society; when his name becomes dirty, he should hide himself away from people." Because of that strict attitude, she was willing to deny her attraction to her teacher and to accept the unwanted marriage to keep her name pure.

During this stage of therapy, there were some hints that a positive transference was taking place. She displayed dependency on the weekly sessions and mentioned, in various ways, how eager she was to come to each session. Because of the conservative values of Arabic society, I usually do not address the transference with female clients. But it became visible to me how she managed her feelings toward men within an acceptable context, such as relations with a teacher or therapist or a family friend, which was disclosed in later stages of the therapy.

Her strict values (superego) about her romantic needs made her fear a loss of control over them, which might explain the anxiety attack that occurred on Land's Day that seemingly evoked repressed romantic memories and emotions related to her teacher. During this stage of therapy, she started to express feelings of anger toward her father and husband.

Insight Stage: Sessions Twenty Through Thirty-Seven

It was not easy for Bushra to admit her love for the teacher on one side and her anger toward her family on the other. When she mentioned her father's behavior in the beginning of the therapy, she added excuses or justifications for it. Later on, in the beginning of the insight stage, she projected her feelings toward her father on me as her therapist. For instance, when I asked her to describe her feelings at the times her father did something, she answered, "What do you want me to say?" and added with an angry expression, "Do you want me to say that he was a dictator? Criminal? Gangster?" After a couple of sessions in which she expressed her anger and hatred indirectly, she gained insight and became ready to express these emotions directly without guilt.

Bushra expressed enthusiasm for her high school days when she had romantic feelings. With many tears, she expressed her need for a romantic, warm, and supportive relationship with a man. In the same breath, she expressed her hatred for and aversion to her husband. As an attempt at compensation, she planned to enroll again in school. She decided to learn, in a community college, to be a kindergarten teacher. She talked about her academic plans with much emotion and eagerness that could not be understood solely on academic terms. For Bushra, learning and books were associated with the romantic period in secondary school.

The first time she admitted her feelings about the teacher, she questioned the idea: "What! Is it forbidden to love a teacher?" After that, she admitted her love but made it clear that it was "innocent love" without an intimate relationship. She described him in idealistic terms and recalled his behavior and conversations that they had. "What prevented you from marrying him?" I asked. She said that he had not mentioned marriage clearly, and she was not able to ask him about his intentions. She waited until her class trip when he could say things clearly, but she was not allowed to go on the trip unless she agreed to the proposal of marriage. During the trip, she was confused, and he did not know what was going on with her.

During her marriage, she tried to forget that relationship. Anniversaries of Land's Day were very difficult, but, somehow, she was able to manage. In the last year before the onset of the symptoms, the tension between Bushra and her husband reached a climax; she felt lonely and isolated, which made that Land's Day very difficult to bear. Extreme frustration over her marriage, together with conflicts that Land's Day evoked, caused the outburst of anxiety. Her relationship with her husband continued to be tense. Unlike her first report about her marriage, in this stage of therapy she described her husband as childish and irresponsible, which forced her to bear all the responsibilities of the household and with their children. Obviously, he was not the man of her dreams.

Open-Wound Stage: Sessions Thirty-Eight Through Fifty-Four

Bushra became conscious of her need for a romantic love that she had never found with her husband. Furthermore, she became aware of her hatred of her husband and her anger toward her parents. At this stage of therapy, the symptoms of anxiety diminished, and she was able to go out by herself and to drive four times a week to her college. To be congruent with her feelings, she avoided intimate contact with her husband and decided to stop the weekly visits that she had made to her parents. This change in her behavior was not understood by either her husband or her family. A new tension was added to her relationships. Her husband became suspicious and pressured her to stop her study at college; he then asked her to terminate therapy. Her parents asked why she ceased to visit them. After they insisted on knowing what was going on, she confronted them with her real feelings toward them. They were shocked and denied her claims and told her that she was an "arrogant daughter." They thought that there was something wrong with her mind, which worsened her situation.

Bushra's wish for a romantic, intimate relationship intensified. She expressed it many times in sessions with much eagerness and tears. It was clear for her that she could not actualize that wish because it contradicted her own values and because she could not withstand the sanctions that her family and society might use against her. This wish became a frequent part of her dreams. Romantic dreams of social settings in which she was attracted to men became obvious triggers that temporally evoked her anxiety about losing control over her drives.

Solutions designed to sublimate her feelings were not successful for Bushra. She tried several options: going back to school, becoming active in social movements and women's clubs that worked toward gender equality and justice, and writing in magazines about her experiences. Her husband threatened to terminate her study and prevent her graduation as a kindergarten teacher. He restricted her movements, which prevented her from becoming involved in any social activity. Also, when invited to take part in the therapy, he did not cooperate.

Therapy ended when Bushra became well aware of her deep frustration over her marriage and of her hatred and anger toward her husband and parents. She became aware of her wish to have a romantic, supportive relationship, but, on the other hand, she realized that she was unable to fulfill her wishes. Free from agoraphobic symptoms, she continued to live with a sense of helplessness and hopelessness.

Commentary

Bushra's story represents many Arabic women who grew up in a restricting social environment. Personal or romantic relationships between the two genders are prohibited before and after marriage. Many women are forced to marry husbands they do not like or love. Wishes and fantasies of love remain secrets that they are afraid to reveal. Some of them find some satisfaction after their marriage, while many others bury their romantic wishes and invest in their new roles as wives and mothers. Often, they identify with the oppressive norms and values from which they suffered and take part in an oppressive education of their children.

Abandoning unacceptable wishes enables women to gain social status. Actually, they enjoy the happiness that comes from the social status while they give up the happiness that comes from self-actualization. Many of them do believe that they are happy, and they present this happiness in the first session of psychotherapy. I learned from my experience as a therapist in Arab society that a description of a happy family, together with a significant symptom such as agoraphobia, usually hides the opposite reality, which is revealed after addressing personal experiences. After that, repressed, forbidden needs are revived. In cases such as Bushra's, who had a rigid superego and strictly identified with conservative values, lacked the ego strength to withstand the interpersonal conflicts that emerge after revealing forbidden needs, and had an inattentive family that rejects behavioral changes, psychodynamic therapy is questionable.

With all sympathy and respect for Bushra's rights, after the event, I wonder if I could have accomplished the alleviation of her anxiety by focusing on the symptoms and patiently sticking to cognitive-behavioral techniques without pursuing repressed needs that could never be fulfilled. In summary, the psychodynamic therapy successfully made the unconscious conscious and alleviated the symptoms. Bushra became aware of intrapsychic conflicts and tried to resolve them by making her behavior congruent with her authentic feelings, which caused familial conflicts she could not bear. The successful therapy for her anxiety left her in a depressed state in which she became aware of basic needs and feelings that she was not able to fulfill. The operation was successful, but she was left with an open wound.

CASE 2: AHMAD

Psychodynamic Therapy Made Him Relinquish Medical School

Ahmad, eighteen years old, was the oldest son among four brothers and three sisters. His father was an ambitious and successful high school teacher and poet. The father was considered a progressive social leader in one of the southern Palestinian townships inside Israel. He was known for his articles in local magazines calling for social change. The mother was an uneducated housekeeper who was described by her son as warm and caring. As in many Arab families, the oldest son was expected to be the fulfiller of his family's dreams. For such an ambitious father, to make his son a medical doctor was a modest dream.

Ahmad and his father came to my clinic one month before the date that Ahmad was expected to travel to Rome to start medical school. Ahmad complained of incessant anxiety and obsessive thoughts. Both were worried about missing that date and ruining a plan that the father had worked hard to reach.

Ahmad had not been able to function for two weeks because of a scene that repeatedly replayed in his mind about a fight that had taken place two years before between him and a friend on the soccer field. This scene paralyzed him and prevented him from thinking or doing anything, even sleeping. Ahmad appreciated the sympathy that his father had shown him during the last two weeks. He seemed more anxious about his father than about himself. Both asked me to do whatever was possible to help him regain his health within a month to allow him to travel to Rome and start medical school.

Crisis Intervention Stage: First Three Sessions

At this stage, I tried to control the symptoms by means of cognitive techniques and "thought stopping." The symptoms persisted, and no progress was achieved. Therefore, it became obvious to all of us that longer therapy was needed, which would postpone the medical school plan.

Exploration Stage: Sessions Four Through Sixteen

This stage is typical with Arab clients. I tend to call it "everything is OK but me" because, usually, clients describe everything in their lives and families in idealistic and perfect terms except themselves. More than many other clients, Arabs are concerned about saving the family's face. They describe happy, warm, and supportive families. In this stage, clients deny any oppression, rejection, restrictions, or abuse. In relation to that ideal life, the symptoms seem unreasonable. It takes several sessions to help a client feel comfortable about touching on oppressive experiences or forbidden feelings. From my experience, I have learned that this process has its own pace. Pushing too fast in this stage may cause either an intensifying of the symptoms or dropping out of therapy.

In this stage, Ahmad told me that he was always the best at school. As the son of a high school teacher, he could not allow himself not to be a good student. He was a member of the soccer team at school and a popular student. Because of his father who preached of high achievement, he invested all of his energy in studying and graduated with high grades, which enabled him to study medicine. From his description, it seemed that he was always observed by and under the control of his father. Every morning he traveled to school with his father, ate lunch with him, and came back home with him which gave Ahmad the feeling of closeness. His father was a help to him in any academic problem. With delight, Ahmad mentioned how his father had him read poetry and Arabic literature. His social life seemed to be limited to school, but he seemed satisfied.

A Critical Turning Point: Session Seventeen

He started this session telling me that, on his way to the clinic, he had seen a group of young delinquents gathered in a bar, and, suddenly, he had a wish to be like them. This wish was very significant, and he continued to talk about it for half an hour. He wished to be careless and rebellious like them and to do what came into his mind without restrictions or fear. He seemed to identify with their oppression and with their antagonism of authorities. After he had become immersed in this idea and seemed to be in touch with his own oppressed feelings, I said, "It seems that you have suffered from many restrictions that you feared to rebel against in the past." Suddenly, he burst into uncontrollable crying that lasted for a few minutes, without being able to talk. This was his first cry and the first time that he was able to feel any negative feelings toward his father. With many tears, he described how his father had undermined his talents in soccer and ridiculed his need to play soccer with his peers in the neighborhood. His father prevented him from spending time with his friends after school. Studying was the only thing that Ahmad was expected to do. Even over the holidays, he was given books to read to be prepared for the next year. Because this pushing had been done by a father who wanted the best for his son and for the sake of becoming a doctor, it was difficult for Ahmad to refuse.

As a child, Ahmad remembered that he was not permitted to play with kids other than his cousins. When he behaved in a childish way, he was told that it was not fitting for an older son. As an adolescent, he was already expected to behave as an adult. He had been asked to carry out social duties and to discipline his younger siblings. When he made mistakes, he was moralized to and punished. He still remembered, with much pain, how his father yelled at him and slapped him because he forgot to give his uncle a certain message from his father.

Insight Stage and a New Turn in Life:
Sessions Eighteen Through Thirty-Three

At this stage, he was clear about the suppression by his father. He expressed anger toward him without hesitation. He seemed to mourn the loss of his talent in soccer and felt pity for himself. He realized that learning medicine was his father's wish but not his own. He decided to quit the plan to study and decided to work as a traveling merchant, selling shoes in the surrounding villages. This change in his life plan was not easily accepted by his family. For him, it was a matter of independence and freedom of choice. He struggled for his right to make personal decisions, even when it contradicted his father's wishes. The relationship with his family, especially his father, became tense and conflicted even though he was happy in regaining his self-mastery.

As for that fight with his friend on the soccer field, he recalled that his father used the provocation of that friend to convince Ahmad to give up soccer. Ahmad had expected his father to support and protect him and was astonished by his father's identification with his friend. It was a very tough episode for Ahmad. He remembered, that night after the fight, crying in his bed. Then, the episode had been forgotten for about two years, until it reemerged in obsessive thoughts. It became clear, at this point in therapy, that the obsessive thoughts represented displaced anger that Ahmad held toward his father but did not dare to express directly. Instead, he expressed them in the form of obsessive thoughts, again and again, of a person (the friend) with whom the father had been identified. For Ahmad, the friend was the symbol of his father's oppression.

In this stage of therapy, he became completely free from anxiety and obsessive thoughts. He started to play soccer on his township's team, an act that had been rejected before by his father. He spent little time at home with his parents and developed new social relations with people that he met at the soccer games or in his new job. Only in this stage of therapy did he start to talk about girls. He mentioned a girl that he knew from school, but he did not dare to talk to her. Because of conservative social norms, it was difficult for them to meet. After he knew from a friend's sister that the love was mutual, he decided to write to her. They started dating secretly out of the township.

In a follow-up session two years later, Ahmad was free of symptoms. His job had developed, and he had opened a shoe store. He seemed happy and was emotionally and economically independent. He was planning to be married and had become known as a soccer player in his township. He gradually regained the respect of his family. The conflicts with his father had ceased. He stated, "My mother is proud of my occupational success. My father is dissatisfied with my vocational choice but doesn't dare express his opinion. I don't particularly care what he thinks. He keeps a distance."

Commentary

Unlike Bushra, forbidden feelings (anger and love) that had been revealed in therapy did not leave Ahmad with an open wound. What enabled Ahmad to gain happiness after therapy?

The three factors mentioned in Chapter 8 worked to Ahmad's benefit. First, he had better ego strength and emotional stability. His anxiety was alleviated after a couple of sessions, and he was able to explore and examine his personal life, then devote his energy to change. Second, Ahmad did not have a strict, overly rigid value system. The change in his life was easily accepted by his superego at the time that he became aware of his authentic feelings and real wishes. Third, his fight for change was less difficult than Bushra's. To relinquish medical school, by all means, is not as difficult as getting a divorce or having affairs for a woman in a traditional society. Besides, by virtue of the progressive values of Ahmad's father, the resistance of the family to his changes did not last long. The father ceased pushing, and this enabled his son to gain independence.

In fact, gender played an important role here. Despite the oppression, Ahmad, as a male, had grown up with better support than Bushra, which strengthened his ego. Rebellion of male youngsters is much more accepted than of females. Therefore, it was easier for his family to accept the change. We still do not know how Ahmad's family would have reacted if one of the daughters had asked for a divorce or wished to have an affair!

CASE 3: RADIA

Conversion Reaction to Handle Conflictual Romantic Wishes

Arabic society holds very strict attitudes toward sexuality. Dating is completely forbidden in the vast majority of the Arab world. Many marriages are arranged or forced. Women's sexual misconduct is thought to abuse the so-called "honor of the family" and is cause for severe punishment (see Chapter 2). Not surprisingly, unfulfilled romantic feelings and wishes among women are kept secretly in fantasies. Some women, who find themselves in unfortunate marriages, continue to hold unresolved romantic feelings toward an idealized male from their past. These feelings, if not rejected by their own superego, would certainly be rejected by the society. In Bushra's case, we saw how agoraphobia functioned to keep her at home to prevent any dangerous steps away from her marriage. In Radia's case, a conversion reaction fulfilled that role.

Radia, thirty-one years old, came to my clinic with her husband. She had suffered from a paralysis in her left leg for three weeks. This was the third time that she had experienced this paralysis, which had appeared for the first time five years before. It lasted for six weeks and then vanished spontaneously. A similar paralysis had appeared eighteen months before they came to me. During the course of the paralysis, Radia was unable to walk independently or to do her job in the household. But the most painful part for her, as she stated, was that she could not visit her family in the next village. Physical examinations did not reveal any organic explanation, and medications proved unsuccessful.

The couple had been married for thirteen years and had four daughters and three sons. She was a religious woman, wearing traditional Islamic clothes that covered all of her body except her hands. Her husband was not religious and expressed discomfort over her religious behavior; he said that he wished she would give up those clothes. Both reported normal, warm relationships with their extended families and expressed satisfaction with their marriage and their relationship with the family.

"Everything Is OK but Me": First Seven Sessions

During these sessions, Radia focused on her successes in life. She was the best student at school. Her father was proud of her. When they had visitors at home, he used to ask her to recite poems that she had memorized. In fact, she was among the few women in her village who read books and magazines. On a daily basis, she read verses from the *Qura'an*. She tried to be up-to-date on the new methods of education so as to raise healthy and successful children. Her children were the best at school as well.

She was always proud of her family of origin. Her father was a wealthy and respectable man in his village. When people knew that she was his daughter, she always got special treatment. She mentioned, with much pride, the achievements of her brothers. When she mentioned her mother, she expressed love mixed with pity. She said that her mother was a victim of her father's strict rules. When she was asked to explain more, she showed some distress and changed the subject.

In the first session, she said that her marriage was arranged, but she had agreed to it. In the late sessions of this stage, she added that she had not had any choice but to submit to her father's will. Surprisingly, when she was in high school, she had had a romantic, intimate relationship with a classmate. After graduation, he traveled to Paris to study but not before both agreed to marry after his return. Immediately after she had graduated from high school and a year after her lover left the country, her father arranged the marriage to her current husband. Because of short notice and the pressure of the family, she could not contact her lover who was still a student and felt that there was nothing to do but to submit to that proposal. In the back of her mind was the fear that her family might discover her forbidden relationship and kill her.

Unlike Bushra, Radia was not focused on her symptom, and there was no manifest concern for her health. She seemed happy to explore her personal life but still was not able to see any relationship between her life and her symptom. Unexplainedly, her paralysis spontaneously vanished in the third week of therapy, but she remained motivated to discuss her life with me.

Insight Stage: Sessions Eight Through Fifteen

More information was revealed in this stage about her relationship with her former classmate. During the years after her marriage, she maintained a secret relationship with her lover. They talked together on the telephone on a weekly basis and exchanged presents. The content of their talk was very romantic, as were their gifts. He sent her underwear and bras. She sent him aftershave lotion and ties. She kept the relationship alive in fantasy during her marriage. He was in her fantasies during the day and during intimate relations with her husband. This kind of relationship was a complete contradiction to her culture and her religious behavior. This was the arrangement that she made as a compromise between her romantic needs, on one side, and her family compulsion, on the other side. She seemed to be living in peace with these contradictions.

After he graduated from college, the lover decided to remain in France. During thirteen years, he visited the country only three times. These were the times when Radia's paralysis appeared. She eagerly looked forward to his first visit, five years earlier. She thought about a plan to see him secretly and fantasized about that meeting and what she would say to him. For a moment, she even thought about flying away with him but immediately recalled the fatal consequences of such a reckless step. The eagerness turned to severe anxiety, and, at that moment, she felt her leg become paralyzed. I believe it was the wisdom of the unconscious that generated this paralysis to prevent that step and to save her from worse consequences.

Because her romantic feelings were not unconscious before therapy, it was quite easy to bring them up in therapy. The insight that she got in therapy was the unconscious connection between her wish to fly away and the paralysis. Her current paralysis started two days before her lover arrived in the country. It was news for her to realize how strong this wish was. When she started to discuss it in therapy, she experienced severe anxiety. She imagined losing her children, being dishonored and humiliated, and put to death. The anxiety continued for a couple of weeks.

Examining Choices Stage: Sessions Sixteen Through Twenty-Seven

After she realized the strength of the wish to abandon her marriage and be with her lover, new issues became problematic in her life. Hatred substituted for the pride that she had in her family, especially toward her father. She became unable to be intimate with her husband. She felt the house was a "cage" in which she was enclosed. She ceased to enjoy her relationships with her children. "I see my house like a prison, and my husband like a jailer," she said. At this stage, a new symptom emerged. In certain times during the day, she lost her vision and became blind. Blindness occurred mainly in the evenings when her husband came home from work and especially when he initiated sexual intercourse. At this stage, she felt that she was losing control and that her family was coming apart. She expressed dissatisfaction with the therapy and some anger toward the therapist. She thought about terminating the therapy, but she did not have any other option.

For me, the blindness indicated how unbearable her marriage was. Naturally, she started to examine her options, which ranged from flying away with her lover to remaining in the status quo. The more she discussed the choices, the more helpless she felt. Within six weeks, the blindness diminished and then disappeared completely. She returned to normal functioning as a mother and a wife.

All through therapy, she remained in contact with her lover in France, but she lost the imaginative quality of romance. The calls became anxiety-evoking as did the romantic fantasies. In Radia's case as well, the "successful treatment" revealed the unconscious processes but left her helpless, hopeless, and realizing that she was caught in an inescapable "cage."

Commentary

In Radia's case, neither her values (superego) nor her ego strength were the reason for backing off from the fulfillment of her wish. This wish could have coexisted with her value system, and her ego was strong enough to enable her to understand correctly what was going on and to examine the choices realistically. She was able to withstand a difficult situation in her marriage. The only factor that sabotaged her plans was her extremely strict family and society. She was not allowed to leave her home without the company of her husband or other members of the family. Money was not under her control. She did not dare to share her secret with anybody because she knew that nobody would understand her. It was clear to her that, if her secret was revealed to her family, she would be killed to protect "the honor of the family."

Psychotherapy, in this case, made her lose that psychological arrangement that had allowed her a corner of romantic fantasy under the cover of being religious and a good mother. Despite the symptoms, by virtue of this arrangement, she functioned in her life and tasted some happiness. Retroactively, I think it could have been better if she had received help that focused on the symptom, such as relaxation and imagery. Medications and placebo also would be helpful with such cases, which are usually highly suggestible.

CASE 4: NAJ'IA

In Certain Circumstances, Some Women Can Achieve Changes Too

In an emergency, Naj'ia's older sister called me because Naj'ia, thirty-three years old, had not been able to sleep for about a week. She was obsessed by "fantasies, as if" she had had intercourse with a man during her five-day trip to Elat, one of the southern tourist resorts in Israel, six months before. The sister emphasized that nothing like that had happened. During the trip, she was with a group from her village and accompanied by her teenage sister. I made an appointment for them the same day.

Both appeared in my clinic. Unlike her sister who dressed in modern clothes, Naj'ia dressed in black traditional clothes that covered her head and body. She seemed tired and depressed. Her head was down, she avoided eye contact, and her tone of voice was very low. She said that the fantasies had started days after she watched a program about Elat, in which they reported about the romantic experiences that tourists had there. They showed nude beaches and night clubs and tourists under the effect of drugs. Immediately, she started to imagine that she had slept with the man who was the receptionist of the hotel. Although she was sure that it did not happen, day after day she became obsessed with that idea and started to be afraid of losing control and sleeping with men. Because of that, she kept her eyes open day and night to keep that from happening.

At this stage it was not clear yet whether the "as if experience" in Elat was a depersonalization indicating a wish, or a leakage of amnesia over a conflictual real event. Therefore, it was important to collect the facts that she remembered about the trip.

Exploration of the Facts: First Three Sessions

Naj'ia was an unmarried woman and daughter of a well-known, respected family that consisted of six daughters and two sons. Her older brother was the leader of the major party in the village. The second one was the only medical doctor in the village. She emphasized the reputation of the family and her concern about hurting that reputation. She invested a lot of time and energy to prove that she could not have committed such an act. She told me how she had been educated to behave in a modest way and how she was appreciated by everybody because of her modest behavior. "To have sexual relationships is the most remote thing that could have happened," she said. Because of her conservative values, the family opposed her plan to work. They permitted her to work as a tailor only for females at home. With much dignity, she mentioned that her family was well known as a conservative family. After a moment of silence, she recalled that she had been surprised to hear her brother, the political leader, mention during a radio interview some weeks before that he supported women's right to equality. Although she had been consumed for a while with her brother's talk, she considered it political and not representative of his real attitudes.

During these three sessions, she told me in detail how she had spent the time on the trip to Elat. She described every place, mall, and restaurant they visited. She brought photos, showing her with the group in different places. She told me about presents that she bought for every person in her family. In the hotel, she shared a room with her sister. She emphasized that she had never been alone with any man during the trip. The only memory that she had about the receptionist was when first they entered the hotel and took their room key from the reception desk. To make sure that nothing had happened, recently, she had asked her sister who accompanied her whether she was alone with any man, and her sister assured her that she was always with the group.

Exploring the Unconscious: Sessions Four Through Seven

I suggested to her that we explore the unconscious by means of hypnotic techniques. She assertively rejected that proposal. Therefore, I continued with therapeutic conversations. During these sessions, she moved from the talk about her modest behavior to talk about her brother's ideas expressed on the radio, and discussed social values and norms. With time, she seemed to accept the idea of equality between genders. Rhetorically, she asked several times, "In what aspects is a woman different from a man?" and "Why does she not deserve what he gets?" After a couple of conversations in which she elaborated on the idea of equality, she became less rigid about her modesty. Her anxiety was gradually alleviated, and she returned to normal sleep. At the end of the seventh session, she said that she might be ready for a hypnotic exploration in the next session.

Hypnotic Exploration: Session Eight

In Ericksonian hypnosis, the client is led to be in touch with and explore inner mind-body experiences. He or she reserves the right whether or not to share those experiences with the therapist. After the trance, only content that could be integrated in the consciousness would be recalled.

Naj'ia was led, by Ericksonian hypnosis, to explore her mind-body state and memories associated with that state. She kept silent during the trance, which lasted for thirty-five minutes. Based on her body language, she obviously had a very significant experience and came in touch with deep emotions and memories. Her facial expressions indicated a mixture of fear and enjoyment. In some moments, her face indicated a hidden smile, then fear and tension, then a frozen face without any expression. Her respiration was not even. In some moments, it became slow and deep, then fast and shallow, then stopped for some seconds, then resumed normally.

After the trance, she did not remember anything; she reported "a peculiar, nice experience that was difficult to explain." Time distortion indicated a deep trance. She asked, "What was that for?" but did not wait for an answer.

Insight Stage and Change of Status: Sessions Nine Through Twelve

In the ninth session, she reported a feeling of confusion and anxiety. She became overwhelmed with the topic of equality between genders. She thought about it day and night. She continued to elaborate on it for a couple of sessions and sounded more assertive and angry about social values. While talking, she said many times, "Why not?" In one session, all of a sudden, I heard her say, "Why not? Should they hang me because I slept with the receptionist?" She said that in a usual tone without realizing that she was revealing important news to me. She continued to talk about the abuse that Arab women face and about the injustice of depriving women of love and romantic relationships while men are secretly enjoying intimate relationships before and after marriage. She expressed anger about the double standards of men and about the false modesty that they claim for themselves. She recalled many incidents in which men from her family, who claimed modesty in public, tried to seduce her.

It became clear to both of us that the "as if" experiences were real. She reported that, one day during the trip, she stayed in the hotel room while her sister went shopping with the rest of the group. The receptionist visited her in her room and offered her candy with white powder on it. Retroactively, she suspected that it was a drug. She remembered him patting her, then she had a vague memory about intercourse.

In this stage of therapy, she became completely free from anxiety and sleep problems. She reexamined her status in the family. She confronted her brother and claimed her right to equality. She insisted on opening a tailor shop. The family rejected that, but Naj'ia was assertive. Remarkably, she did not permit the men of her family to intervene in her life. When it became necessary, she threatened to reveal her brother-in-law's attempts to seduce her.

The therapy ended at this stage when she was assertive about her rights and felt strong enough to face her family. It seemed that she had gotten some understanding from her brother. In the last session, she came to therapy with her head uncovered. It seemed that she did not need any of the traditional clothes to cover her human needs.

Commentary

It seems that Naj'ia had had intercourse with the receptionist under unclear circumstances (perhaps drugs were involved). Because this behavior conflicted with her values, this experience had been dissociated from her memory. The combination of the show about Elat and the talk that her brother gave on the radio evoked this dissociated memory of an event that had taken place six months before the onset of the symptoms.

During the early stages of therapy, she spent much energy on preserving her modesty. She talked a great deal about that aspect. Her conservative clothes, which were different from her sister's, may have served her need to undo "sinful" behavior that she had committed and to hide her human needs. Only in later stages of the therapy was she able to admit her need for intimacy.

Naj'ia's case is one of few female cases in which they were able to fulfill, in one way or another, the desires that were repressed before therapy. It seems that the attitude of her brother played a significant role in her recovery. Because he was considered an authority on values, his attitude was very significant to her and became a very good support to lean on and to justify her desires for herself. Only after she revised her attitudes toward modesty was she able to accept that memory in her conscious. It was in this stage that she agreed to hypnosis. Unlike Bushra and Radia, Naj'ia had all three factors that helped her accomplish success: ego strength, flexible value system, and flexible family who allowed the change to happen.

Naj'ia's case demonstrates three issues in Arabic society:

1. This case depicts an unsolved problem in Arabic society, which forbids out-of-wedlock sexual relationships. Any intimate relationship, or even friendship between genders, is forbidden. These strict norms do not give answers to women who are not able to marry. Not only are they deprived of intimate relationships, but they are strictly observed and controlled to prevent any behavior that hurts the so-called "honor of the family." In many cases, they become "servants" to their brothers who take responsibility for them.
2. Contradictions in the attitudes of Arab leaders are not uncommon. Concerning political and social issues, Arab leadership is progressive and fights for equality, justice, democracy, and freedom on the political level. At the same time, they remain regressive concerning their families and other social issues. Many of them are authoritarian toward their children and their female family members. I have learned that the therapist can use this contradiction to promote changes in the family. If the therapist joins family authorities in their nonabusive parts, and avoids any threat to their position, many of them will be ready to move toward progressive changes in their families and to ease oppression.
3. As mentioned in Chapter 2, external control in Arabic society overrides internal self-control; many problems may emerge once a person is far away from that external control, such as during trips. In many clients, the onset of their problems is related, in one way or another, to a trip during which they missed the security and stability that the external control serves. In this sense, the case of Naj'ia is not uncommon.

CASE 5: SALEM

Latent Oppression of a Single Male Son

Salem, seventeen years old, was brought to me by his parents, two rural peasants who seemed very concerned about the health of their son. For six months, Salem had been suffering from seizures lasting thirty to fifty minutes, several times a week, in which he would lose consciousness, lay down, and talk in strange, chanting ways, and seem not to recognize the people around him. Sometimes during the seizures, he would become aggressive and extremely rude. "Three men could not have controlled him," said the father. Medical examination ruled out any organic etiology. The last neurologist they visited referred them to psychotherapy. The same day, they came to me as a last resort. Wiping away her tears, the mother begged me to do all that I could to restore her son's health. "He is our whole life; we are ready to afford all that is needed to cure him," she said.

Exploring Childhood and Family Relationships: First Six Sessions

The major impression that Salem made was of a polite and mannerly young man. He wore a special skullcap and was unshaven, indicating that he was religious. His family was a traditional Muslim one, but not so religious. Salem, on the other hand, had been attracted to religion since the age of fourteen and had started praying on a daily basis. His parents appreciated that change and saw it as a sign of righteousness. In the last few months, he had become extremely orthodox. At school, he was the best from first grade until twelfth grade. He was highly appreciated by his teachers because of his respectful behavior.

He was the only son after five sisters and the first grandson for both families. As with many other Arab families, his parents longed for his arrival. Since early childhood, he had been pampered with much love and protection. He had been bought the best clothes and toys in the village. Books were purchased for him and he was taken to a variety of cites in the country to broaden his experience. When he described his relationship with his parents, he left no doubt about their extraordinary love. "I have always felt I owe them my life," he said.

In the happy childhood that he described, infantile or childish behavior was missing. According to his description, he always was accompanied and observed by adults and motivated with much love to meet their expectations and wishes. He told me that he was not allowed to play with peers or to meet his classmates after school. When I asked about the way his parents reacted to his misbehavior, he said that he never misbehaved at any time in his life. I asked if he ever felt any kind of distress or anger and how he expressed it. He denied any such experience.

When I repeatedly addressed the existence of negative feelings or misbehavior, he vaguely recalled an episode at age fourteen in which he remembered packing his clothes in a bag, intending to leave the house. When he left the door of the house, his father met him and asked him where he was going. Salem was frightened to tell him the truth and ran back home to unpack his clothes. His father did not realize anything was wrong, and life continued as usual. At this stage in therapy, he did not recall any distress and was not able to figure out what brought him to attempt leaving home. Certainly, the episode was a strong indication of distress that co-existed with the happy childhood he described.

Insight Stage: Sessions Seven Through Sixteen

I arrived at the seventh session thirty minutes late because of a family emergency, which was unusual. When I arrived, Salem was waiting in the lobby and seemed nervous, walking back and forth. When he saw me, he smiled and welcomed me politely. As a response to my apology, he said that it was OK, claimed he actually enjoyed the time, and seemed not to be interested in talking about his feelings anymore. This was an unplanned opportunity to watch his passive way of expressing anger or distress toward authority figures.

At my request, he brought a tape to the next session of his talk during the seizures that his family had recorded. On the tape, he moralized to his father in his chanting voice: "You should obey God; you are a bad man; you need to clean up your sins. . . . " When the father tried to make him realize that he was talking to his father, Salem sounded aggressive and swore at his father. He continued to chastize his father and his mother, then the principal of the school, citing verses from the *Qura'an*. Salem told me that when he heard the tape, he could not believe he had said such dreadful things. "It sounds as if it is not me. I would not say such things," he said.

The contradiction between his daily behavior and his behavior during the seizures became obvious to both of us. Unlike his daily behavior, during the seizures he was aggressive and rude toward his parents and other authority figures, such as the school principal. At this stage of therapy, he seemed more rigid in emphasizing his virtuousness and denying any negative feelings. In the twelfth session, he again recalled that episode of leaving home but, this time, with much rage over an insult from his father the day before. He recalled his father hushing him when he attempted to express his opinion when his father was arguing one evening with Salem's uncle about politics. The father said, "Shut up boy; go talk with your cousins." Salem went to his bed, cried for hours, and remained there until the next day, when he decided to leave home. During childhood, he recalled himself gazing for hours at his books and daydreaming because his parents forced him to spend the time reading rather than playing. Despite these tough experiences, he never expressed any overt anger. For him, anger was considered very rude behavior that he should avoid. In stressful times in his life, depression substituted for anger. In the thirteenth session, he brought me a composition that he had written after his attempt to leave home. He wrote:

> Pessimism attacked my life and turned it upside down. Destroyed every beautiful thing. I wish to die. I do not find anybody who understands me. I lost everything, even the smile. Darkness occupied my life and turned it to a deadly silence, to suffocating repressed talk, to extinguished torch, to sadness and depression, even in holidays. I hate all the people and revenge becomes my only dream. My frozen dream. At last, I decided to forget even my name. I ridiculed everything. I laughed in sad situations. I did that to forget not to ridicule.

Obviously, he had experienced depression at that time, that he never revealed to anybody. On the surface, he continued to function normally and to meet the expectations of his family. During the fourteenth to sixteenth sessions, he recalled, with many tears, a series of oppressive experiences that he had in his childhood and adolescence.

The onset of the seizures helped to clarify the psychodynamics of the symptom. The first seizure occurred during a two-day trip with his class. On that trip, his classmates started to ridicule him. They stole his food and his sleeping bag. They laughed at him, and he was unable to defend himself. It continued on the second day. He became upset but continued to pretend to enjoy the trip. When he asked for his teachers' help, they did not take it seriously. He broke when his cousin joined the class in the ridicule. With tears, he said, "He was my only family member there. I expected him to be on my side and to protect me." In one of the recreation areas in which they stopped, he left the group and walked away alone for some kilometers. The last thing he recalled from that walk was that he was very angry, full of rage, and was repeatedly cursing the class and the teachers. He was found after a couple of hours and brought back by the police. Obviously, the onset of the seizures had been associated with anger.

The "New Salem" Stage: Sessions Seventeen Through Twenty-Two

In this stage, the seizures ceased completely. He referred to himself as "new Salem." When asked what he meant, he said that he was now able to express anger that he never expressed before. Fortunately, his parents continued to be committed to their first declaration to afford everything that would help their only son. They absorbed his reactions and continued to be loving and supporting even when he was rude at home.

At this stage, he continued to talk about his oppression. For several sessions, he verbally expressed his anger toward his parents and his teachers. He resumed creative writing in which he released his anger. In one of his last writings, he wrote, "Challenge and courage were revived in my blood, after it was buried in my chest for a long time. It revolted and faced the reality. This is how the *ward* [*ward* has double meaning: rose or lion] became a giant, facing the oppression."

Only in this stage of therapy did he mention his sisters. He realized that they, too, were victims of oppression. He started to empathize with them and became close to them. He said that they were new people for him since he did not really know them before. He felt guilty for being the distinguished son. He initiated communication with them about his feelings and theirs. The parents were satisfied with this move between their son and daughters, even at the expense of their closeness to him.

Therapy ended when he felt strong enough to face many issues that needed to be faced as "new Salem," such as his feelings toward his parents and his academic plans. In follow-up six months later, he was in college and living away from home, and he was completely free of seizures. He continued to be religious, but with much more flexibility. Romantic relationships had started to occupy part of his interest.

Commentary

With an overflow of parental love and support, it becomes hard for children to express negative feelings toward their parents that may emerge. Therefore, feelings of distress and anger had been kept "in the chest" of Salem for a long time. When he decided to run away from home at age fourteen, he discovered that he was not able to do so. He continued to live in latent depression. He was able to tolerate this situation by virtue of his family's love and support. On his class trip he attempted to leave again, and he left the class and ran away with much rage and anger. He did so when he was away from his family's support and when his cousin, "the only family member," had joined the ridiculers. At that time, losing consciousness was the only refuge. Because expressing negative feelings, according to his value system, was not permitted, expressing anger unconsciously through seizures was the only reasonable way. This arrangement allowed him to express anger and rage without taking responsibility for his actions. In daily life, he continued to be polite, while his rage found release in seizures.

Two major factors allowed him to get in touch with his repressed rage and to express it. First, the authentic care of the family absorbed his aggressive behavior. Second, ego strength was apparent in his high level of self-control, and his verbal creativity helped him sublimate his rage into creative forms.

As in the case of Naj'ia, the onset of Salem's problem was associated with a trip in which he lost the stability and security of his normal environment. The other issue that Salem's case illustrates is the ridiculing behavior that is common among Arab teenagers. It is the way that teenagers earn their social status within the group, and a way that helps them develop their egos. Certainly, this way turns some members of the peer group into victims of ridicule, which hurts their self-esteem and their psychosocial development. Salem was one of these victims.

CASE 6: ABBAS

Forced Marriage, Sexual Reluctance

One day I got a call from a man asking if I could treat his "child" (*al walad*). "What is the problem?" I asked. He said, "This child (*hada alwalad*) is not successful (*mesh nafie'*) with his wife." This story about a "child" and his wife seemed strange to me until I understood that the father meant his son, Abbas, twenty-six years old, who had married a month before and had an erectile problem. When I asked to talk with Abbas, he sounded shy and depressed and verified to me that he had an erectile problem and wished to seek treatment. I scheduled an appointment for him and his wife.

First Meeting with the Couple

The bride wore new, fancy clothes that Palestinian brides wear during the early months of marriage. Compared to other Palestinian women, she seemed open and assertive. Abbas, who works as a plumber, came in his work uniform. He was shy and avoided eye contact. Both seemed as if they were in a competition in which the husband was the loser.

Abbas told me that when he attempted intimate contact with his wife he felt pain in his stomach and would have no erection. Both of them were stressed and wanted to overcome the "husband's problem" because their families were waiting for them to have a full sexual relationship, as is expected from a newlywed couple. The bride expressed her readiness to do everything that could help her husband. Answering my questions about the way they married, they told me that it was an arranged marriage that both families, as well as the bride and the bridegroom, had agreed on. They were engaged for eight months, but they did not meet much during that period. Their wedding ceremony was very special, because both families were prominent in their village. Abbas's father built a new house for the couple and furnished it with the best furniture. The bride's jewelry and clothes had been the talk of the whole village since the wedding.

Massive involvement of the families in the intimate relationships of Arab couples after the wedding is very common. Both families usually wait for a report from the couple to be sure that everything is okay in the sense that the bride was a virgin and the bridegroom was able to penetrate. After that, the families start pushing the couple to conceive as soon as possible. Couples who have problems, such as this one, or do not conceive face huge social pressures that sabotage, many times, efforts to work out their problems. Therefore, the stress that Abbas and his wife experienced was not a surprise.

To eliminate external pressure on Abbas and to understand his own experience, I invited him to come alone to the next session.

Sessions Two and Three with Abbas

This time, Abbas was less depressed, more open, and more active. He told me that he had never had this problem before. He had had occasional sexual relationships that were successful. He felt attraction to women and had normal sexual desire and arousal. When he would masturbate, he had a normal erection. Abbas expressed his wish to solve his problem soon. He told me that his father visited him several times during the last week and asked about the treatment; he had expressed disappointment that no progress had taken place yet. When I asked him to discuss his feeling about the involvement of his father, he answered, in short, that he felt okay. His body language and his reluctance to express his feelings led me to assume that he was avoiding disclosure of some significant issue concerning their relationship. My assumption was strengthened when Abbas mentioned "some problems" that occurred during the engagement period. He was not ready to talk about these problems, believing that they were irrelevant. His reluctance was eliminated only after I made it clear to him that this information was pertinent to his problem and was crucial for the treatment.

To justify the behavior of his father, Abbas told me that his father intervened in the life of everybody in the village. People got used to his style and respected him. I kept the focus on his personal experience with his father. He told me that his father was very authoritarian and strict with him. He wanted Abbas to be like his older brother, with whom the father was completely satisfied. Abbas had been verbally humiliated and physically punished for disobedience. He dropped out of school at age fifteen and went to work as a plumber, far away from the village. This was the first time that he got away from his father's interventions and punishments. In the beginning, he came home every weekend. Later on, he visited the village barely every month. At age twenty, after a period of unemployment, his father offered to equip a shop for him in the village. Because he had no other options, Abbas agreed, and, since then, he had been working in the village.

One day, the father told Abbas that he had arranged a marriage for him. Abbas was astonished and immediately expressed his opposition. What made him more angry was that his father did not care and continued to disregard Abbas's feelings and attitudes. To make his opposition clear, he decided not to go back home and slept on the roof of the house for six months (by virtue of the nice weather in the summer, it is not unusual for people to sleep on the roofs). This rebellious act did not change the stubbornness of his father; instead, Abbas was exposed to recurrent and intensive pressure from family members and others, who disapproved of his reluctance and considered it rude and disrespectful to the father and the family name. All of them tried to convince him that his father was concerned about his best interests and that the right attitude was to submit to his father's will. During those six months, Abbas found no ally, seldom worked, and lost nine kilograms (about twenty pounds).

The stress that Abbas experienced was huge. After six months, it became unbearable. He realized that nothing could be accomplished if he continued his protest. His anger turned gradually to sadness, and he had no choice but to submit to his father. When I suggested that it was a forced marriage, he said, "No, I was really convinced that this was the right thing to do. I went to my father myself and apologized to him." Of course, the father was delighted and wanted to set a date for the marriage the next week, but Abbas asked him to wait several months to allow him to know and get used to the bride. The first visit to the bride's family was formal. Abbas's family brought valuable presents and asked formally for "the hand of the bride." That was the first time that Abbas felt a pain in his stomach. He had been treated with medication without any improvement. The pain had intensified during the visits to his bride. On one visit, the bride's family had rushed him to the doctor because of intense pain. Both families were understanding about his problem and agreed several times to postpone the marriage date. Eight months after the first visit to the bride's family, the couple got married.

Abrupt End of Therapy

It was obvious to me that I could not achieve any progress unless we worked out the unfinished business between Abbas and his father. According to my professional judgment, behavioral techniques of desensitization would not have worked because the erectile problem had to do with anger, rather than anxiety. It was his passive aggressive reaction to his father's oppression. The absence of erection was, in fact, the authentic expression of Abbas's wish to oppose his father, a decision that had been made by Abbas's ego and/or superego, totally ignoring his feelings and wishes. In other words, his agreement to the marriage was his mind's decision rather than his body's decision. Therefore, it seemed unwise for me to apply any behavioral techniques before discussing this issue and allowing him to reexamine his decisions and his relationships with his father and wife.

Unfortunately, the push for immediate results and the fear of examining Abbas's relationships and his decision prevented him from continuing in therapy with me. He did not keep his appointment for the fourth session. In a phone conversation, he told me that they (he and his father) had decided to seek medical treatment because they believed that the problem was medical rather than psychological.

Commentary

It is obvious that Abbas's ego strength was not great enough to face his strict authoritarian family. His beliefs (superego) had conformed, after the failure of Abbas's protests, to the wishes of his unconquerable father. In light of these conditions, there was no chance for psychodynamic therapy. On the other hand, I still believe that behavioral intervention would not have succeeded either. I question whether any medical treatment would help him to enjoy a normal sexual relationship with his wife.

Abbas's case is one of the sad cases that I doubt any treatment would have resolved. After his marriage, he found himself in a trap in which any move would involve a high price. Divorce would leave his innocent wife in misery because of the negative attitude toward divorced women in Arabic society. He was not able, economically and emotionally, to free himself from the oppression of his father and, at the same time, to change the situation in his marriage unless he got psychotherapy. As mentioned, his attitude and that of his father prevented him from getting that therapy.

Abbas's case demonstrates identification with the oppressor (mentioned in Chapter 4) in its extreme form. After he realized that he was unable to be independent economically and could no longer stand the social pressure, his mind adopted the attitude of his oppressor and left the body to "talk" for him. In this case, we can observe how the individual family conflict is transferred to the somatic field (pain and absence of erection). Abbas's body, more specifically his penis, was able to express what he was unable to do consciously. It was a passive-aggressive expression of his anger and his reluctance to his father. His family was much more understanding about his physical pain than his emotional pain. It is likely that his stomach pain will continue to bother him throughout his marriage.

As is obvious from all the cases mentioned in this chapter, authoritarian cultures, specifically authoritarian fathers, seem to be behind the bulk of psychological distress of Arab clients. Within this system, the oppression of women is obvious. Abbas's case exemplifies the oppression of men as well. It shows how Arabic men, in a traditional community, are expected to play at least two contradictory roles. For their fathers, they are considered children; hence, Abbas's father referred to him as a child (*walad*) when he first talked to me. To their wives and children, as well as the community, they are expected to be men in the traditional, phallic sense of masculinity. In Abbas's case, his father wanted the impossible; he wanted his *walad* to be a man in bed.

The economic dependence of Abbas on his father, more than the emotional dependence, was behind his submission to his father's will. Emotionally, he was able to be independent, when he was also economically independent between the ages of fifteen and twenty, after he had found work away from his family and his village. In this case, we can observe, on the personal level, how the lack of state institutions that allow independence (see Chapters 2 and 4) maintains the family as the main provider, the authority from which the individual can not free him- or herself. When the state still does not carry the responsibility for its citizens, individualism cannot be expected.

Appendix

Conclusive Comparison of Modern Western Culture with Medieval and South/Eastern Cultures

Sociocultural differences	**Medieval and South/ Eastern cultures**	**Modern Western cultures**
Sociopolitical system	Feudal, totalitarian, and unindustrialized	Capitalist, democratic, and industrialized
Citizen-state relationship	The state and the citizens are the ruler's property	The state serves the needs of the citizens (interdependence)
Individual-family relationship	Interdependence	Independence Personal freedom
Basic needs provider	Mainly the family	Mainly the state
Smallest socio-economic unit	Family	Individual
Cultural features	Authoritarian/Collectivism	Liberalism/Individualism
Socialization methods	Mainly moralization and punishments	Mainly democratic
Scientific perspective	Holistic: • oneness between the individual and the family • no clear-cut differentiation between mind and body • subjective experiences (e.g., visions and dreams) considered as part of the reality, if not the real reality	Dualistic: • the self emerged as an entity independent from the body as well as from others • psychology emerged to understand the individual • tendency toward objectification and undermining subjective experience

Sociocultural differences	Medieval and South/ Eastern cultures	Modern Western cultures
Scientific perspective (continued)	Holistic: • distress manifested in physical or holistic/ subjective terms	Dualistic: • psychologization of distress (anxiety and depression) • physical manifestation of distress is considered somatization
Psychological differences		
Psychological development	Development within the family unit	Individuation and development as independent identity
Personality	Collective: values, needs, and control are collective rather than personal	Intrapsychic constructs (self, ego, and superego) and processes (conflict, repression, and thoughts) conduct a person's life
Main source of control	More social control, family and community control	More self-control, ego and superego control
Main conflict and main source of repression and anxiety	More social/interpersonal	More intrapsychic
Main source of happiness	Social approval	Self-actualization
Coping	More social and cultural skills	More defense mechanisms
Prediction of behavior	Norms predict more	Personality predicts more
Consistency of personality	More contextual	More consistent across situations
Treatment	Psychotherapy explores the wrong intrapsychic area and evokes forbidden drives that generate new, tough conflict with the family. Biopsychosocial approach is recommended.	Psychotherapy makes new intrapsychic changes that help to accomplish self-actualization.

References

Abdel-Khalik, A. M., and Eysenck, S. B. G. (1983). A cross-cultural study of personality: Egypt and England. *Research in Behavior and Personality*, 3, 215-226.

Abdelrahman, A. I., and Morgan, S. P. (1987). Socioeconomic and institutional correlates of family formation: Khartoum, Sudan, 1945-1975. *Journal of Marriage and the Family*, 47, 401-412.

Abu Baker, K. (in press). *Arab women in politics*. Israel: Bet Birl.

Acosta, F., Yamamoto, J., and Evans, L. A. (Eds.). (1982). *Effective psychotherapy for low-income and minority patients*. New York: Plenum Press.

Ahlawat, K. S. (1989). Psychometric properties of the Yarmouk Test Anxiety Inventory. In R. Schwarzer, H. M. van der Ploeg, and C. D. Spielberger (Eds.), *Advances in test anxiety research* (Volume 6, pp. 263-278). Lisse, Netherlands: Swets and Zeitinger.

Al-Awad, A. M. E., and Sonuga-Barke, E. J. S. (1992). Childhood problems in Sudanese city. A comparison of extended and nuclear families. *Child Development*, 63, 906-914.

Al-Haj, M. (1989). Social research on family lifestyle among Arabs in Israel. *Journal of Comparative Family Studies*, 20(2), 175-195.

Al-Issa, I. (1966). Psychiatry in Iraq. *British Journal of Psychiatry*, 112, 827-832.

Al-Issa, I. (1989). Psychiatry in Algeria. *Psychiatric Bulletin*, 13, 240-245.

Al-Issa, I. (1990). Culture and mental illness in Algeria. *International Journal of Social Psychiatry*, 36, 230-240.

Al-Issa, I. (1995). The illusion of reality or the reality of illusion: Hallucination and culture. *British Journal of Psychiatry*, 166, 368-373.

Al-Issa, I., and Al-Issa, B. (1969). Psychiatric problems in developing country: Iraq. *International Journal of Social Psychiatry*, 16, 15-22.

Al-Jabiri, M. A. (1991a). *Takween el-a'ql el A'rabi* (fourth edition). Beirut: Al-markiz al-thaq'afi al-Arabi (in Arabic).

Al-Jabiri, M. A. (1991b). *Al-a'ql al-siasi el-A'rabi* (second edition). Beirut: Al-markiz al-thaq'afi al-Arabi (in Arabic).

Al-Khani, M. A. F., Bebbington, P. E., Watson, J. P., and House, F. (1986). Life events and schizophrenia: A Saudi Arabia study. *British Journal of Psychiatry*, 148, 12-22.

Al-Sabaie, A. (1989). Psychiatry in Saudi Arabia: Cultural perspectives. *Transcultural Psychiatric Research Review*, 26, 245-262.

American Psychiatric Association. (1994). *Diagnostic and statistical manual of mental disorders* (fourth edition). Washington, DC: American Psychiatric Association.

Ammar, H. (1964). *Fee binaa' el-bashar*. Cairo: Manshurat Sars ellaian (in Arabic).

Atkinson, D. R., Morten, G., and Sue, D. W. (1989). *Counseling American minorities: A cross cultural perspective* (third edition). Dubuque, IA: W. C. Brown Publishers.

Baasher, T. (1962). Some aspects of the history of the treatment of mental disorders in the Sudan. *Sudan Medical Journal,* 1, 44.

Baker, A. M. (1990). The psychological impact of the intifada on Palestinian children in the occupied West Bank and Gaza: An exploratory study. *American Journal of Orthopsychiatry*, 60, 496-505.

Bandura, A. (1986). *Social foundations of thought and action. A social cognitive theory.* Englewood Cliffs, NJ: Prentice Hall.

Barakat, H. (1993). *The Arab world: Society, culture, and state.* Los Angeles: University of California Press.

Bazzoui, W. (1970). Affective disorders in Iraq. *British Journal of Psychiatry*, 117, 195-203.

Bazzoui, W., and Al-Issa, I. (1966). Psychiatry in Iraq. *The British Journal of Psychiatry*, 112(489), 827-832.

Berne, E. (1961). *Transactional analysis in psychotherapy.* New York: Grove Press.

Bresler, D. (1984). Mind-controlled analgesia: The inner way to pain control. In A. A. Sheikh (Ed.), *Imagination and healing: Imagery and human development series* (pp. 211-230). New York: Baywood Publishing Company, Inc.

Budman, C. L., Lipson, J. G., and Meleis, A. I. (1992). The cultural consultant in mental health care: The case of an Arab adolescent. *American Journal of Orthopsychiatry*, 62(3), 359-370.

Burckhardt, J. (1921). *The civilization of the renaissance in Italy.* New York: The Macmillan Co.

Cederblad, M., and Rahim, I. A. (1989). A longitudinal study of mental health problems in a suburban population in Sudan. *Acta Psychiatrica Scandinavica*, 79, 537-543.

Chaleby, K. (1986). Psychological stresses and psychiatric disorders in an outpatient population in Saudi Arabia. *Acta Psychiatrica Scandinavica*, 73, 147-151.

Chaleby, K. (1987). Social phobia in Saudis. *Social Psychiatry,* 22, 167-170.

Chaleby, K. (1988). Traditional Arabian marriage and mental health in a group of outpatient Saudis. *Acta Psychiatrica Scandinavica*, 77, 139-142.

Chien, C., and Yamamato, J. (1982). Asian-American and Pacific Islanders patients. In F. X. Acosta, J. Yamamato, and L. A. Evans (Eds.), *Effective psychotherapy for low-income and minority patients* (pp. 117-145). New York: Plenum Press.

Chimienti, G., and Abu-Nasr, J. (1992-1993). Children's reactions to war-related stress. II. The influence of gender, age, and the mother's reaction. *International Journal of Mental Health*, 21(4), 72-86.

Cooper, J. E., Jablensky, A., and Sartorius, N. (1990). WHO collaborative studies on acute psychosis using the SCAAPS schedule. In C. N. Stefanis (Ed.), *Psychiatry: A world-wide perspective*. New York: Elsevier Science.

Corsini, R., and Wedding, D. (1989). *Current psychotherapies*. Itasca, IL: F. E. Peacock Publishers, Inc.

Cote, J. E., and Levine, C. (1988). A critical examination of the ego identity status paradigm. *Developmental Review,* 8, 147-184.

Cotler, B., and Guerra, J. (1976). *Assertive training*. Illinois: Research Press.

Donovan, D. M. (1988). Assessment of addictive behavior: Implications of an emerging biopsychosocial model. In D. M. Donovan and G. A. Marlatt (Eds.), *Assessment of addictive behavior* (pp. 3-48). New York: Guilford Press.

Dwairy, M. (1992a, August 5,6). How can we ask for freedom of expression when we do not have the right to possess opinions. *El-Ettihad* (in Arabic).

Dwairy, M. (1992b, April 2). Abolition of the self. *El-Ettihad* (in Arabic).

Dwairy, M. (1992c, October 2). The relationship between the individual and his society. *El-Ettihad* (in Arabic).

Dwairy, M. (1997a). Addressing the repressed needs of the Arabic client. *Cultural Diversity and Mental Health*, 3(1), 1-12.

Dwairy, M. (1997b). *Personality, culture, and Arab society.* Jerusalem: Ministry of Education (in Arabic).

Dwairy, M. (in press). Mental health in the Arab world. In A. S. Bellack and M. Hersen (Eds.), *Comprehensive clinical psychotherapy: Sociocultural and individual differences* (Volume 10). New York: Pergamon Press.

Dwairy, M. (1997). A biopsychosocial model of metaphor therapy with holistic cultures. *Clinical Psychology Review,* 17(7), 719-732.

Dwairy, M., and Van Sickle, T. (1996). Western psychotherapy in traditional Arabic societies. *Clinical Psychology Review,* 16(3), 231-249.

El-Athem, G. S. (1969). *A self criticism after the defeat.* Beirut: dar Ettaliaa (in Arabic).

El-Islam, M. F. (1979). A better outlook for schizophrenics living in extended families. *British Journal of Psychiatry,* 135, 343.

El-Islam, M. F. (1982). Arabic cultural psychiatry. *Transcultural Psychiatric Research Review,* 19, 5-24.

El-Islam, M. F., and El-Deeb, H. A. (1968). Marriage and fertility of psychotics. *Social Psychiatry,* 3, 24.

Ellis, A. (1974). Rational-emotive therapy. In A. Burton (Ed.), *Operational theories of personality* (pp. 308-344). New York: Brunner/Mazel.

Ellis, A. (1986). *Effective self-assertion.* Cassette recording. Washington, DC: Psychology Today Tapes.

Ellis, A. (1989). Rational-emotive therapy. In R. J. Corsini and D. Wedding (Eds.), *Current psychotherapies* (fourth edition, pp. 197-240). Itasca, IL: F. E. Peacock Publishers, Inc.

El-Rufaie, O. E., and Absood, G. H. (1993). Minor psychiatric morbidity in primary health care: Prevalence, nature and severity. *The International Journal of Social Psychiatry,* 39(3), 159-166.

El-Rufaie, O. E., Albar, A. A., and Al-Dabal, B. K. (1988). Identifying anxiety and depressive disorder among primary care patients: A pilot study. *Acta Psychiatrica Scandinavica*, 77, 280-282.

El-Rufaie, O. E., and Mediny, M. S. (1991). Psychiatric inpatients in a general teaching hospital: an experience from Saudi Arabia. *The Arab Journal of Psychiatry*, 2, 138-145.

El-Sarrag, M. E. (1968). Psychiatry in the Northern Sudan: A study in comparative psychiatry. *British Journal of Psychiatry*, 114, 946-948.

El-Sayed, S. M., Maghraby, M. M., Hafeiz, H. B., and Buckley, M. M. (1986). Psychiatric diagnostic categories in Saudi Arabia. *Acta Psychiatrica Scandinavica*, 74, 553-554.

El-Zahhar, N. E., and Hocevar, D. (1991). Cultural and sexual differences test anxiety, trait anxiety, and arousability: Egypt, Brazil, and the United States. *Journal of Cross-Cultural Psychology*, 22(2), 238-249.

Erikson, E. H. (1963). *Childhood and society* (second edition). New York: Norton.

Everett, F., Proctor, N., and Cortmell, B. (1983). Providing psychological services to American Indian children and families. *Professional Psychology,* 14, 588-603.

Farrag, M. F. (1987). Dimensions of personality in Saudi Arabia. *Personality and Individual Differences*, 8(6), 951-953.

Festinger, L. (1957). *A theory of cognitive dissonance*. Palo Alto, CA: Stanford University Press.

Finkelhor, D., Hotaling, G., Lewis, I. A., and Smith, C. (1990). Sexual abuse in a national survey of adult men and women: Prevalence, characteristics, and risk factors. *Child Abuse and Neglect*, 14, 19-28.

Foley, V. D. (1989). Family therapy. In R. J. Corsini and D. Wedding (Eds.), *Current psychotherapies* (fourth edition, pp. 455-502). Itasca, IL: F. E. Peacock Publishers, Inc.

Freire, P. (1970/1995). *Pedagogy of the oppressed* (new revised twentieth anniversary edition). New York: Continuum.

Freire, P. (1992/1994). *Pedagogy of hope: Reliving pedagogy of the oppressed.* New York: Continuum.

Freud, A. (1936/1966). *The ego and the mechanisms of defense* (revised edition). In Volume 2 of *The writings of Anna Freud*. New York: International Universities Press.

Freud, S. (1935/1960). *A general introduction to psychoanalysis.* New York: Washington Square Press.

Freud, S. (1949). *An outline of psycho-analysis*. New York: W. W. Norton.

Fromm, E. (1941). *Escape from freedom*. New York: Henry Holt and Company.

Fromm, E. (1976). *To have or to be*. New York: Harper and Row.

Ghubash, E. H., and Bibbington, P. (1994). The Dubai community psychiatric survey: Acculturation and the prevalence of psychiatric disorder. *Psychological Medicine*, 24, 121-131.

Ghubash, E. H., Hamdi, E., and Bibbington, P. (1992). The Dubai community psychiatric survey: I. Prevalence and sociodemographic correlates. *Social Psychiatry and Psychiatric Epidemiology*, 27, 53-61.

Goldberg, D. P., Cooper, B., Eastwood, M. R., Kedward, H. B., and Shepherd, M. (1970). Standardised psychiatric interview for use in community surveys. *British Journal of Preventive and Social Medicine*, 24, 18-23.

Gorkin, M., Masalha, S., and Yatziv, G. (1985). Psychotherapy of Israeli-Arab patients: Some cultural consideration. *The Journal of Psychoanalytic Anthropology*, 8(4), 215-230.

Griefat, Y., and Katriel, T. (1989). Life demands Musayara: Communication and culture among Arabs in Israel. In S. T. Toomey and F. Korzenny (Eds.), *Language, communication, and culture* (pp. 121-138). London: Sage Publication.

Gross, D. A. (1981). Medical origins of psychiatric emergencies: The systems approach. *International Journal of Psychiatry in Medicine*, 11(1), 1-24.

Gulick, J. (1976). The ethos of insecurity in Middle Eastern culture. In G. A. DeVos (Ed.), *Responses to change, society, culture and personality*. New York: Van Nostrand Comp.

Hafeiz, H. B. (1980). Hysterical conversion: A prognosis study. *British Journal of Psychiatry*, 136, 548-551.

Haj-Yehia, M. M. (1991). *Perceptions of wife-beating and the use of different conflict tactics among Arab-Palestinian engaged males in Israel*. Unpublished doctoral dissertation. Minnesota: The University of Minnesota.

Haj-Yehia, M. M. (1995). Toward culturally sensitive intervention with Arab families in Israel. *Contemporary Family Therapy*, 17(4), 429-447.

Haley, J. (1967). Marriage therapy. In H. Greenwald (Ed.), *Active psychotherapy* (pp. 189-223). Chicago: Aldine.

Harding, T. W., De-Arango, M. V., Baltazar, J., Climent, C. E., Ibrahim, H. H. A., Ignacio, L. L., Murthy, R. S., and Wig, N. N. (1980). Mental disorders in primary health care: A study of their frequency and diagnosis in four developing countries. *Psychological Medicine*, 10, 231-241.

Hatab, Z., and Makki, A. (1978). *Al-solta el-abawia wal-shabab*. Beirut: Ma'had El-Inmaa' El-Arabi (in Arabic).

Hofestede, G. (1991). *Cultures and organizations: Software of the mind*. London: McGraw-Hill.

Hourani, A. (1991). *A history of the Arab peoples*. New York: Warner Books, Inc.

Ibrahim, A. S. (1977). Dogmatism and related personality factors among Egyptian university students. *The Journal of Psychology*, 95, 213-215.

Ibrahim, A. S. (1979). Extroversion and neuroticism across cultures. *Psychological Reports*, 44, 799-803.

Ibrahim, A. S. (1982). The factorial structure of the Eysenck personality questionnaire among Egyptian students. *The Journal of Psychology*, 112, 221-226.

Ibrahim, A. S., and Al-Nafie, A. (1991). Perception and concern about sociocultural change and psychopathology in Saudi Arabia. *The Journal of Social Psychology*, 13, 179-186.

Ibrahim, A. S., and Ibrahim, R. M. (1993). Is psychotherapy really needed in nonwestern cultures? The case of Arab countries. *Psychological Reports*, 72, 881-882.

Ibrahim, R. M. (1991). Sociodemographic aspects of depressive symptomatology: Cross-cultural comparisons. *Dissertation Abstracts International*, 51(12).

Isaui, A. (1994). *Psychosomatic disorders*. Beirut: Dar El-Nahda Al-Arabia (in Arabic).

Israeli Ministry of Education Report. (1994). Jerusalem: Psychological services department.

Ivey, A. E. (1995). Psychotherapy as liberation. In J. G. Ponterotto, J. M. Casas, L. A. Suzuki, and C. M. Alexander (Eds.), *Handbook of multi-cultural counseling* (pp. 53-72). London: Sage Publication.

Katchadourian, H. (1980). The historical background of psychiatry in Lebanon. *Bulletin of the History of Medicine*, 54, 544-553.

Kinzie, J. D. (1985). Overview of clinical issues in the treatment of Southeast Asian refugees. In T. C. Owan (Ed.), *Southeast Asian mental health treatment, prevention services, training, and research* (pp. 113-135). Washington, DC: National Institute of Mental Health.

Kirmayer, L. J. (1984). Culture, affect and somatization, Part I. *Transcultural Psychiatry Research Review*, 21, 159-188.

Koll El-Arab (October 11, 1996). A parent is reluctant to complain to court against a teacher. Volume 461, p. 3 (in Arabic).

Kopp, R. R. (1995). *Metaphor therapy: Using client-generated metaphors in psychotherapy.* New York: Brunner/Mazel.

Kunzendorf, R. G., and Sheikh, A. A. (Eds.). (1990). *The psychophysiology of mental imagery.* New York: Baywood Publishing Company, Inc.

Laing, R. D. (1959). *The divided self.* Baltimore: Penguin.

Lambert, R. G., and Lambert, M. J. (1984). The effects of role preparation for psychotherapy on immigrant clients seeking mental health services in Hawaii. *Journal of Community Psychology,* 12, 263-275.

Laval, R. A., Gomez, E. A., and Ruiz, P. (1983). A language minority: Hispanics and mental health care. *The American Journal of Social Psychiatry,* 3, 42-49.

Levitt, E. E., and Truumaa, A. (1972). *The Rorschach technique with children and adolescents: Application and norms.* New York: Grune and Stratton.

Liebert, R. M., and Spiegler, M. D. (1994). *Personality: Strategies and issues* (seventh edition). Pacific Grove, CA: Brooks/Cole Pub.

Mahler, M. (1968). *On human symbiosis and the vicissitudes of individuation: Infantile psychosis* (Volume 1). New York: International Universities Press.

Mahler, M., Bergman, A., and Pine, F. (1975). *The psychological birth of the infant: Symbiosis and individuation.* New York: Basic Books.

Maslow, A. H. (1970). *Motivation and personality* (second edition). New York: Harper and Row.

McGoldrick, M., Pearce, J. K., and Giordano, J. (1982). *Ethnicity and Family Therapy.* New York: Guilford Press.

Meleis, A. I. (1981, June). The Arab American in the health care system. *American Journal of Nursing*, 1180-1183.
Meleis, A. I., and La Fever, C. W. (1984). The Arab American and psychiatric care. *Perspective in Psychiatric Care,* 22(2), 72-86.
Minuchin, S. (1974). *Families and family therapy.* Cambridge: Harvard University Press.
Mischel, W. (1986). *Introduction to personality* (fourth edition). New York: Holt, Rinehart and Winston.
Mohamad, A. M. (1985). *Al-shabab el-Arabi wal-tag'ier el-ig'timaa'i*. Beirut: Dar El-Nahda El-Arabia (in Arabic).
Monte, C. F. (1995). *Beneath the mask: An introduction to theories of personality.* New York: Harcourt Brace College Publishers.
Nassar, C. (1991). *The reality of war and its reflections on the child*. Tarablus, Lebanon: Gros Bryce (in Arabic).
Nasser, M. (1986). Comparative study of prevalence of abnormal eating attitudes among Arab female students of both London and Cairo universities. *Psychological Medicine*, 16, 621-625.
Nisio, K., and Bilmer, M. (1987). Psychotherapy with Southeast Asian American clients. *Professional Psychology: Research and Practice,* 18, 342-346.
Okasha, A. (1968). Preliminary psychiatric observation in Egypt. *British Journal of Psychiatry,* 114, 949-955.
Okasha, A. (1977). Psychiatric symptomatology in Egypt. *Mental Health and Society,* 4, 121.
Okasha, A. (1993). Psychiatry in Egypt. *Psychiatric Bulletin*, 17, 548-551.
Okasha, A., and Demerdash, A. (1975). Arabic study of cases of functional sexual inadequacy. *British Journal of Psychiatry,* 126, 446-448.
Okasha, A., Kamel, M., and Hassan, A. (1968). Preliminary psychiatric observations in Egypt. *British Journal of Psychiatry,* 114, 494.
Okasha, A., Saad, A., Khalil, A. H., Seif El Dawla, A., and Yehia, N. (1994). Phenomenology of obsessive-compulsive disorder: A transcultural study. *Comprehensive Psychiatry,* 35(3), 191-197.
Okasha, A., Seif El Dawla, A., Khalil, A. H., and Saad, A. (1993). Presentation of acute psychosis in an Egyptian sample: A transcultural comparison. *Comprehensive Psychiatry,* 34(1), 4-9.
Ornstein, R., and Sobel, D. (1987). *The healing brain: Breaking discoveries about how the brain keeps us healthy.* New York: Simon and Schuster.
Palestinian Authority Report. (1994-1995). Gaza: Ministry of Health.
Paniagua, F. A. (1994). *Assessing and treating culturally diverse clients*. Thousand Oaks, CA: Sage Publications.
Parhad, L. (1965). The cultural-social conditions of treatment in psychiatric outpatient department in Kuwait. *International Journal of Social Psychiatry,* 11, 14-19.
Pedersen, P. B. (1986). The cultural role of conceptual and contextual support systems in counseling. *Journal of the American Mental Health Counselor Association,* 8(1), 35-42.

Pedersen, P. B., Draguns, J. G., Lonner, W. J., and Trimble, J. E. (1989). *Counseling across cultures* (third edition). Honolulu: University of Hawaii Press.

Pedersen, P. B., Fukuyama, M., and Heath, A. (1989). Client, counselor, and contextual variables in multi-cultural counseling. In P. B. Pedersen, J. G. Draguns, W. J. Lonner, and J. E. Trimble (Eds.), *Counseling across cultures* (third edition) (pp. 23-52). Honolulu: University of Hawaii Press.

Pedersen, P. B., and Ivey, A. (1993). *Culture-centered counseling and interviewing skills: A practical guide*. Westport, CT: Praeger.

Putnam, F. W. (1989). *Diagnosis and treatment of multiple personality disorder*. New York: Guilford Press.

Racy, J. (1970). Psychiatry in Arab East. *Acta Psychiatrica Scandinavica*, 221, 1-171.

Racy, J. (1977). Psychiatry in Arab East. In C. L. Brown and N. Itzkowitz (Eds.), *Psychological Dimensions of Near Eastern Studies* (pp. 279-329). Princeton: Darwin Press.

Racy, J. (1980). Somatization in Saudi women: A therapeutic challenge. *British Journal of Psychiatry*, 137, 212-216.

Racy, J. (1985). Commentary on "psychotherapy of Arab-Israeli patients." *The Journal of Psychoanalysis Anthropology*, 8(4), 231-233.

Rahim, S. I., and Cederblad, M. (1989). Epidemiology of mental disorders in young adults of newly urbanized area in Khartoum, Sudan. *British Journal of Psychiatry*, 155, 44-47.

Raskin, N. J., and Rogers, C. R. (1989). Person-centered therapy. In R. J. Corsini and D. Wedding (Eds.), *Current psychotherapies* (fourth edition, pp. 155-196). Itasca, IL: F. E. Peacock Publishers, Inc.

Raundalen, M., and Melton, G. B. (1994). Children in war and its aftermath: Mental health issues in the development of international law. *Behavioral Science and the Law*, 12(1), 21-34.

Rayhida, J., Shaya, M., and Armenian, H. (1986). Children health in a city at war. In J. Bryce and H. Armenian (Eds.), *Wartime: The state of children in Lebanon*. Beirut: American University of Beirut.

Rogers, C. R. (1961). *On becoming a person*. Boston: Houghton Mifflin.

Rogers, C. R. (1965). *Client-centered therapy*. Boston: Houghton Mifflin.

Rossi, E. L. (1993). *The psychobiology of mind-body healing: New concepts of therapeutic hypnosis*. New York: W.W. Norton.

Rossi, E. L., and Ryan, M. O. (Eds.) (1992). *Mind-body communication in hypnosis: The seminars workshops and lectures of Milton H. Erickson*. New York: Irvington Publishers, Inc.

Ruiz, P., and Ruiz, P. P. (1983). Treatment compliance among Hispanics. *Journal of Operational Psychiatry*, 14, 112-114.

Satir, V. (1967). *Conjoint family therapy*. Palo Alto: Science and Behavior Books.

Schwartz, G. E. (1982). Testing the biopsychosocial model: The ultimate challenge facing behavioral medicine. *Journal of Consulting and Clinical Psychology*, 50, 1040-1053.

Schwartz, G. E. (1984). Psychophysiology of imagery and healing: A systems perspective. In A. A. Sheikh (Ed.), *Imagination and healing* (pp. 35-50). New York: Baywood Publishing Company, Inc.

Schwartz, G. E. (1989). Dysregulation theory and disease: Toward a general model for psychosomatic medicine. In S. Cheren (Ed.), *Psychosomatic medicine: Theory, physiology, and practice* (Volume 1, pp. 91-118). Madison, CT: International Universities Press.

Sharabi, H. (1975). *Moq'adimat ledirasat el-mojtamaa' el-Arabi.* Jerusalem: Salah El-Deen (in Arabic).

Sharabi, H. (1977). Impact of class and culture on social behavior: The feudal bourgeois family in Arab society. In L. C. Brown and N. Itzkowitz (Eds.), *Psychological Dimensions of Near Eastern Studies*. Princeton: The Darwin Press.

Sharabi, H. (1992). *Al-nith'am al-a'bawi waa'shkaliat takhaluf el-mojtamaa' al-A'rabi.* Beirut: Markiz Derasat El-Wehda El-Arabia (in Arabic).

Shq'er, A. (1996, October 11). Nurses are justifying violence against women. *Koll El-Arab*, 461, 7 (in Arabic).

Skinner, B. F. (1953). *Science and human behavior.* New York: Macmillan.

Skinner, B. F. (1974). *About behaviorism.* New York: Knopf.

Story, R. D. (1985). Health patterns in Saudi Arabia and in the Islamic world: A pharmacist's perspective. *Anthropology UCLA*, 53-61.

Sue, D. W., and Sue, D. (1990). *Counseling the culturally different: Theory and practice* (second edition). New York: John Wiley and Sons.

Swagman, C. (1989). Fija': Fright and illness in highland Yemen. *Social Science and Medicine*, 28(4), 381-388.

Timimi, S. B. (1995). Adolescence in immigrant Arab families. *Psychotherapy*, 32, 141-149.

Tuma, J. M. (1989). Mental health services for children: The state of the art. *American Psychologist*, 44, 188-199.

Walker, M., Trimboli, A., and Trimboli, C. (1995). Parental discipline in Anglo, Greek, Lebanese, and Vietnamese culture. *Journal of Cross-Cultural Psychology*, 26(1), 49-64.

Webster's encyclopedic unabridged dictionary of English language (1983). New York: Gramercy Books.

West, J. (1987). Psychotherapy in the eastern province of Saudi Arabia. *Psychotherapy*, 24(1), 8-10.

Zeig, J. K. (1995). Experiential approaches to clinician development. In J. K. Zeig (Ed.), *The evolution of psychotherapy: The third conference* (pp. 161-181). New York: Brunner/Mazel.

Zucker, R. A., and Gomberg, E. S. L. (1986). Etiology of alcoholism reconsidered: The case for biopsychosocial process. *American Psychologist,* 41, 783-793.

Index

Page numbers followed by the letter "f" indicate figures; those followed by the letter "t" indicate tables.